The Anthropology of Corporate Social Responsibility

DISLOCATIONS

General Editors: August Carbonella, *Memorial University of Newfoundland,* Don Kalb, *University of Utrecht & Central European University,* Linda Green, *University of Arizona*

The immense dislocations and suffering caused by neoliberal globalization, the retreat of the welfare state in the last decades of the twentieth century, and the heightened military imperialism at the turn of the twenty-first century have raised urgent questions about the temporal and spatial dimensions of power. Through stimulating critical perspectives and new and cross-disciplinary frameworks that reflect recent innovations in the social and human sciences, this series provides a forum for politically engaged and theoretically imaginative responses to these important issues of late modernity.

For full series listing, please see back matter.

THE ANTHROPOLOGY OF CORPORATE SOCIAL RESPONSIBILITY

Edited by Catherine Dolan & Dinah Rajak

berghahn
NEW YORK · OXFORD
www.berghahnbooks.com

First published in 2016 by
Berghahn Books
www.berghahnbooks.com

Library of Congress Cataloging-in-Publication Data
A CIP cataloging record is available from the Library of Congress.

British Library Cataloguing in Publication Data
A catalogue record for this book is available from the British Library

ISBN 978-1-78533-071-1 (hardback)
ISBN 978-1-78533-750-5 (paperback)
ISBN 978-1-78533-072-8 (ebook)

CONTENTS

ILLUSTRATIONS

ACKNOWLEDGMENTS

First and foremost we would like to thank the authors of the book's chapters for their compelling and thought-provoking contributions, which build on complimentary themes while drawing from diverse cases to address key questions concerning the discourse and practice of corporate social responsibility (CSR) in contemporary capitalism.

This volume joins an innovative collection of books in Berghahn's Dislocations series, edited by Don Kalb, which critically confronts contradictions, inequalities and frictions in the new millennium. We are very grateful to Don for his advice and support in the evolution of this volume.

At Berghahn, we wish to thank Molly Mosher, Adam Capitanio, Dhara Patel, Charlotte Mosedale and Sarah Sibley for their enthusiastic support and expert guidance in the development of this manuscript. We are also most grateful to the three anonymous reviewers for Berghahn for their particularly insightful and detailed comments on the manuscript.

This volume grew out of a special section of *Focaal* (volume 60) on "Ethnographies of corporate ethicizing." Sincere thanks are owed to Luisa Steur, editor of *Focaal*, who shepherded that initial special section that formed the seed for this volume, and to Christina Garsten, our co-editor of the special section. We thank *Focaal* for permission to reprint the essays by Cross, Dolan and Johnstone-Louis, Hardin, Li and Rajak (which constitute chapters 1, 3, 5, 8 and 9 of this volume). Chapter 4, "Power, inequality, and corporate social responsibility: The politics of ethical compliance in the South Indian garment industry" by Geert De Neve first appeared in *Economic and Political Weekly* (volume 44, issue 22, 2009). We are grateful to Geert De Neve and *Economic and Political Weekly* for granting permission to reprint this article as a contribution to the present book. The Afterword, "Big men and business: Morality, debt, and the corporation: A perspective" by Robert Foster has also appeared as an article in *Social Anthropology* (volume 20, issue 4, 2012). We are grateful to *Social Anthropology* for permission to use his article in this volume. We are grateful to

Chicago University Press for permission to reprint Stuart Kirsch's essay "Virtuous language in industry and the academy" which was first published in *Corporate Social Responsibility? Human Rights in the New Global Economy*, edited by Charlotte Walker-Said and John D. Kelly.

We would like to express our gratitude to Mick Blowfield and Samuel Knafo for their tireless support and commitment to our work; and to Lucy, Raphael and Noa for providing a joyful respite from it.

INTRODUCTION

Toward the Anthropology of Corporate Social Responsibility

Catherine Dolan and Dinah Rajak

As corporations confront new social and environmental challenges to their operations—from concerns about labor productivity to community resistance, climate change, or saturated markets—the corporate social responsibility (CSR) movement has demonstrated a powerful capacity to offer itself up as a solution. Today, ethical initiatives—from certification and labeling schemes to cause-related marketing and inclusive business programs—are ubiquitous, circulating new regimes of accountability that aim to institute ethics and social responsibility in global business practice. Indeed, while ethics were once the province of philosophy and religion, they are increasingly insinuated into corporate capitalism as the market supplants politico-judicial and religious domains as society's ethical arbiter. It is now the global brand—whether Coca-Cola, Nike, Wal-Mart, or L'Oréal—that serves as a guarantor of social welfare and environmental stewardship, uniting financial profit with social good in the localities in which companies operate across the globe, and giving rise to a contemporary expression of what has become known as "enlightened self-interest."

Two decades ago James Ferguson, in making his case for an anthropology of development, wrote that the study of development had been dominated by an "ideological preoccupation with the question of whether it is considered to be a 'good thing' or a 'bad thing'" (Ferguson 1994 [1990]: 14). The study of CSR has been similarly polarized, drawing supporters and critics in equal measure. While advocates extol CSR as a radical reorientation of business for the twenty-first century, heralding a new era of "humane capitalism,"[1] critics have sought to expose CSR as "a Band Aid over deep capitalist scars" (Jones 1996: 8), a smokescreen that can be blown away to reveal an unchanging capitalist order (Sharp 2006). Yet, this normative preoccupation with whether corporations are a "good" or "bad" thing for society obscures not only the ideological fault lines along which the study of CSR has run, but also the ambivalences, contradictions and potentialities that inhere in the morality of the corporate form. How then do we make sense of the emergence of these new forms of ethical corporate capitalism, encapsulated in the discourse and practice of corporate social responsibility?

Over the past decade, as corporate social responsibility has become established as orthodoxy within the arena of both development and multinational business and enshrined within a web of standards, auditors and certifiers that make up a burgeoning ethical industry, anthropologists have begun this process of sense-making, tracing how "responsibility" is practiced in the everyday routines of organizations and differentially grounded in particular social and material realities. They have trained the ethnographic lens on CSR's moral economy in industries around the world, including garments (De Neve 2009), soft drinks (Foster 2008), oil and gas (Shever 2008; Appel 2012; Gardner 2012; Weszkalnys 2014), mining (Rajak 2011a; Kirsch 2014a; Welker 2014), tobacco (Benson 2012), pharmaceuticals (Ecks 2008), consumer goods (Cross and Street 2009; Dolan and Roll 2013), sporting goods (Moeller 2013), and humanitarian objects (Redfield 2013; Cross 2013; Dolan and Rajak forthcoming).[2] In doing so, anthropologists have explored CSR from two vantage points; on the one hand focusing on the apparatus and architecture of CSR (see, for example, Garsten and Jacobsson 2007; Welker 2009; Benson and Kirsch 2010; Cross 2011; Rajak 2011a), and on the other exploring CSR's local effects, contestations and responses, etc. (see, for example, Sawyer 2004; Kirsch 2006; De Neve 2009; Dolan and Scott 2009; Li 2010; Gardner 2012; Gilberthorpe 2013). This volume, which has grown out of a special section of *Focaal* (2011, volume 60) on "Ethnographies of corporate ethicizing," brings the two together, tracking the production, circulation, deployment and outcomes of CSR from boardrooms to operations and back again in a variety of social, cultural, and geographical locations (Bangladesh, Cameroon, Chile, the Democratic Republic of Congo, Ghana, India, Peru, South Africa, the UK, and the USA).[3]

In the years since the special issue came out, the anthropological study of corporate social responsibility has expanded and developed — pushing the boundaries of enquiry to new geographies, industries, and confrontations. The goal of this larger collection is to bring together many of the key scholars involved in that enterprise, who have been tracking the processes and outcomes of CSR ethnographically in diverse contexts across the globe. In drawing together research at the vanguard of this exciting and dynamic field, we hope that this volume will open new avenues of enquiry into the morality of the corporate form and highlight the contributions of anthropological knowledge to the contemporary social and economic transformations CSR tenders. Indeed, as more transnational corporations step in, so it seems, to fill the ethical void, as it were, left in the wake of neoliberal capitalism, there is a growing need to grapple with the myriad configurations of CSR and the expectations, contradictions and frictions the movement is generating.

The book raises several questions concerning the ethical turn of corporate capitalism, including: how does the embedding of ethics within commercial rationalities blur the boundaries between moral and market forms of exchange? In what ways do systems of ethical and environmental governance introduce new forms of management, control and discipline that alienate rather than empower? To what extent do CSR standards and protocols replace human forms of sociality with a virtual "transnational economy of inspectability" (Mutersbaugh 2005: 391)? Does corporate responsibility challenge existing patterns of inequality, or is it implicated in the reproduction of power inequalities, creating new geographies of inclusion and exclusion? Crucially, a little over a decade since CSR was heralded as a new panacea to underdevelopment at the 2002 World Summit on Sustainable Development, we ask how CSR has evolved and mutated as it navigates the fault lines between the exigencies of capital and social obligation. The book addresses these questions through ethnographic accounts of "ethical" practices in a range of transnational corporations—Anglo American, Chevron, De Beers, ExxonMobil, Barrick Gold, Newmont Mining, and Avon—revealing the local realignments and reorderings of social relations produced through the contemporary reign of corporate responsibility. The chapters in this volume subject the "win-win" claims of CSR to sustained empirical research, scrutinizing the intended and unintended outcomes of CSR in practice in a variety of settings. In doing so they go a long way toward untangling the hopes, ambivalences and contradictions of CSR—bringing its unalloyed promise of empowerment through business into sharp relief against the empirical realities of exclusionary corporate-sponsored welfare, enhanced inequality, and conflict and contestation. Crucially, a key insight that emerges collectively from the chapters is that while the benefits of CSR may genuinely be enjoyed by some of its stakeholders (to borrow the corporate jargon), they are inevitably contingent on the inherent contradictions of a doctrine that claims social responsibility for corporations while eschewing obligation and entitlement. The promise of inclusion for some almost invariably comes at the cost of exclusion, precarity or disempowerment for others. As the ethnographic insights collected here demonstrate, this fundamental contradiction—the capacity of CSR discourse to enable corporations to simultaneously assert and displace responsibility—is manifest most clearly in the mutually involved rise of CSR and subcontracting in corporate strategy, the former claiming responsibility in the same moment that the corporation works to outsource, offshore or displace responsibility down the supply chain (a theme to which we later return).

In this introduction, we trace the emergence of CSR in broad brushstrokes, summarizing its trajectory and translations, and alignments and disjunctures, as it travels from nineteenth-century paternalism to twenty-first- century bottom billion capitalism. We suggest that far from emulating a Latourian immutable mobile, an object whose meanings and forms remain stable as they engage diverse networks and geographies (Latour 1987), CSR continually reinvents itself, as corporations mobilize new material practices, forms of affect and discursive strategies in pursuit of new markets and novel techniques for heading off new social and political challenges. However this capacity for adaptation and reinvention has meant that CSR tends to be represented as a novelty of millennial capitalism, birthed in a post-Washington consensus era. Here, we briefly trace its rise and evolution in order to contextualize and historicize the apparent ethical turn in corporate capitalism, highlighting the deeper roots and longer legacies of the corporate responsibility movement.

The shifting morphology of CSR

The contemporary wave of CSR came into focus in the 1990s as allegations of corporate malfeasance, from financial scandals to human rights abuses, swept across the US and Western Europe, airing the moral failings of business to public scrutiny. As media exposés and non-governmental organization (NGO) campaigns highlighted the sweatshop conditions, ecological disasters and human rights abuses wrought by global multinationals, many companies sought to recoup credibility and avert brand-damaging attacks by incorporating social and environmental concerns in business operations. Though

CSR is often associated with the distinct standards, protocols and principles adopted during this period, its scope is both temporally and spatially broader, situated in a lineage of efforts to "moralize" or "humanize" capitalism (Jenkins 2005; Hopkins 2007). Attempts to regulate, harness and tame corporate power have taken shape since the rise of the "modern" corporation and the antitrust movements of the late nineteenth century (Jenkins 2005): from the nineteenth-century boycotts of slave-produced sugar, the industrial paternalism of Unilever's Port Sunlight and Cadbury's Bourneville, and the corporate philanthropy of Andrew Carnegie and John D. Rockefeller (Blowfield and Frynas 2005; Carroll 2008), to the enlightened self-interest model of the 1970s, ethical audits of the 1990s, and the current emphasis on entrepreneurialism, self-empowerment, and bottom of the pyramid (BoP) business, CSR is perpetually reasserted and rewritten as it seeks to broker the uneasy relationship between market and social imperatives.

Looking back over the past century, CSR has shown a chameleon-like capacity (Gond and Moon 2011) to respond to and incorporate new ideas, embodying a shape-shifting character that finds currency in response to the particular political-economic and social currents in which it is deployed. Over the past decade CSR has shown itself to be particularly adaptable, encompassing (and mainstreaming) movements that often start out as alternative or even oppositional to the corporate world, such as fair trade, as well as drawing on new management frameworks/philosophies that promise to turn development imperatives into business opportunities, such as BoP business and cause-related marketing. Equally, as fair trade, ethical consumption, and more recently, social business movements, have been progressively mainstreamed and subject to corporate capture, they should be seen within this broad, evolving landscape of CSR; as part and parcel of the same apparatus with which corporations have monopolized and deradicalized what were once seen as alternative economic models and political movements (Shamir 2004). Indeed, rather than reframing business interests to reflect social imperatives or community needs, CSR can have the counter effect: reframing the interests of communities and government to fit the priorities of corporations.

CSR is thus best seen as protean and multiply enacted—an evolving and flexible and overlapping set of practices and discourses (as opposed to a distinct set of initiatives or principles) through which business (re)makes and asserts itself as an ethical actor, claiming to elide the frictions between principles and profit by reframing (if not actually reinvigorating) the responsibilities, interests and priorities of the corporation. Like the corporate form itself, CSR confounds stability; it transmogrifies, mutating, dividing and recombining (Welker, Patridge and Hardin 2011: S4) through encounters with diverse configurations of actors and institutions. Through its "capacity for decontextualization and recontextualization, abstractability and movement," CSR materializes what Ong and Collier term a "global assemblage," circulating and taking on new meanings, artifacts and practices of capitalism as it travels through and becomes emboldened by corporations, business schools, development institutions, think tanks, social enterprises, certification bodies, and consultancy organizations (Thrift 2005 [1997]; Ong and Collier 2005: 11).

Equally, the empirical study of CSR in practice reveals how there is often little intentionality or cohesion in the dispersion of CSR practices, "no central, controlling corporate apparatus" or clear-cut rationality that directs its course (Welker n.d.: 7). It often emerges reactively rather than systematically, rolled out in fits and starts by particular actors and sets of interests. Indeed, CSR can seem as mercurial as it is coherent: corporations bait and switch in response to external pressures (for example, Shell's turn from philanthropy toward corporate citizenship in the wake of the Brent Spar Oil Disaster (Shever 2010)) or deploy CSR programs in parallel that are disjointed, disparate or contradictory to one another, as Sydow's chapter (this volume) evocatively shows. Even during the classic CSR period of the 1990s and early 2000s, CSR assumed a polyvalent character; on the one hand functioning as a proxy state, assuming responsibility for job provision, social welfare, infrastructure, and environmental stewardship (Welker 2014), and on the other hand functioning as a form of technocratic governance exercised through the rationalist instruments of corporate codes, global compacts, and "best practice" guidelines; a pastoral ethics of care lying side by side with the detachment of the "audit culture" (Power 1997; Strathern 2000).

When viewed over a longer historical perspective we can see how CSR has evolved from its earlier incarnation of corporate philanthropy and paternalism to a contemporary rejection of that paternalism and on toward an emphasis on promoting local enterprise, entrepreneurialism, self-empowerment and BoP business as the cornerstones of sustainable development, very much mirroring shifts in the agendas of the international development arena more broadly. Today, corporate actors are seen less as patrons and stewards than as catalysts, championing the mundane everyday workings of the market as the solution to social problems through what Roy terms "bottom billion capitalism" (Roy 2010). Here, too, different instantiations are at play: we find the mainstreaming of fair trade regimes, underwritten by the dual promise of corporate responsibility for producers and ethical consumption for shoppers, and the mushrooming of cause-related marketing, which leverages the power of the brand to mobilize consumer-corporate-NGO "partnerships" for development ends. We also find the ascent of social enterprise and the rapid rise of the BoP concept of the poor as a profitable market, which are extending the territory of CSR through a new cadre of "enterprising" businesses and "self-reliant" entrepreneurs. All these models, however, share a guiding telos: to leverage and capitalize on the moral terrain of development, repositioning poverty, disease, hunger and so forth as a font of profit and accumulation for business (Roy 2012: 106). Here we briefly review the evolving landscape of these market-based, corporate-led social initiatives, from ethical trade and corporate efforts to "responsibilize" supply chains, to "social business" campaigns that target those at the "bottom of the pyramid" as consumers and "entrepreneurs." All, in different ways, solicit corporate responsibility beyond the economic; all aim (or claim) to transform corporations into agents (and architects) of development. Sketching out this wider architecture of ethical economies highlights the focus and scope of this volume. For, as we highlight below, while fair trade and ethical consumption have been the subject of a significant body of ethnographic and sociological research, much less focus has been devoted to corporations as ethical agents themselves, and the practices, processes and partnerships they engage in the deployment of CSR.

The anthropology of ethical economies: An emerging field

The anthropology of fair trade and ethical consumption has drawn significant ethnographic attention in recent years (see ethnographic collections of Lyon and Moberg 2010; De Neve et al. 2008; Carrier and Luetchford 2012). Though the fair trade movement consists of both an idealist orientation toward trade justice and human solidarity and an instrumentalist focus on certification and market expansion (Jaffee 2007: 31; Dolan 2010), recent anthropological work has honed in on the latter, tracking the deepening marketization or "mainstreaming" of fair trade as the movement, birthed in opposition to the logic of capital, increasingly conforms to its logic, embracing corporate participation as a way to ameliorate poverty among a wider swathe of producers (Barrientos and Dolan 2006:181; Raynolds 2009). Though hardly seamless, the incursion of global retail giants such as Starbucks, Dunkin' Donuts, McDonalds and Sam's Clubs (Wal-Mart) (Schmelzer 2007) into the spaces of "alternative trade" marks a radical break in the ethos of the movement as corporations morph from adversaries to allies (Dolan 2010) and capture increasingly large portions of the fair trade market under the banner of their corporate responsibility to both producers and consumers.

Broadly speaking, anthropologists have tracked this process at two scales, one focusing on the "impact" of mainstreaming and how its material artifacts (standards, audits) mediate perceived benefits for producers and workers in the South; and the other focusing on the discourses and aesthetics of fair trade, exploring how the moral pact that fair trade rests upon is constituted and made meaningful for consumers. In both cases, we see long-standing anthropological themes—alienation, commoditization, and defetishization (De Neve et al. 2008)—invoked to explain the entanglements of affect and economic action entailed in fair trade's ethical economies.

The interplay between corporate brand strategy and the ethical dispositions of consumers also lies at the heart of cause-related marketing (CRM). CRM, where a company or brand aligns with a non-profit organization to realize business and societal benefits, is often held up as a form of market-savvy philanthropy—a corporate gift bestowed upon a deserving proximate cause, such as breast cancer or homelessness. In the last decade, however, CRM has morphed beyond local and national "charitable" causes into a form of "humane" capitalism, deploying branded goods such as Pampers diapers, a Product Red iPod or an Always sanitary pad as tools of global development. These initiatives, which Richey and Ponte (2011) term "Brand Aid" and others describe as "marketized philanthropy," peddle the sale of branded products to mitigate pressing social concerns like HIV/AIDS, neonatal tetanus, or girls' education, parlaying the mundane purchase of consumer goods into a political act. This theme—how corporations reformat the realm of development—is also taken up by Moeller's (2013) ethnographic study of Nike's flagship program "The Girl Effect," which portrays how women have been moved to the front line of CSR as corporations like Nike seek to extend their power and influence, simultaneously bolstering their social credentials while activating new frontiers of growth. Like fair trade and related forms of ethical consumption, CRM aligns development with consumer choice, replacing "conviction with consumption" by tethering the moral self to the purchase of the "right" product or cause. The causes pursued are increasingly spun out of a celebrity-charity-corporate complex (Brockington 2014), an assemblage that twins the celebrification of development with corporate branding. For instance, CRM casts "A-list" celebrities like Angelina Jolie, Bono and Annie Lennox as arbiters of morality; brand ambassadors who mediate the encounter between Western consumers and those in need by mobilizing the emotion and affect of the former. Like fair trade, CRM traffics in what Tsing (2000) terms an "economy of appearances"—that is, how celebrity spectacle conjures the "possibility of economic performance" (Tsing 2000: 118), a speculation that impels ethical consumption.

Recently, CSR has undergone another paradigmatic shift as corporations seize the new terrain of "inclusive business," "shared value," and BoP business (Blowfield and Dolan 2014; Dolan and Johnstone-Louis this volume), each of which claims a symbiosis between social and financial value (Roy 2010). The BoP concept, in particular, has enjoyed a meteoric rise among corporations and development professionals alike, moving CSR from the margins to the mainstream of business strategy. Born from the vision of the late management scholar C. K. Prahalad (2005), the BoP model seeks to marry a corporate logic of profit maximization with development aspirations for poverty reduction by bringing the "poor" into the sphere of transnational economic circulation as consumers for low-cost goods and services, and into productive activity as entrepreneurs. Though the model holds the market sacrosanct, it also turns on an ideology of inclusion (what Roy (2010) terms "neoliberal populism"), seeking to democratize access to markets by enveloping those who have been excluded (or included on unfavorable terms) from the productive possibilities of the global economy. From transnational corporations like Danone distributing fortified food through Bangladeshi "micro-entrepreneurs" and Hewlett-Packard's "digital brokers" delivering electronic services in Costa Rica, to social enterprises promoting low-cost health and energy solutions in East Africa (see review by Kolk, Rivera-Santos and Rufín 2014), the BoP is at the coalface of inclusive capitalism, celebrating social dividends as a natural by-product of capital accumulation (World Business Council for Sustainable Development 2005).

Though lauded in global development circles, anthropologists have explored the ambiguities BoP's union of profit and possibility rests upon as geographies of poverty are recast as loci of unmet consumer needs (Roy 2012; Elyachar 2012; Dolan and Roll 2013). Dolan and

Roll's (2013) exposition of corporate expansion into the BoP in Africa, for example, describes how business maps and marshals the cultural and knowledge assets of the poor, converting inchoate consumers into viable markets and harnessing the affective relations of the poor as infrastructure for entrepreneurial innovation. Similarly, Cross and Street (2009) show us how Unilever's marketing of "accessible" hygiene products (soap) in India reshapes consumer habits through the regulation of everyday consumption practices, rendering the spaces at the bottom of the pyramid primed and predictable to capital.

Corporations engaging the BoP, anthropologists suggest, not only scan untapped markets, looking to capitalize on the underutilized assets of the poor; rather, they seek to convert "that knowledge as a capacity, resource or a commodity in new ways" (Cross 2014: 4; Elyachar 2005; Dolan and Roll 2013). Like other "new approaches to development," such as microcredit, which mobilize affective ties, social collectivities and the intimate domain of kin as a source of economic value (Rankin 2001; Elyachar 2005), the knowledges, cultural practices and social relations of the poor are the raw material of BoP capitalism; seedbeds for growing profit and poverty reduction. Here we see an ethic of CSR purveyed not through pastoral programs of community care but through the neoliberal motif of self-reliance as entrepreneurial futures are conjured from economic disenfranchisement. Echoing the archetypal "self-regulating," "responsible" subjects of neoliberalism (Welker 2014; Dolan and Johnstone-Louis this volume; Dolan and Rajak forthcoming), BoP initiatives cast entrepreneurs as emissaries for the corporate economy of mutuality, encasing the bodily, social and economic capital needed to animate the power of the corporation and the vision of global development. As Dolan and Rajak's (forthcoming) ethnography of Catalyst—a social enterprise that provides unemployed youth with entrepreneurial opportunities in Nairobi's slums—suggests, it is a moral mission that not only impels the transformation of the individual into an industrious entrepreneurial citizen, but charges them with the responsibility of bringing about a second order of moral transformation—that is, serving the wider societal project of "good growth," a double moral injunction for the "poor to help themselves [in order to help] the economy" (Elyachar 2002: 500; see Dolan and Rajak forthcoming).

Through all of these renditions and expressions of corporate responsibility we find continuities, as well as interruptions, as CSR strives to mediate business-society relations and mitigate the contradictions of corporate capitalism. What we see from emergent ethnographic work in this field — from the work on resource extraction in Indonesia, Papua New Guinea, or sub-Saharan Africa (Welker 2014; Kirsch 2014a; Rajak 2011a), to soft drinks, big tobacco, apparel and cosmetics (Foster 2008; De Neve 2009; Dolan 2011; Benson 2012) — is, time and again, the various ways in which corporations use the language and practice of ethics to contain and respond to different kinds of challenges and conflicts generated by their activities — from ecological/environmental crises to labor rights and local expectations of jobs; from dependency and Dutch disease to corruption and conflict over resources — and CSR's immense flexibility to offer itself up as the solution to all of them. This points to a key dimension of CSR that this book underlines — that is, how the various mutations of CSR, from philanthropy to cause-related marketing, signal its Darwinian capacity to adapt to and exploit the unpredictability of global markets as it remakes and reproduces capitalism.

Ethnographies of CSR: An emergent field

As anthropologists have turned their attention to this emergent field of enquiry they have applied classic anthropological tropes as heuristic devices to analyze how CSR reconstitutes social relations between corporate actors and their consumers, producers, and wider "stakeholders" (to borrow from corporate jargon), and to investigate how the politics of CSR create new domains for the exercise of corporate power. At the same time, corporate discourse has appropriated anthropological concepts in a bid to "humanize" the corporate machine: it has become common to hear corporate actors describe the corporation in terms of culture, personhood, and kinship, while describing CSR in relation to notions of the gift, social contract, and even reciprocity. As described below, anthropologists of CSR have responded by interrogating ethnographically these renditions of the anthropomorphic corporate form and its claims to personhood, citizenship and family to reveal the power relations that the corporate use and abuse of these concepts engender (Kirsch 2014b; Rajak 2014; Foster 2014).

One of the most salient of such claims is the evocation of "reciprocity," which circulates through the new corporate currency of partnership, community engagement, and shared value. Anthropologists have explored the apparent capacity of CSR to bring about a shift from combat to collaboration between the diverse constellations of actors, who are drawn into complex, multilevel processes of production and extraction, creating novel partnerships and alliances between corporations, global NGOs, local civil society organizations, government officials, and even trade unions (Rajak 2011b). At the same time, building on the much longer history of anthropology of development, these ethnographic enquiries have set out to reveal what lies behind claims to mutuality and consensus around supposedly universal orthodoxies of sustainable development and global ethics (Sharp 2006; Garsten and Jacobsson 2007; Benson and Kirsch 2010), and the conflicting interests that can at times be masked by them (Gardner 2012). Other scholars have focused on the capacity of such corporate-community partnerships to provide new channels/vehicles for patronage, elite pacting/corruption, dependency and control (Jones 2007; Welker 2009; Rajak 2011a).

Another notable strand of analysis running through the anthropological contribution to the study of CSR concerns the corporate gift. Advocates of CSR claim it to be a radical departure from old-school industrial philanthropy—defined by its integration into core business DNA as opposed to a moral bolt-on. Yet, as the chapters in this volume underline, the practice of CSR confounds stock polarities between the corporate "gift" and economic interest; between human affect and market imperatives, and the modernist teleology on which they are based. Rajak (2009, 2011a), for example, describes how the transnational corporation (TNC) Anglo American seeks to sever its CSR programs from a legacy of philanthropic largesse and charitable "gifts" by casting corporate ethics in a new register of "social investment," "community empowerment," and "self-reliance." She found, however, that the specter of the Maussian gift continued to animate Anglo's CSR programs, sustaining corporate authority and control through long-held patterns of dependency and patronage. In the same vein, Dolan's (2009) study of Kenyan Fairtrade flowers problematizes fair trade's calculation of equivalence, embodied in the mantra of "equal exchange," suggesting that fair trade tenders less an economic than a social contract that carries ideological continuities with charity and international development, thus rendering the commensurability of exchange less clear and the proximity to the Maussian gift more apparent. The gift motif has been recently picked up by Gardner (2012), who considers how in the case of Chevron the corporation's conception of the gift clashes with a local Bangladeshi, Islamic conception of charity and gifts; by Muñoz and Burnham (this volume), who describe how ExxonMobil construes its "standards of business conduct and ethics" as a gift from multinational to local enterprise; and by Cross

(2014), whose ethnographic portrayal of industrial workers in India examines the moral, economic and political logics that motivate the "corporate gift." Cross calls for a reimagining of these transactions beyond a corporation's calculus of capitalist value; one that considers how giving might position "donor and recipients, their capacities and assets, in a relational way" (Cross 2014: 124). In each of these cases we see the ways the corporate gift constellates around a set of recurring conceptual tensions: between attachment and detachment (Cross, and Muñoz and Burnham this volume); connection and disconnection (Gardner this volume); patron and client (Rajak 2009); entanglement and disentanglement (Appel 2012); and intimacy and estrangement (Dolan 2009).

The tension between affect and economic action expressed in the Maussian gift also appears in the material artifacts of CSR— the ethical standards and auditing protocols that undergird CSR's new ethical economy. Building on the work of Scott, who described how states deployed technical procedures to render human and territorial subjects more "visible," legible, and governable, a number of ethnographic accounts show us how CSR technologies (standards, protocols, "best practice" guidelines) embed a supra-cultural ethic to govern disparate spaces and actors, drawing them into the regulatory province and moral fold of the corporation (Blowfield and Dolan 2008; M. Goodman, D. Goodman and Redclift 2010: 11; Welker 2014; De Neve this volume). CSR technologies are construed as "travelling rationalities" (Craig and Porter 2006: 120), instruments that distill the messy and unbounded social realities of the factory floor (Dunn 2005; De Neve 2009), mineshaft (Rajak 2011a), oil fields (Shever 2012; Gilberthorpe 2013) or plantations (Blowfield and Dolan 2008) into standardized and categorical forms, a process of "decoupling" (Power 1997) and disembedding (Miller 1998) that solidifies, if not deepens, hierarchical relations between CSR agents and their "beneficiaries." Others have explored how the separations that are thus entailed unsettle the language of partnership, reciprocity and collaboration that circulates through CSR. Berlan and Dolan (2014), for example, writing of cocoa production in Ghana, describe how standards transgress and invert CSR's relational ethic, mediating face-to-face relations between producers/consumers, suppliers/ buyers and workers/management through the phenomenal form of the CSR standard. Similarly, Rajak (2011a) describes how CSR instruments serve as mechanisms of containment and exclusion, confining their moral purview to certain spaces, fields and actors and rendering "them distinct from those areas and people who are not in its line of vision" (Rajak 2010: 567). Others (Dunn 2005; Freidberg 2007; Gilberthorpe 2013) have focused on the processes of information-gathering and surveillance, materialized and routinized in contemporary audit cultures (Strathern 2000), and how these practices lay claim to moral credentials through representations of doing good. Analyzing export production zones in India, the chapters by Cross and De Neve (this volume) point to the frictions and power asymmetries the audit and its surveillance practices produce, as the audit's routinized exchanges of codified information become a proxy for the sociality CSR implies, a variant of Cross's ethic of detachment (this volume). A key theme here is how CSR audits manufacture an illusion of transparency, as staged performances are choreographed and ritualized to "represent" compliance and cover-up untoward practices, generative of concealment as much as revelation (Freidberg 2007; De Neve et al. 2008; Dolan 2010). They become, to borrow from Poovey's analysis of accounting, a "self-actualizing fiction" (Poovey 2008: 58); a performance that reproduces the conditions the audit describes.

The anthropology of CSR has also drawn traditional anthropological concerns with personhood into the realm of corporate capitalism (Mauss 1990; Strathern 1999; Kirsch and Benson 2014), exploring how CSR is woven into the corporate form through the "legal fiction" of corporate personhood, often in unexpected ways. Sawyer's analysis of a legal suit challenging the deleterious practices and effects of Chevron Texaco's operations in Ecuador, for example, describes how the reification of corporate personhood underscored both opposition to and defense of the transnational giant (Sawyer 2006: 34). On the one hand, ascription of human form and agency was critical to plaintiff strategies to hold Chevron-Texaco to account for environmental and health damages. On the other hand, Sawyer describes how corporate personhood was also appropriated by Chevron to contest the plaintiffs' argument, as the company claimed that as part of a corporation headquartered in the US it bore no responsibility for the actions of employees in its Ecuadorian subsidiary. Shever (2010), in contrast, describes how Shell flexibly deployed the notion of corporate personhood to rebrand its public persona as a good citizen and CSR leader, exchanging the detachment of philanthropy for the intimacy of affect, articulated in the aptly named "Creating Bonds" program. Welker and Wood (2011), too, describe how shareholder activism, materialized in socially responsible investment (SRI), construes shareholder personhood variously, drawing on both relational and bounded notions of the self. In this volume, Foster considers the notion of corporate personhood through the lens of long-running debates in Melanesian anthropology about the nature of personhood, to highlight just how problematic the idea of the corporate person is. Comparing corporate discourses of personhood with anthropological analyses of the Melanesian "Big Man," as both assume a role as arbiter of debts, gifts and moral responsibility over the community or clan, Foster shows how what is at stake in both is a question of authority.

A related site of ethnographic inquiry concerns kinship. Shever's (2012) analysis of corporate practice in the oilfields of Argentina, for example, shows us how kinship sodalities work in (and are intrinsic to) the process of oil privatization. Like Yanagisako's (2002) ethnography of the Como silk industry, Shever is concerned with the generative power of affect; how it shapes and produces business and the economy, transgressing prescribed boundaries between "affective desires and economic goals" (Shever 2012: 19). Similarly, Gilberthorpe (2013) shows how the technologies of CSR in the oil operations of Papua New Guinea serve to objectify social relations, "abstracting them from the rules of kinship ... and exchange that ensure social and economic security." In all cases, kinship, or kin-like relations, is shown to be a resource that is exploited by the technologies of corporate responsibility, yet leaves the targets of corporate policies weaker.

Finally, a growing field of interest extends attention beyond the enactment and assumptive logics of CSR to how workers and communities resist corporate modes of governance and control, whether contesting the coercive effects of corporate largesse or the disciplinary force of codes of conduct or corporate security apparatuses. Here, the empirical frailty of CSR's claim to mutuality and consent becomes apparent, as purported beneficiaries challenge the surveillance, authority and inequality wrought through CSR initiatives and thus refuse the inexorability of its logic (see for example, Blowfield and Dolan 2008; De Neve 2014; Ruwanpura 2013 and 2014; Sydow, this volume; Dolan and Rajak, forthcoming).

As the brief review of the literature above illuminates, while anthropological engagement with CSR has grown over the past decade, greater attention has been paid to the local impacts and outcomes of so-called ethical economies than to the actual corporate structures that produce them. With the exception of a handful of cases (Garsten and Jacobsson 2007; Welker 2009; Benson and Kirsch 2010; Rajak 2011a), corporations, and CSR in particular, thus form part of the backdrop, rather than the direct objects of study themselves.

Corporations emerge as synonymous with global capital—part of the structure rather than agents and actors themselves—while CSR is portrayed as a reified set of global structures, principles, or frameworks, rather than a constantly evolving range of practices that corporate actors deploy in pursuit of particular goals. The authors collected in this volume aim to redress the balance—subjecting corporations, corporate actors and their various constellations of partners and panoply of tools to ethnographic scrutiny. What unites the contributions in this volume is a particular focus on the corporation as direct arbiter of social and ethical goods. This role takes many forms: from claiming a duty of care over workers, to environmental stewardship, or asserting guardianship over a particular community. What is of particular interest to us is the power and authority that corporations accrue through their assumption of these roles. The key concern running through these chapters is, then, a question of power—a classic anthropological preoccupation focused here on the various ways in which corporate power is rendered, exercised, limited or resisted through the discourse and practice of CSR. Our aim in bringing these contributions together is, therefore, to highlight how CSR works as a functional resource for corporations, responding to a broad spectrum of challenges, contradictions and even crises produced by millennial capitalism.

Aims and scope of the volume

The chapters in this collection bring new perspectives to the diverse forms of ethical corporate capitalism, engaging how ethics are defined, authorized and performed across companies, commodities, and countries. Rajak opens the account by introducing the ritualized performance of CSR in what she terms "theatres of virtue," the cosmopolitan arenas in London in which dominant discourses of CSR are produced and authenticated as transnational corporations (TNCs) and which stake their claims to global corporate citizenship. Similarly, Kirsch interrogates another element in the production of corporate virtue: the particular power of "virtuous language" as a corporate asset. Moving from the sites of discursive construction to that of material production, Cross and De Neve explore the intersection of CSR and management regimes on the shop floors of diamond-polishing (Cross) and apparel (De Neve) factories in India, while Dolan and Johnstone-Louis describe how Avon's organizational practices repurpose "poor" women as the instruments of ethical capitalism in the "New South

Africa." Li and Hardin, exploring the seemingly incommensurable worlds of Chilean gold mining and wildlife conservation in the Congo Basin, draw our attention to a common theme: how regimes of power and vested interests mediate CSR's exercise of responsibility. Across various extractive sites (Newmont's mining concessions in Ghana and Peru, Chevron's gas fields in Bangladesh, and the Chad-Cameroon pipeline), Sydow, Gardner, and Muñoz and Burnham show how corporations deploy CSR in pursuit of local compliance, collaboration, and consent. In each case, however, CSR produces division and disconnection as much as, if not more than, cohesion and inclusion. Finally, Foster wraps up the collection by reflecting on the relationship between CSR, corporate personhood and authority by juxtaposing classic anthropological interest in the status and role of the Melanesian "Big Man" and the power of corporations. In all of these contexts, corporations are practicing CSR and deploying ethics in different ways and to different ends, from the mundane to the ritualistic and from the discursive to the material. Thus, we see how new ethical schemes are routinized in novel management practices as well as long-standing business models (Cross, Dolan, and Johnstone-Louis), how they are instrumentalized in response to particular local or global challenges (Cross, De Neve), and how they are marketed in cosmopolitan arenas to celebrate and naturalize corporate virtue (Rajak, Kirsch). Yet across these diverse sites certain continuities in the practice and discourse of CSR emerge, a set of common themes on which these contributions reflect.

First, the chapters attend to a broad empirical concern with how companies practice responsibility, exploring what people do when they engage with ethics in organizational contexts (Clegg, Kornberger, and Rhodes 2007). This emphasis on "ethics" as process foregrounds the "making" and "doing" of CSR in situated contexts, shifting the focus to how moral strategies are made, mobilized and diffused through specific material and discursive practices. Several chapters address the question of how these processes of corporate ethicizing and social responsibility mold the subjects they seek to transform: whether as Avon's army of empowered entrepreneurs (Dolan and Johnstone-Louis), or in the attempt to create a disciplined and "modern" workforce (Cross); as active participants in corporate processes of "stakeholder engagement" (Li) and local partnership (Gardner), or the right kind of NGO collaborators for corporations (Rajak, De Neve). The focus on how companies shape the targets of their ethical actions also points to another critical theme that runs through the collection. The CSR movement projects an inclusive vision of empowerment and social responsibility through corporate investment, partnership, and market mechanisms.[4] But in practice, as the chapters in this collection highlight, they often prove to be exclusive, privileging certain actors, agendas and interests while marginalizing others, despite a rhetorical, if not often institutional, commitment to principles of collaboration and participation. In fact, as the chapters illustrate, defining the boundaries of participation— that is, designating who is and who is not included in the moral fold of CSR—transforms not only the targets of CSR initiatives, but its agents. For example, Dolan and Johnstone-Louis show how Avon's empowerment initiatives require participants to embody the model of the successful entrepreneur. Similarly, the chapters by Gardner and Rajak illustrate that the performance of corporate-civil society partnership (the mainstay of good corporate citizenship) often demands that NGOs and communities conform to a hegemonic conception of the "perfect partner," one that accords with dominant corporate interests, norms, and ideologies.

A second, related concern running through the collection is the uneasy fusion between the spheres of affective ties and self-interested calculation that underlies the CSR mission to remoralize the economy. At one level, the discourse and practice of CSR draws on elements of morality and affection not usually associated with the workings of corporate capitalism, penetrating the technocratic world of mineral extraction or the supposedly pure free-market rationalism of the free-trade zone, and unsettling the accepted wisdom that such corporate spaces institutionalize asociality in its most detached form. Yet as Dolan and Johnstone-Louis' chapter shows, the intimate world of social attachments and moral obligations drives not only Avon's CSR agenda, but also its commercial success. From another vantage point, both Cross's and Gardner's chapters underline the productive work that distance, dissociation and detachment perform. Cross, for example, illuminates how diamond multinationals operate as much through disconnection as relationality, as companies are "constantly engaged in establishing the limits and endpoints to relationships in their supply chain" to sustain a foothold in global markets, whilst Gardner considers the ways detachment is constitutive of CSR itself—what she terms "disconnect development," as Chevron's "partnerships" with a small cadre of labor contractors works to exclude (often with inimical outcomes) the broader community. The tension between detachment and inclusion also informs Muñoz and Burnham's analysis of subcontracting in the Chad-Cameroon pipeline, where ExxonMobil sees its industry standards as both a technical way to smooth the functioning of modular supply chains as well as a gift to local subcontractors, who are skilled-up and professionalized through the effort of complying with them. As an ethic, detachment thus assumes both human and technical forms. On the one hand, we see how the global firm and CSR standards sustain non-binding attachments to suppliers, producers, and communities, circumscribing the boundaries of relationships in order to short-circuit obligation and dependence. CSR's claim to partnerships, stakeholder alliances and mutuality do not foreclose disconnection, but rather, as Gardner's chapter suggests, can serve as a cover for their power to disengage at any time; the back door is always open. On the other hand, in De Neve's study we witness how the contemporary modalities of ethical governance, such as standards, protocols, compacts, and auditing technologies described earlier, embody a derivative value, serving as a strategic resource through which firms deflect the risk of obligation and attachment "offshore" (Appel 2012), in effect detaching them from the sociality they purport to create.

Third, the eleven chapters engage collectively with questions concerning the interrelation of global discourse and local practice that constitutes corporate social responsibility. As a global ethical regime, the CSR movement appears as a marriage of "global" values and "local" practice, systematized in technical reporting frameworks and international corporate codes or compacts that claim to be simultaneously globally applicable and locally responsive. Yet the claim to global values is far from neutral, just as the technologies employed to embed these corporate ethics in practice are much more than just technical mechanisms. The discourse and practice of CSR attempts to standardize, categorize, measure and routinize different forms of value (economic, ethical, legal) in a supposedly "win-win" marriage of social and commercial objectives that works for all parties involved, even those with apparently conflicting interests, as the chapters in this collection show: for example, the community and the corporation (Gardner), environmental activists and mine engineers (Li), workers and managers (Cross), buyers and suppliers (De Neve), multinationals and subcontractors (Muñoz and Burnham), and a cosmetics firm and its door-to-door sellers (Dolan and Johnstone-Louis). As the collection reveals, this equation glosses over the tensions and disjunctures among the different ethical values and interests of actors drawn into the transnational networks of CSR. Companies do not simply extend universal ethics to operational localities. Rather, ethics take shape within the particularities of place as commercial imperatives, social relations, knowledge forms, and cultural meanings, to name but a few, come together to create different "ethical formations," or in Li's words new "logic[s] of equivalence" that arbitrate the conflicting values inherent in CSR. This demands that researchers examine different points, intersections and levels within these processes, tracing connections (and conflicts) between local micropolitics of corporate engagement and global movements of CSR. The chapters in this collection go some way to capturing these multiple scales, from the ritualized performance of corporate citizenship in London conference suites, to business strategy devised in corporate headquarters in London, Johannesburg, or Toronto; from the routines of the factory floor in an Indian diamond-polishing factory, the gas fields of Bangladesh, or a prospective Ghanaian gold mine, to the sales conventions of an "Avon Lady" selling door to door in Soweto.

Just as the production systems of most industries operate through globally diffused webs of subcontracting, so getting a grip on what CSR does in practice requires that we track it through a complex chain of interlocking contractors and partnerships from high street consumer brand names (Avon, De Beers, Coca Cola, Gap) and global mineral and energy giants (ExxonMobil, Chevron, Newmont, and Anglo), to the local contractors recruited to lay pipelines, the small supply firms contracted to manufacture garments, or even the individual front-line "entrepreneurs" enlisted to sell cosmetics door to door. A number of the chapters in this volume set out to do just that, training the ethnographic lens precisely onto those processes of subcontracting (Cross, De Neve, Muñoz and Burnham, and Dolan and Johnstone-Louis). They explore the role of CSR in lubricating and facilitating these relations—to shed light on what De Neve terms the politics of "ethical compliance." In the extended supply chains of the garment industry, De Neve shows us how codes of conduct, as artifacts of CSR, act not as we might expect as repositories of corporate ethics, but as conduits of power, providing Western clothing retailers with yet more leverage over their small, local suppliers. Here we see a similar set of processes at work in the diamond-polishing factories of India's special economic zone and in the construction of the Chad-Cameroon pipeline, which are the focus of the chapters by Cross and Muñoz and Burnham. They show us how, within the intricate chain of subcontracting, CSR serves to reinforce rather than challenge existing hierarchies, while affording companies a protective mechanism that paradoxically works to limit (rather than extend) their ethical liability and displace risk down the chain of contractors to those at the bottom. As the chapters by Cross, Gardner and Muñoz and Burnham underscore, while the "soft fuzzy language of CSR" (Gardner this volume) seems to invoke connectivity and collectivity, it in fact works to render the opposite effect: corporate detachment, displacing responsibility even as it is claimed by corporations. After all, it is no coincidence that the rise of CSR has paralleled the rise of rampant subcontracting across global industry.

Ultimately, each of the chapters reflects on the mystification CSR performs; how the discourses and practices of empowerment, partnership, mutuality and so forth sideline issues of power and profit. The chapters by De Neve, Kirsch, Sydow and Rajak probe CSR's depoliticizing effects—that is, how it sops critique by bathing the corporation in a virtuous hue that masks the pathologies of capitalism. While De Neve reveals the capacity of ethical audits to abstract labor from local politics, Sydow similarly highlights the "anti-political" effect of Newmont's community engagement and investment apparatus as a set of uniform technologies imposed to discipline diverse localities and social contexts to corporate agendas. As with Gardner's study of Chevron in Bangladesh, and Muñoz and Burnham's research on the Chad-Cameroon pipeline, Sydow reveals how, while the technologies of CSR and community investment serve to depoliticize corporate action in Ghana and Peru, CSR becomes implicated in particular kinds of state violence. But, as Sydow notes, this is not always the case. Her comparative analysis of Newmont Mining's CSR programs in Peru and Ghana reveals that CSR's capacity to suspend politics is contingent, implicated in local resistances and agency. In Rajak's chapter it is morality itself that acts as an "anti-politics machine," by reframing political concerns and conflicts as moral matters amenable to apparent acts of corporate virtue. The language and performance of corporate virtue are key concerns of both Kirsch and Rajak's contribution, which explore, in different ways, how the discourse of virtue acts as a vital corporate resource that can be adapted, instrumentalized and deployed to respond to external challenges and audiences. As these chapters stress, this language and performance of corporate virtue goes beyond rhetoric to endow corporations not with ethics, but with a source of power in relation to new social and political problems. The crucial point that these chapters collectively demonstrate is that the grammar of CSR does not operate at a merely rhetorical level, but is part of a deeper and broader set of tools (both at the level of discourse and practice) mobilized to respond to and absorb opposition, enabling them to survive and expand.

From the gas fields of Bangladesh to the mines of Papua New Guinea and the corporate boardrooms of London, the chapters by Kirsch, Gardner, Hardin and Rajak all variously demonstrate how the discourse of CSR affords corporations new currency to forge (or compel) collaboration from diverse corners, where previously we would have expected to find combatants, underlining the performativity of CSR language, as it enables corporations to shape the terms of development to their interests. In the so-called "global" arenas of CSR policymaking, Rajak shows how these alliances are forged between multinationals and international NGOs. This is reinforced by Hardin's analysis, which reveals similar, surprising alliances between conservationists and corporations, while Gardner highlights the capacity of "partnership" discourse to claim collaborators of local leaders. Finally, it is the academy itself where Kirsch shows CSR to have gained traction to the extent that universities and mining companies claim to speak the same language. The discursive effect of these appeals to and performances of partnership is evident in the ethnographies collected here, compelling consent and marginalizing dissent, or, as Gardner puts it, "'partnership' does not merely look good for global shareholders, it creates compliance" (this volume) while, as the chapter by Rajak shows, helping them to gain entry into new spheres of policymaking. Strategically deployed buzzwords—partnership, sustainability, consensus—give the impression that these diverse groups with divergent values and interests, as Kirsch notes, "suddenly seem to be speaking the same language" (this volume). Indeed, as the contributions to this volume show, the power of CSR often lies precisely in its capacity to invoke ethics as a source of corporate legitimacy in a great variety of geographical and political-economic contexts, as well as across the full spectrum of industries. This is highlighted by Sydow, who uses a comparative approach to reveal the striking uniformity in the techniques deployed by Newmont in the radically different settings of an old mine in Peru and a prospective greenfield operation in Ghana. Yet, as well as Gardner, and Muñoz and Burnham show, there are limits to the power of this corporate apparatus. Their ethnographic evidence from the Chevron gas fields, Newmont mines and Chad-Cameroon pipeline reveals disjuncture, disconnection and even dissent beneath the claims to partnership.

As a whole, however, the ethnographic encounters that unfold across the various sites of inquiry in the book demonstrate the powerful ways CSR simultaneously sanitizes and fuels the production of capital. Whether through "empowering" Avon's door-to-door sellers (Dolan), offering employment to disenfranchised Bangladeshis (Gardner), or skilling up local enterprise in Cameroon (Muñoz and Burnham), the locus of benefit remains skewed in the interest of capital. CSR may, to quote Gardner, extend the "corporation a pass into Development World," but the seductions of that world still pale against the imperatives of the market.

In her contribution to this collection, Fabiana Li quotes a mine engineer remarking that "few people get to see the 'the complete picture.'" This is of course equally true of the anthropologists who attempt to capture these new ethical forms within corporations, constituted as they are by multiple social relations and transnational economic processes connecting centers at diverse points on the globe. But, while the full picture is always unattainable, this collection contributes to building a fuller understanding of the shifting, ambiguous and dynamic field of CSR and the constellation of actors, interests and agendas that are drawn into or become subject to new forms of corporate ethicizing.

Acknowledgments

The authors thank Luisa Steur and two anonymous reviewers for their advice in the writing of this chapter.

Notes

1. See, e.g., Hopkins 2007; McIntosh, Murphy, and Shah 2003; and Zadek 2001.
2. See also De Neve et al. 2008 and Garsten and Hernes 2009 for anthropological critiques of CSR discourse and practice.
3. The chapters in this book were originally prepared for the panel "Ethnographies of corporate ethicizing" organized for the Canadian Anthropological Society and American Ethnological Society Conference in Vancouver, British Columbia in May 2009.
4. Cf. the forum on De Soto's *Mysteries of capital* in *Focaal* 41: 179–201.

References

Appel, Hannah. 2012. Offshore work: Oil, modularity, and the how of capitalism in Equatorial Guinea. *American Ethnologist* 39(4): 692–709.

Barrientos, Stephanie, and Catherine Dolan, eds. 2006. *Ethical sourcing in the global food system*. London: Earthscan.

Benson, Peter. 2012. *Tobacco capitalism: Growers, migrant workers, and the changing face of global industry*. Princeton: Princeton University Press.

Benson, Peter, and Stuart Kirsch, eds. 2010. Corporate oxymorons: Entry points into the ethnography of capitalism. *Dialectical Anthropology* 34(1): 45–48.

Berlan, Amanda, and Catherine Dolan. 2014. Of red herrings and immutabilities: Rethinking fair trade's ethic of relationality among cocoa producers. In M. Goodman and C. Sage, eds., *Food transgressions: Making sense of contemporary food politics*, pp. 39–60. Aldershot, UK: Ashgate.

Blowfield, Michael, and Catherine Dolan. 2008. Stewards of virtue? The ethical dilemma of CSR in African agriculture. *Development and Change* 39(1): 1–23.

Blowfield, Michael, and Catherine Dolan. 2014. Bottom billion capitalism: The possibility and improbability of business as development actor. *Third World Quarterly* 35(1): 22–42.

Blowfield, Michael, and Jedrzej George Frynas. 2005. Setting new agendas: Critical perspectives on corporate social responsibility in the developing world. *International Affairs* 81: 515–524.

Brockington, Daniel. 2014. The production and construction of celebrity advocacy in international development. *Third World Quarterly* 35(1): 88–108.

Carrier, James, and Peter Luetchford, eds. 2012. *Ethical Consumption: Social value and economic practice*. Oxford: Berghahn.

Carroll, Archie B. 2008. A history of corporate social responsibility: Concepts and practices. In A Crane, A. McWilliams, D. Matten, J. Moon, and D. Siegel, eds., *The Oxford handbook of CSR*, pp. 19–46. Oxford University Press.

Clegg, Stewart, Martin Kornberger, and Carl Rhodes. 2007. Business ethics as practice. *British Journal of Management* 18(2):107–122.

Craig, David, and Doug Porter. 2006. *Development beyond neoliberalism: Governance, poverty reduction and political economy*. London & New York: Routledge.

Cross, Jamie. 2011. Detachment as a corporate ethic: Materializing CSR in the diamond supply chain. *Focaal: Journal of Global and Historical Anthropology* 60: 34–46.

Cross, Jamie. 2013. The 100th object: Solar lighting technology and humanitarian goods. *Journal of Material Culture* 18(4): 367–387.

Cross, Jamie. 2014. The coming of the corporate gift. *Theory, Culture, Society* 31: 121–145.

Cross, Jamie, and Alice Street. 2009. Anthropology at the bottom of the pyramid. *Anthropology Today* 25(4): 4–9.

De Neve, Geert. 2009. Power, inequality and corporate social responsibility: The politics of ethical compliance in the South Indian garment industry. *Economic and Political Weekly* 44(22): 63–72.

De Neve, Geert. 2014. Fordism, flexible specialisation and CSR: How Indian garment workers critique neoliberal labour regimes. *Ethnography* 15(2): 184–207.

De Neve, Geert, Peter Luetchford, Jeff Pratt, and Donald Wood, eds. 2008. *Research in economic anthropology: Hidden hands in the market: Ethnographies of fair trade, ethical consumption and corporate social responsibility*, p. 28. Bingley: Emerald Group.

Dolan, Catherine. 2009. Virtue at the checkout till: Salvation economics in Kenyan flower fields. In K. Browne and L. Milgram, eds., *Economics and morality: Anthropological approaches*, pp. 167–185. Lanham, MD: Altamira Press.

Dolan, Catherine. 2010. Virtual moralities: The mainstreaming of fairtrade in Kenyan tea fields. *Geoforum* 41(1): 33–43.

Dolan, Catherine. 2011. Branding morality. In M. Warrier, ed., *The politics of fairtrade*, pp. 37–52. London: Routledge.

Dolan, Catherine, and Dinah Rajak. Forthcoming. Remaking Africa's informal economies: Youth, entrepreneurship and the promise of inclusion at the bottom of the pyramid. *Journal of Development Studies*.

Dolan, Catherine, and Kate Roll. 2013. Capital's new frontier: From "unusable" economies to bottom-of-the-pyramid markets in Africa. *African Studies Review* 56(3): 123–146.

Dolan, Catherine, and Linda Scott. 2009. Lipstick evangelism: Avon trading circles and gender empowerment in South Africa. *Gender and Development* 17(2): 203–218.

Dunn, Elizabeth. 2005. Standards and person making in East Central Europe. In A. Ong and S. Collier, eds., *Global assemblages: Technology, politics, and ethics as anthropological problems*, pp. 173–193. London: Blackwell.

Ecks, Stefan. 2008. Global pharmaceutical markets and corporate citizenship: The case of Novartis' anti-cancer drug Glivec. *Biosocieties* 3: 165–181.

Elyachar, Julia. 2002. Empowerment money: The World Bank, non-governmental organizations, and the value of culture in Egypt. *Public Culture* 14(30): 493–513.

Elyachar, Julia. 2005. *Markets of dispossession: NGOs, economic development, and the state in Cairo*. Durham: Duke University Press.

Elyachar, Julia. 2012. Next practices: Knowledge, infrastructure, and public goods at the bottom of the pyramid. *Public Culture* 24(1): 109–129.

Ferguson, James. 1994 [1990]. *The anti-politics machine: "Development," depoliticisation and bureaucratic power in Lesotho*. Minneapolis: University of Minnesota Press.

Foster, Robert. 2008. *Coca-globalization: Following soft drinks from New York to New Guinea*. New York: Palgrave Macmillan.

Foster, Robert. 2014. Corporations as partners: "Connected capitalism" and the Coca-Cola Company. *PoLaR* forthcoming.

Freidberg, Susanne. 2007. Supermarkets and imperial knowledge. *Cultural Geographies* 14(3): 321–342.

Gardner, Katy. 2012. *Discordant development: Global capitalism and the struggle for connection in Bangladesh*. London: Pluto Press.

Garsten, Christina, and Tor Hernes. 2009. Beyond CSR: Dilemmas and paradoxes of ethical conduct in transnational organizations. In K. Browne and L. Milgram, eds., *Economics and morality: Anthropological approaches*, pp. 189–210. Lanham, MD: Altamira Press.

Garsten, Christina, and Kerstin Jacobsson. 2007. Corporate globalization, civil society and postpolitical regulation: Whither democracy? *Development Dialogue* 49:143–158.

Gilberthorpe, Emma. 2013. In the shadow of industry: A study of culturization in Papua New Guinea. *Journal of the Royal Anthropological Institute* 19: 261–278.

Goodman, Michael, David Goodman, and Michael Redclift. 2010. Introduction: Situating consumption, space and place. In M. Goodman, D. Goodman, and M. Redclift, eds., *Consuming space: Placing consumption in perspective*, pp. 3–40. Aldershot: Ashgate.

Gond, Jean-Pascal, and Jeremy Moon. 2011. Corporate social responsibility in retrospect and prospect: Exploring the life-cycle of an essentially contested concept. Discussion paper 59–2011. Nottingham: International Centre for Corporate Social Responsibility.

Hopkins, Michael. 2007. *Corporate social responsibility and international development: Is Business the solution?* London: Earthscan.

Jaffee, Daniel. 2007. *Brewing justice: Fair trade coffee, sustainability, and survival*. Berkeley, CA: University of California Press.

Jenkins, Rhys. 2005. Globalization, corporate social responsibility and poverty. *International Affairs* 81(3): 525–540.

Jones, Marc T. 1996. Missing the forest for the trees: A critique of social responsibility concept and discourse. *Business and Society* 35(1): 7–41.

Jones, Bryn. 2007. Citizens, partners or patrons? Corporate power and patronage capitalism. *Journal of Civil Society* 3(2): 159–177.

Kirsch, S. 2006. *Reverse anthropology: Indigenous analysis of social and environmental relations in New Guinea*. Palo Alto, CA: Stanford University Press.

Kirsch, Stuart. 2010. Sustainable mining. *Dialectical Anthropology* 34: 87–93.

Kirsch, Stuart. 2014a. *Mining capitalism*. Berkley, CA: University of California Press.

Kirsch, Stuart. 2014b. Imagining the corporate person. *PoLaR* 37(2): 207–217.

Kirsch, Stuart, and Peter Benson, eds. 2014. Special section of *PoLaR* on corporate personhood. *PoLaR* 37(2).

Kolk, Ans, Miguel Rivera-Santos, and Carlos Rufín. 2014. Reviewing a decade of research on the "base/bottom of the pyramid" (BOP) concept. *Business & Society* 53(3): 338–377.

Latour, Bruno. 1987. *Science in action: How to follow scientists and engineers through society*. Cambridge, MA: Harvard University Press.

Li, Fabiana. 2010. From corporate accountability to shared responsibility: Dealing with pollution in a Peruvian smelter-town. In Ravi Raman, ed., *Corporate social responsibility: Discourses, practices, perspectives*. London: Palgrave Macmillan.

Lyon, Sarah, and Mark Moberg, eds. 2010. *Fair trade and social justice*. New York University Press.

McIntosh, Malcolm, David F. Murphy, and Rupesh A. Shah. 2003. *Something to believe in: Creating hope and trust in organisations: Stories of transparency, accountability and governance*. Sheffield: Greenleaf Publishing.

Mauss, Marcel. 1990. *The gift: The form and reason for exchange in archaic societies*. New York; London: W. W. Norton.

Miller, Daniel. 1998. Conclusion: A theory of virtualism. In J. G. Carrier and D. Miller, eds., *Virtualism: A new political economy*. Oxford: Berg.

Moeller, Kathryn. 2013. Proving the girl effect: Corporate knowledge production and educational intervention. *International Journal of Educational Development* 33(6).

Mutersbaugh, Tad. 2005. Just-in-space: Certified rural products, labor of quality, and regulatory spaces. *Journal of Rural Studies* 21(4): 389–402.

Ong, Aihwa, and Stephen Collier. 2005. *Global assemblages: Technology, politics, and ethics as anthropological problems*. London: Blackwell.

Poovey, Mary. 2008. *Genres of the credit economy: Mediating value in eighteenth and nineteenth-century Britain*. Chicago: University of Chicago.

Power, Michael. 1997. *The audit explosion*. London: Demos.

Prahalad, Coimbatore Krishnarao. 2005. *The fortune at the bottom of the pyramid: Eradicating poverty through profits*. Upper Saddle River, NJ: Wharton School Publishing.

Rajak, Dinah. 2009. I am the conscience of the company: Responsibility and the gift in a transnational mining corporation. In K. Brown and L. Milgram, eds., *Economics and morality: Anthropological approaches*, pp. 211–232. Lanham, MD: AltaMira Press.

Rajak, Dinah. 2010. HIV/Aids is our business: The moral economy of treatment in a transnational mining company. *JRAI* 16: 551–571.

Rajak, Dinah. 2011a. *In good company: An anatomy of corporate social responsibility*. Stanford: Stanford University Press.

Rajak, Dinah. 2011b. Theatres of virtue: Collaboration, consensus and the social life of corporate social responsibility. *Focaal: Journal of Global and Historical Anthropology* 60 (summer): 9–20.

Rajak, Dinah. 2014. Corporate memory: Historical revisionism, legitimation and the invention of tradition in a multinational mining company. *PoLaR* 37(2): 259–280.

Rankin, Katherine. 2001. Governing development: Neoliberalism, microcredit, and rational economic woman. *Economy and Society* 30 (1): 18–37

Raynolds, Laura. 2009. Mainstreaming fair trade coffee: From partnership to traceability. *World Development* 37(6): 1083–1093.

Redfield, Peter. 2013. *Life in crisis: The ethical journey of doctors without borders.* Berkeley: University of California Press.

Richey, Lisa Ann, and Stefano Ponte. 2011. *Brand aid: Shopping well to save the world.* Minneapolis: University of Minnesota Press.

Roy, Ananya. 2010. *Poverty capital: Microfinance and the making of development.* London: Taylor and Francis.

Roy, Ananya. 2012. Ethical subjects: Market rule in the age of poverty. *Public Culture* 24(1): 105–108.

Ruwanpura, Kanchana N. 2013. Scripted performances? Local readings of "global" health and safety standards (the apparel sector in Sri Lanka). *Global Labour Journal* 4(2): 88–108.

Ruwanpura, Kanchana N. 2014. The weakest link? Unions, freedom of association and ethical codes: A case study from a factory setting in Sri Lanka. *Ethnography* 16(1): 118–141.

Sawyer, Suzana. 2004. *Crude chronicles: Indigenous politics, multinational oil and neoliberalism in Ecuador.* Durham, NC: Duke University Press.

Sawyer, Suzana. 2006. Disabling corporate sovereignty in a transnational lawsuit. *Political and Legal Anthropology Review* 29(1): 23–43.

Schmelzer, Matthias. 2007. Fair trade – in or against the market? *Institute of Social Threefold,* http://www.threefolding.org/essays/2007-01-001.html

Shamir, Ronen. 2004. The de-radicalization of corporate social responsibility. *Critical Sociology* 30(3): 669–689.

Sharp, John. 2006. Corporate social responsibility and development: An anthropological perspective. *Development Southern Africa* 23(2): 213–222.

Shever, Elana. 2008. Neoliberal associations: Property, company and family in the Argentine oil fields. *American Ethnologist* 35(4): 701–716.

Shever, Elana. 2010. Engendering the company: Corporate personhood and the "face" of an oil company in metropolitan Buenos Aires. *PoLAR: Political and Legal Anthropology Review* 33(1): 26–46.

Strathern, Marilyn. 1999. *Property, substance and effect: Anthropological essays on persons and things.* London: Athlone Press.

Strathern, Marilyn. 2000. *Audit cultures: Anthropological studies in accountability, ethics and the academy.* London: Routledge.

Thrift, Nigel. 2005 [1997]. *Knowing capitalism.* London: Sage.

Tsing, Anna. 2000. Inside the economy of appearances. *Public Culture* 12(1): 115–144.

Welker, Marina. 2009. "Corporate security begins in the community": Mining, the corporate responsibility industry and environmental advocacy in Indonesia. *Cultural Anthropology* 24(1): 142–179.

Welker, Marina. nd. Notes on the difficulty of studying the corporation, http://www.law.seattleu.edu/Documents/berle-center/Welker.pdf

Welker, Marina. 2014. *Enacting the corporation: An American mining firm in post-authoritarian Indonesia.* Berkeley: University of California Press.

Welker, Marina, Damani Patridge, and Rebecca Hardin, eds. 2011. Corporate lives: New perspectives on the social life of the corporate form. *Current Anthropology* 52(S3): S3–S16.

Welker, Marina, and Donald Wood. 2011. Shareholder activism and alienation. *Current Anthropology* 52(S3): S57–S69.

Weszkalnys, Gisa. 2014. Anticipating oil: The temporal politics of a disaster yet to come. *The Sociological Review* 62(S1): 211–235.

World Business Council for Sustainable Development (WBCSD). 2005. *Business solutions in support of the millennium development goals,* http://www.wbcsd.org/web/publications/biz4dev.pdf

Yanagisako, Sylvia. 2002. *Producing culture and capital: Family firms in Italy.* Princeton: Princeton University Press.

Zadek, Simon. 2001. *The civil corporation: The new economy of corporate citizenship*. London: Earthscan.

Catherine Dolan is on the faculty of anthropology at SOAS, University of London, and holds fellowships at the James Martin Institute, Green Templeton College and Said Business School, all at University of Oxford. Her research centers on contemporary forms of moral capitalism, including Fairtrade, inclusive development and bottom of the pyramid business in Africa. She is a co-founder of the Centre for New Economies of Development (www.responsiblebop.com).

Dinah Rajak is a senior lecturer in Anthropology and International Development at the University of Sussex. She is the author of *In good company: An anatomy of corporate social responsibility* (Stanford University Press, 2011) and the co-founder of the Centre for New Economies of Development (www.responsiblebop.com).

– Chapter 1 –

THEATRES OF VIRTUE

Collaboration, Consensus, and the Social Life of Corporate Social Responsibility

Dinah Rajak

Who better than Coca-Cola, a firm with a better distribution network in sub-Saharan Africa than any aid agency, to get materials out to needy populations? ... Exhortation not regulation!

> —David Cameron, British Prime Minister (then Conservative Party Leader), Annual Business in the Community Conference, 9 May 2006.

In the past decade, transnational corporations have become increasingly important players on the landscape of international development, under the banner of corporate social responsibility (CSR)—a movement promising to harness the *global* reach and resources of corpo-rations in the service of *local* development and social improvement. This movement projects corporations not only as self-disciplining moral actors, but as leaders in a new orthodoxy of business-led development which promises empowerment through "the market." The primacy of the market as the panacea for poverty has been proclaimed by leaders of transnational corporations and multilateral development institutions alike, encapsulated in Kofi Annan's statement at the launch of the Global Compact between business and civil society: "Let us choose to unite the power of markets with the authority of universal ideals. Let us choose to reconcile the creative forces of private entrepreneurship with the needs of the disadvantaged" (World Economic Forum, Davos 1999). The powerful populism of the "Make poverty history" campaign, which captured the imagination of celebrities and school children across the UK, has been respun to reflect the prominence of business in this mission with the catchy, yet perhaps unintentionally ambivalent message: "Make poverty business" (Wilson and Wilson 2006: 1). Meanwhile the United Nations Development Programme reminds readers of the *Financial Times* that "the poor need business to invest in their future. Business needs the poor because they are the future" (14 September 2005). Drawing on idioms of emancipation through the market, CSR has thus demonstrated an apparent capacity to unite disparate actors (and former combatants), creating coalitions between unexpected partners eager to realise this union of global markets and universal ideals.

This exuberance in the public arena has been matched (and reinforced) within much of the academic literature, with scholars heralding CSR as nothing less than the dawn of a new era of development in which global corporations transcend the pitfalls of state-led development: "Never before has a partnership been created between the highest levels of the UN, business, NGOs and labour representatives.... The stakes are high ... the potential gains are immense" (Zadek 2001: 102).

Frequently the subject of panegyric or polemic but less often critical analysis, the normative preoccupation with whether CSR is a force for good or a cynical corporate ploy obscures the discursive capacity of CSR to reshape development agendas according to corporate values and interests. However, in the past couple of years, anthropologists have begun to reveal the effects of these corporate social initiatives in diverse contexts around the world (see, e.g., Benson and Kirsch 2009; De Neve 2008; Shever 2010). They have done so primarily from the perspective of the intended targets, rather than the architects of these ethical regimes on which this article focuses.

One theme emerges most strongly from the literature on CSR, whether from insiders or analysts, advocates or critics: that CSR is a truly *global* phenomenon, exercised through supranational networks of ethical governance (see, e.g. Garsten and Jacobsson 2007; Shamir 2008). Norms and standards thus appear as components of a global moral regime. But this preoccupation with the global dimension of CSR—whether as an instrument of social improvement worldwide or a tool of global governmentality—has resulted in an analysis of CSR disembedded from its social practice. We are left asking, how is this new orthodoxy of compassionate corporate capitalism forged? And what actors and interests work (directly or indirectly) toward sustaining, reinforcing, and extending its power?

The purpose of this article is to shed light on these processes, and in particular the ritualized and performative dynamics of CSR, which

I argue are crucial to establishing it as development orthodoxy. These rituals are elements in the construction of narratives that structure the processes of the CSR world. As Bloch (1992) argues, ritual can serve to constrain contestation while inviting participants to share in and thus validate a particular world view. Put another way, they compel consensus while mystifying the dynamics of power at work. Rituals of corporate morality thus play an important role in generating particular ways of seeing and understanding on the part of people involved in the CSR industry and, I argue, should be seen as a new and significant dimension of corporate power.

The article is based on fieldwork tracking the performance of CSR through the circuit of conventions, policy forums, and award ceremonies that constitute the elite "global" arena of corporate citizenship, or put another way the "social life" of CSR. For it is here that we begin to disentangle the agency of various actors—from captains of industry to representatives of the "grass roots," from business schools to UN agencies—involved in the production of this powerful discourse; and we begin to see how the shift from agonistic to collaborative, from conflictual to consensual is achieved. Within these arenas corporate executives come together with representatives of global NGOs, the growing army of CSR consultants, and dozens of small firms or nonprofits (the boundary between which is often blurred). Participants extol the virtues of bi-, tri- or multisector partnerships, develop standards, and present case studies recounting their engagement with the local communities who represent the targets of their ethical behaviour. Such gatherings unfold as highly ritualistic theatres of virtue, in which awards for the best corporate citizen are presented and inspiring stories of social responsibility are told. Here, a moral register of compassionate capitalism summons the ghosts of Rowntree and Cadbury, and the paternalistic philanthropy of Victorian industrialists. Yet at the same time, commitment to the supposed amorality of market rationality is claimed through the language of "the business case for CSR," "enlightened self-interest," and not least "the fortune at the bottom of the pyramid."

The ethnographic focus of this article is London—global financial capital, home to some of the world's largest multinationals, and central hub of the booming CSR industry. As in cities worldwide, one is continuously met with testaments to corporate citizenship. The rhetoric of sustainable development is emblazoned on bus stops advertising BP (newly incarnated as "*Beyond* Petroleum"). Standard Bank promises to "bank the unbanked" across Africa. And even BAE

Systems (the world's second biggest defense contractor) advertises its social responsibility on the London underground beneath the slogan "making the world a safer place."[1] Thus a senior economist and CSR advisor for the OECD's CSR unit remarked: "I have always viewed London as being the CSR capital of the world.... [T]he London CSR community has done a great service to the world, getting governments, business, and NGOs to work together."

The exhortation to "partnership" is of course nothing new in the development industry. Nor is the power of the partnership paradigm to assert equality and consensus where in fact inequality and difference reign, as anthropologists of development have shown. In the case of CSR, however, the concept of partnership has demonstrated even broader appeal, and greater discursive power, in its capacity to unite parties in an apparently shared enterprise, proclaiming a collaborative venture for a collective goal of sustainable development and elevating "the global market" as the fundamental mechanism through which this can be achieved. For as CSR recruits support from distant corners it asserts a global, national, and indeed local alliance between business and society, and thus a congruence of values between the logic of maximization and the moral imperatives of development.

Theatres of virtue

In October 2005, senior executives from a number of the world's biggest corporations (including Shell and Coca-Cola) came together with numerous consultants in search of contracts, and with NGO representatives (those willing or able to pay the £695 conference fee) at the Regent's Park Marriott Hotel in London for a convention hosted by Ethical Corporation on "The New Role of Business in Development." "The real reason for being in business is to create wealth," the poster headline announced, "so is it good business to join the fight against poverty?" As if in response, the conference was opened by the director of the Shell Foundation, Kurt Hoffman, who asserted the new orthodoxy of a business-led development agenda:

> The challenge in 2005 is not to restate the problems but to apply *business thinking* and come up with solutions.... So Tony Blair's Africa Commission— which has placed a welcome emphasis on the role of the private sector—needs to push the pro-poor enterprise agenda even further.

The underlying theme of Hoffman's speech was the failure of development led by a parochial state sector burdened with a moral mission to uplift—the modern day legacy of, as he put it, "the white man's burden." The solution, according to Hoffman, is to be found in the world of big business, where technocratic efficiency comes together with competitive creativity, driven by the limitless power of the market. "Let us choose to unite the power of markets...," he proclaimed, quoting Kofi Annan.

The next speaker on the conference bill, a representative from the World Business Council for Sustainable Development, echoed this economistic formula: poverty eradication through access to expanding markets, and profit generation through the vast reserve of untapped customers and aspirant entrepreneurs in developing countries:

> What's the point in expanding markets? The market creates opportunities. *When you're cut out of the market, you're cut out of the social system,* you're not empowered.... One unique contribution that business provides is enterprise— enterprising ways out of poverty, this isn't about doing good, it's about providing environments for enterprise.

According to this equation the market comes to stand for the social system as a whole. Questions concerning the inequitable distribution of wealth vanish, as poverty is recast within this depoliticised framework as due simply to a lack of market opportunities.

Implicit within this vision of empowerment is an ideal (entrepreneurial) actor who can respond to the moral exhortation "to help oneself" to a piece of the global market by embracing the opportunities provided by expanding business (Dolan, this volume). However, the promise of CSR goes far beyond the apparent benefits of foreign direct investment and market growth. As David Cameron's statement quoted above exemplifies, corporations are now urged to engage wholeheartedly with the developmental needs and goals of the countries and communities in which they operate, helping to build stable affluent societies with the aim of establishing the conditions for further investment.

Speaker after speaker echoed the same refrain of doing good business to do good, attended by compelling promises of "collective responsibility" and "win-win solutions," or as the representative from the OECD put it: "making profits and protecting our planet!" Positioned at the centre of the capitalist global market, corporations are seen to be perfectly placed not only to implement this agenda but to lead it. This was encapsulated by the director of the Partnering Initiative at the International Business Leaders Forum: "business knows how to operate in certain parts of the world better than development agencies.... [W]e should follow them into Africa...."

This conference was just one in an annual cycle of events, from large-scale conferences such as "Climate change: how to get your message across to consumers" (March 2007) to one-day master classes on stakeholder engagement, hosted by the likes of Ethical Corporation and Business in the Community (BITC), organizations which are part NGO, part CSR consultancy. These events generally take place in top London hotels, at which participants are treated to "business-leaders' breakfasts" and glossy leather-bound conference packs. Common are joint panel presentations by the CSR executive of a multinational enterprise and the representative from a partner NGO, offering "lessons learned" from their shared experience. Such conventions commonly include practical learning forums or training seminars on ethical and social technologies, such as scenario planning or social-impact assessment, that contribute to an ethos of technocratic rationalism. Yet these are combined with "celebrity" speeches by the chairmen of global corporations, government ministers, or aspiring future leaders hoping to attach their names to the optimistic promise of CSR. This was manifest at the convention launching the 2006 BITC Index, which opened with David Cameron's promising a Conservative rule which offered a "lighter regulatory touch" to companies that demonstrate social responsibility; a bid, in his words, "to reclaim corporate responsibility for the political centre-right." Meanwhile the UK government-funded "Beyond CSR?" event held at the National Liberal Club kicked off with a debate between Labour MP and former head of the UK Department for International Development (DFID) Clare Short and Conservative MP and former cabinet minister John Redwood (22 May 2006). But what had been billed as a political debate turned quickly into vocal affirmations of mutual agreement, exemplifying the apparent ability of CSR to replace political partisanship with a competition for who can proclaim collective responsibility the loudest.

Certain events in the CSR calendar are devoted to generating particular products such as codes of conduct, accountability frameworks, and indices. A high point is the launch of BITC's annual CR index, "the UK's leading benchmark of responsible business" (BITC 2006: 4) on which companies vie for top spot. Companies submit detailed reports on their CSR activities to be ranked according to a set of complicated metrics. Each year BITC packs the Millennium Hotel in Knightsbridge with over 400 executives and CSR managers of some of Europe's largest companies for the launch of its index. Yet here the managerial model offered by the Index, as a tool for measuring corporate responsibility, is underpinned by an ethos of zealous moral endeavour. The event unfolds as a highly orchestrated theatre of virtue, with all the ritualised trappings of a speech by the Prince of Wales piped in on video link and awards presented to the companies ranking top of the index, backed by a soundtrack of uplifting music. The presentation of awards is followed by lofty speeches promising to achieve even greater heights of CSR and thanking "the public" for such recognition. Within these arenas, performers take on the mantle of "integrity warriors," demonstrating their commitment to "funding virtue" for the collective good (Sampson 2005: 114).

As companies strive for recognition as the best corporate citizen, awards become a marker of success in this competitive market of social responsibility. While executives stress that "CSR is not about winning awards," the symbolic value of such prizes is significant. Presented by organizations that are seen to represent common societal values or the "voice of the community," and at the same time the result of rigorous metrics, awards act as symbolic proof authenticating the companies' moral claims as agents of social improvement. Thus awards come to symbolize a kind of reciprocal gratitude in return for the benefits provided through the companies' moral endeavors, so unsettling the economistic register of "social investment" and "enlightened self-interest" with the social rituals of gift-giving.

Yet of course such events are not only highly ritualized, they are exclusive. While the rhetoric is one of societal consensus and inclusion, the reality of such gatherings is that only those who are invited by the organizers or those who can afford the prohibitively high admission fee can attend. As Sampson (2005: 114) writes of the Tenth Anti-Corruption Conference, "Underlining the importance of this event were the access conditions: the participation fee for the three days was no less than US$890.... So much for the grassroots element." Likewise the CSR conventions where you would expect to pay a minimum of GBP 895, or as much as GBP 2000 for a two-day function. In this way the CSR industry often excludes from its discussions all but representatives from very well resourced corporations or international bodies. The appearance of consensus between participants, and the allegiance to the shared goals of development through business, is produced by the exclusion of groups with alternative visions, conflicting agendas, or simply smaller budgets. Actors with fewer resources, who tell a different story to that of the common interests that the CSR movement strives to project, are thus marginalized from this hegemonic mainstream.

This was starkly demonstrated at the 2004 Business and Human Rights event entitled "Spheres of influence: Understanding human rights in business" (London, 9 December 2004). Tickets for the one-day conference, which was chaired by Mary Robinson (former president of Ireland and U.N. High Commissioner for Human Rights) cost GBP 400. The conference began with a presentation by the Deputy Chairman of Barclays Bank. He stressed the need for global financial institutions to safeguard human rights through rigorous "stakeholder engagement," and to ensure the "free, prior, and informed consent" of "local communities" before financing large-scale projects such as dams and pipelines. However, the event did not run as smoothly as usual. Outside, representatives from "local communities" in Thailand and India that had been adversely affected by the Trans-Thai-Malaysia Pipeline and a number of big dams—projects financed by Barclays Bank—had flown to London and demanded entry to the conference and a platform from which to put "their side of the story" to the audience.[2] While conference security personnel kept the "gate-crashers" in the lobby (for they had no tickets), executives of transnational corporate giants, along with speakers from Amnesty International and the World Bank, passed by and took their places on the podium. Finally, after much delay, a message came from Mary Robinson that the unexpected guests should be invited into the auditorium and given an opportunity to speak. There was a palpable sense of surprise among the whispering audience as the representatives from Thailand explained that the claims to "free, prior, and informed consent" were fraudulent, and that they were being forcibly removed from their land by government security forces to make way for the pipeline. A representative from BITC turned to me and remarked: "I go to these functions all the time, and I've never seen anything like this! I'm amazed they were given a platform to speak. I wonder what the man from Barclays is going to say now."

Few questions followed the accounts of houses bulldozed and villages relocated. The rest of the conference got under way according to the program as if little had happened. The conference report contains only a very short paragraph briefly mentioning that "representatives on behalf of communities adversely affected by the activities of companies were also given the opportunity to address delegates." The report makes no mention of the fact that this was an unscheduled and uninvited addition to the conference. On the contrary, this addition is recorded as if it had been a planned part of the program. So rather than disrupting the positive ethos of corporate responsibility which the function generated, it serves to create the illusion of an arena characterized by transparency and pluralism.

From combat to collaboration

Corporate social responsibility, it's the badge of honor these days.... [N]obody sensible would say it was a bad thing, how could it be a bad thing?
— James Naughtie, *Radio 4 Today*, 15 January 2007.

The title of the Nineteenth World Trader's Tacitus Lecture, delivered by Mark Moody-Stuart, former Chairman of Shell and Anglo American and figurehead of the CSR movement, was "Business and NGOs in sustainable development—*Common cause or endless wars*?" "Can the two work together to *solve* major sustainable development issues such as climate change?" he asked (Moody-Stuart 2006: 23). It appears that "common cause" is winning out over "endless wars." CSR may initially have arisen from a concern in the public domain about overweening corporate power, born out of a call for companies to become more accountable for their activities. But the CSR movement has been so fully embraced by the big multinationals that it has effected a seamless shift from calls to "do no harm" to an expression of companies as active agents of global improvement, bringing in its wake rapprochement and even a wholehearted marriage between NGOs and big business; a shift viewed by many as rooted in a widespread disillusionment with the failure of governments to regulate corporate behavior, as a result of which NGOs saw a greater possibility for change by, as Doane puts it (2005: 24), "partnering with the enemy." Thus an increasing number of NGOs, such as Oxfam and the World Wide Fund for Nature (WWF), have begun partnering with or advising companies on best practice models for corporate responsibility.

The capacity of CSR to turn former combatants into collaborators was evident at the 2002 World Summit on Sustainable Development in Johannesburg. Even the extractive industries—once seen as the pariahs of capitalism—were congratulated for their leadership on global issues such as HIV and poverty. "One might have expected the mining industry to be the whipping boy of the summit," an executive of a mining multinational told me, "but instead, we actually got a special plug for addressing these issues." Dorsey (2005: 46) argues that the same goes for the environmental agenda: "Since [the] World Summit … championed public and private partnerships … international conservation groups opened their doors to transnational corporate leaders." During the past two decades, when NGOs have been seen to champion pro-poor participation, sustainable livelihoods, and grass-roots change as the cornerstones of development, one might have expected them to be more reserved in supporting the vision of development through business which CSR promotes. So what accounts for this apparent shift?

The answer lies, in part, in the persuasive power of the very concept of collective responsibility. Phrases such as "common good," "shared values," and "societal consensus" are constantly repeated by advocates from both business and civil society at CSR events and in the multitude of reports produced on the subject. Just as Moody-Stuart argued in his speech that global problems can only be addressed by collective action, so a recent paper produced by a trio of leading NGOs (Oxfam, Civicus, and the Global Action Network) stresses that "to have global influence … requires a collective effort" (Waddell 2004: ii). The alliance between business and civil society—from the one side resources and competitiveness, from the other proximity to and knowledge of "the people"—is put forward as a more favorable option than responsibility imposed through "the dead hand of state regulation."

Underlying this declaration of collaborative action is a claim of commitment to common interests: "If you look at what motivates partners, we all have the same interests basically: stable societies, income generation, healthy and educated populations, and strengthening the capacity of local entrepreneurs," the chairman of a mining multinational explained to me during an interview. As the values which are seen to lie at the heart of this collaborative enterprise—those of responsibility, accountability, and sustainability— are enshrined in global covenants and codes, they are projected as universal moral goods, thus further reinforcing the faith in a collective conscience. During interviews, corporate executives commonly stressed that, both as individuals and as part of a corporate body, they shared the same values—and vision of sustainable development— as the rest of society; values which were reflected in the company's business principles. As a mining executive put it:

> If you take a poll of the 100,000 employees of the company around the world, you'd come up with the average number of people who have membership of Amnesty International etc. We care about sustainability and human rights … it's just a question of how we mobilize that spirit.

The common target of this collaborative vision is Southern governments, who are *talked about* at such gatherings yet are rarely present. At the Ethical Corporation event for example, although the conference brochure had promised to reveal "how to avoid becoming a de facto government," representatives from governments in the global South were strikingly absent from the list of participants. In contrast, as is common, experts and policy-makers from Northern bilateral aid agencies including USAID, DFID, and the Danish International Development Agency were all present and prominently positioned on the program. Thus a movement which began with the aim of exposing corporate social *irresponsibility* has shifted to focus on the mismanagement of resources and revenues by Southern governments at the expense of their people, over whom this elite coalition extends its collective guardianship. This was encapsulated by the former chairman of Anglo American at the 2006 annual shareholder's meeting:

> Extractive revenues have sometimes been subject to wholesale embezzlement by government.... Whilst we cannot and should not take on responsibilities that are properly those of governments, *we cannot stand aloof from major governance and social issues in the countries where we operate.*

This should not, we are told, be seen as a usurpation of state powers, but a virtuous act of stepping into the breach left by government's abdication or corruption: "It may not be our responsibility, but it becomes our problem" (Anglo American 2005: 13). This discourse underscored much of what was said by executives and their NGO partners alike at conferences, in interviews, and shareholders meetings. A representative from Care International, for example, commended corporate executives at the Ethical Corporation conference for bringing "best practice" and good governance to the developing countries in which they work:

> In a country like Cambodia where there is so much corruption they need ... companies like you, to keep coming with your standards and principles.... [Y]ou can raise the standards of the country through your investments.

The logic behind this mission is presented as apolitical and market-oriented, with business cast as a neutral party transcending the parochial politics of national governments: "The message from the business sector is blunt. We want to do business with you, but in various ways you make it very difficult. Let us help you do away with those difficulties" (Phaswana 2006: 62). By shifting scrutiny onto governments which are defined, according to such narratives, at best by chronic incapacity at worst by corrupt rapacity, the CSR movement co-opts support not only from NGOs, but also from bilateral development agencies for whom "good governance" has become the latest buzzword.

This is not to say that CSR has effectively stamped out criticism or anticorporate activism, nor that international NGOs operate in a homogenous realm of "global civil society." As the campaigners outside the Human Rights and Business Conference described above demonstrate, people continue to challenge motives and expose fraudulent claims to responsibility. Rather, what this suggests is that as corporations are elevated as instruments of social improvement, rather than exploitation, opposition to this orthodoxy and other alternatives become further marginalized from the development mainstream of policy-making and power. Compelling visions of global partnership in the service of local development have proved a particularly powerful tool for recruiting support from noncorporate actors, while marginalizing dissenters from the arenas in which these cosmopolitan alliances are forged. Particular NGOs emerge as "partners of choice," or as a CSR executive at a multinational extractive company put it:

> I would draw the line between the big and small single-issue NGOs. For example, groups like Earthworks, Care, WWF—with whom (we) [have] a very successful partnership—we can have a rational discussion with. But at the same time, other branches continue to insist on critiquing companies like us whatever we do.

Meanwhile WWF asserts a vision of common values and solutions with companies that once might have been the target of their "clean-up" campaigns: "conservation Partners are multinational companies that contribute substantial funding to WWF's global conservation work. WWF understand that corporations have their share of things to answer for but the solutions to key conservation problems will either be *common solutions* or they won't be solutions at all."

NGOs that do not embrace this new process are accused of being "confrontational, incidental," or "purely opportunistic" (Waddell 2004: i). This was manifest at Chatham House's conference on "Emerging rules and evolving responsibilities" (London, 13–14 March 2006[3]). The atmosphere was triumphant, expressed in the common refrains of "the most effective agent of change is enterprise" and "we believe the only way to achieve change is to trust each other and to dehorn the devil" from corporate, NGO, and even union personnel. Upbeat speeches championing the social role of business were given by Malcolm Wicks (then Minister for Energy and CSR), the Executive Head of the UN Global Compact, and senior executives from various companies. Among these, a presentation was given by Bill Eckhart, Communications Director for the world's largest advertising conglomerate.

Eckhart's presentation focused on a selection of adverts that the firm had produced for Coca-Cola, BP, and Chevron Texaco. He explained how this form of advertising was a central vehicle by which responsible corporations could "educate customers and communities" on responsible living in areas such as the environment and health. A flow diagram with companies and government at the top, media in the middle, and "communities" on the bottom illustrated the flow of ethical expertise. The presentation was followed by a number of comments from the audience in support of this form of "ethical education" through publicity and consumption. No critical questions or comments were made. As a participant at the conference, I somewhat hesitantly asked whether corporations such as BP, Coca-Cola, and Chevron Texaco—all of which had recently been accused of environmental and social misconduct—were well positioned to provide "ethical education." The response was curt, though perhaps not surprising: "These companies are actually trying to *do something*, unlike the reckless NGOs who destroy brand and reputation with unfounded accusations." Much more surprising was that during the next coffee break I was approached by two representatives from WWF London, one of whom said:

> We were so pleased when you asked your question. We were hopping in our seats. It's so difficult when you come from an NGO, because you can't say these things because they just dismiss it as, "Oh you're the reckless NGO" and then the audience think it too. So you have to sit quietly or you risk the credibility of your organization.

Thus norms of appropriate behavior within such collaborations are established, and collaborators (particularly those with the most to lose) are understandably reluctant to transgress them. The expected product of these engagements is at the very least demonstrable collaboration, but preferably consensus, the performance of which is equally ritualized. Clearly, what appears as a process of mutual collaboration depends on the capacity of such forums to impose consensus through silencing dissent. Those who challenge the orthodoxy of collective goals risk being labeled as more interested in "throwing stones" than "making progress." A recent article in the *Ethical Corporation* magazine stated that "for every constructive builder of change, there are more throwing stones from the sidelines" (Baker 2007). Many multinationals have so fully embraced CSR that critique against them appears as a denial of the collective responsibility for which the companies themselves are striving, rising above the fray, putting aside partisanship. Who wants to be seen to undermine that?

The demand for active "win-win solutions" tends therefore to expunge debate and critique as cynical, ideological, or just a waste of precious time. This was evident at BITC's 2004 Annual General Meeting, as Nigel Griffith, another former UK Labor government minister for CSR, stated:

> I want to combat cynicism! I want to make sure that great companies, especially great British companies, are not knocked off their pedestal by some cheap journalism or political activism.... I want to make sure that our NGOs are working with business on a common agenda so that British companies retain their competitive and ethical edge.

Similarly, at an Ethical Corporation conference, a delegate from the World Business Council of Sustainable Development celebrated the "bravery" of six UK-based NGOs that had publicly launched a sustainability strategy in partnership with the former targets of their campaigns.

The spheres of legitimate action (partnership with business for the common cause) and illegitimate action (misguided, anticorporate campaigning) are clearly delineated, one as ethical, the other as unethical:

> Greenpeace, for instance, has an extremely effective and thoughtful policy group on climate. This is far removed from its dinghy and abseiling image, but if Greenpeace does not have some action involving dinghies ... much of their membership ... thinks it's gone *soft*.... Just as in the commercial world, competition for customers and funds, or just over-enthusiasm for a particular cause can lead to behavior which *I consider to be unethical*. (Moody-Stuart 2006: 31)

This has the effect of further reinforcing the parameters for discussion and acceptable action, narrowing the space for critique. Where opposition is voiced, the criticism tends to challenge the sincerity of a claim to corporate responsibility, but not its ideological underpinnings. Anglo American and Survival International, for example, can be seen to draw on a shared register of references and terms in the struggle over responsibility, even if they are on opposite sides of an issue.

Thus the power of CSR lies not simply in its capacity to sideline critical voices, but to *colonize* the language and, in some sense the identities of critics, drawing even vocal campaigners against corporate irresponsibility into its project. Henrietta Moore (2004: 82) notes that: "The very same language, concepts, and images that are used by activists to try and preserve the ozone layer and prevent environmental catastrophe are employed by multinational corporations to promote images of global responsibility."

This is reinforced by the discourse of global values enshrined in codes and conventions such as the U.N. Global Compact, which establish an official canon of concepts and terms to be reproduced in the policy goals and action plans of corporations, NGOs, and consulting firms, lending them further authority in a process of mutual, if unintentional, legitimation.

In order to compete in this elite marketplace of corporate virtue, actors must take on many of the forms and practices of commercial markets upon which this market for corporate responsibility is, ultimately, contingent (Dezalay and Garth 1996). On one side, corporations compete for index rankings, awards, and high profile partnerships, in pursuit of the intangible resource of "moral" capital. On the other, NGOs are in competition for a more obvious resource— money. Moody-Stuart (2006: 31) described one half of this competitive market for humanitarianism as an effective mechanism for imposing a much-needed rigor and professionalism on NGOs: "They compete for funding every bit as aggressively as commercial businesses compete for customers, for their jobs depend on it." Similarly, the head of the Partnering Initiative spoke of the need to apply business drivers to "aid agencies in this competitive marketplace of creative chaos."

Thus the CSR arena is characterized as much by intense competition as by collaboration, as groups strive to be the donor's chosen collaborator and win hard-fought funding. In order to do so, NGOs must compete to be seen as the embodiment of ecological virtue, sustainable development, or human rights by maintaining a high profile through participation in international conferences and corporate domains, together with publications such as practical manuals or position papers. But the relationship between the capital markets and the market for humanitarianism is not simply a dualistic matter of conversion. The picture becomes complicated when we look at the other side of this process of exchange and conversion—the corporate donors.

Just as the director of BITC remarked, "we are a customer-driven organization" (the "customers" being their corporate partners/

clients), so Mark Moody-Stuart, delivering the Tacitus Lecture, described NGOs as "enterprises" that "provide services to their donors and supporters" (2006: 31). Just as the language of partnership obscures the workings of patronage, so the representation of NGOs as enterprises competing in a market for corporate customers denies the relations of power and dependence (and frequently deference) that are generated by these corporate-charity alliances in the service of CSR. Both the partnership paradigm and the market model of competitive responsibility attempt to claim CSR as a radical break from the legacy of corporate philanthropy, the former evoking an ideal of collaboration for common cause, the latter appealing to the economistic discourse of "enlightened self-interest." Both attempt to recast donor and recipient as partners, or as customer and vendor. Yet as is implicit in Moody-Stuart's slippage into the terminology of "donor," the dynamics of benefactor and beneficiary prevail, affirming the hierarchy between donor and recipient: "Without business, there is no development aid, and no money generated to *donate* to NGOs. NGOs did not thrive under communism" (ibid.: 30). The implication is that in order to receive much-needed corporate funding—"donations" as Moody-Stuart puts it—NGOs must strive to endorse the centrality of business. In return, this "alliance" provides corporations with symbolic capital, endowing their influence with a moral authority that is projected and renewed through the performative practices of CSR. Such rituals of corporate virtue thus obscure relations of power and maintain the illusion of mutual independence that sustain the myth of partnership.

Conclusion

The process of co-option, achieved both through the persuasive moral discourse of partnership and the coercive power of giving and withholding funding where the donor sees fit, facilitates the wider acceptance of the business-driven approach to development that CSR advocates. Other alternatives that once might have been the domain of NGOs disappear from the picture, as does the fact that, in many situations, the demands of social and environmental justice require the development movement to challenge rather than endorse corporate interests, so paving the way for development to be redefined according to the interests of corporate elites and their investors (Blowfield 2005).

This is, then, a world of apparently universal virtues, within which CSR professionals take on the mantle of purveyors of this cosmopolitan rationality, sharing a set of globally relevant tools and values. At the base of these values is the market principle, held up to embody a natural and universally valid truth about human and social nature. Kofi Annan's assertion of the primacy of markets as the solution to poverty provides a dominant vision of development through access to markets—a vision which fully accords with the directives and interests of multinational corporations. By claiming the happy coincidence of doing good business and doing good—"what's good for business is good for development!"—commitment to the market logic of maximization is not only maintained, but is endowed with a moral legitimacy and celebrated as the "win-win solution" for which the development industry has been searching. At the same time, the landscape of CSR appears to be made up of transparent arenas of competition, diversity, and political pluralism in which corporate executives "confess" past misconduct or mistakes, and explain the best-practice regimes they have since developed in partnership with NGOs. Indeed the apparent inclusiveness of such arenas, in which a collaborative and confessional ethos appears to reign, serves to create a sense of shared responsibility at work.

I have argued that the performative and ritualistic dimensions of CSR practice serve not only to celebrate corporations as agents of social improvement, but also to establish the rules of participation in this realm of global governance. The commitment to CSR has become shibbolithic, a declaration of common purpose and global citizenship with which corporations win a seat at (the head of) the table of international development planning. Contrary to mainstream critics of CSR, who see such rituals merely as attempts at corporate branding, these theatres of virtue perform a much more vital function in the exercise of corporate power, as they serve to manufacture a form of consensus which marginalizes alternative visions or critique through the discursive mechanisms of collaboration.

Acknowledgments

This article is based on research funded by the ESRC. I am grateful to Catherine Dolan, James Fairhead, Elizabeth Harrison, Samuel Knafo, Geert De Neve, Luisa Steur, and two anonymous reviewers for their advice in the writing of this article.

Notes

1. Porritt 2006: 15.
2. This was organized by the Save the Narmada Movement in India and the Alternative Energy Project for Sustainability.
3. Chatham House rules were not applied at the conference.

References

Anglo American. 2005. *Anglo American—a climate of change. Report to society 2005*. London: Anglo American Plc.

Baker, Mallen. 2007. NGOs and business—spot the difference-makers. *Ethical Corporation*, February: 5.

Benson, Peter, and Stuart Kirsch. 2009. Corporate oxymorons. *Dialectical Anthropology* 34 (1): 45–48.

Bloch, Maurice. 1992. *Ritual, history and power: Selected papers in social anthropology*. London: Athlone Press.

Blowfield, Michael. 2005. Corporate social responsibility: Reinventing the meaning of development. *International Affairs* 81 (3): 515–24.

BITC (Business in the Community). 2006. Reports to Business in the Community's PerCent Standard 2006 and the London Benchmarking Group. *The Guardian: The Giving List*, 6 November: 4.

De Neve, Geert. 2008. Global garment chains, local labour activism: New challenges to trade union and NGO activism in the Tiruppur garment cluster, South India. *Research in Economic Anthropology* 28: 213–41.

Dezalay, Yves, and Bryant G. Garth. 1996. *Dealing in virtue: International commercial arbitration and the construction of a transnational legal order*. Chicago: University of Chicago Press.

Doane, Deborah. 2005. The myth of CSR. *Stanford Social Innovation Review*, Fall 2005: 23–29.

Dorsey, Michael K. 2005. Conservation, collusion and capital. *Anthropology News* 46 (7): 45–46.

Garsten, Christina, and Kerstin Jacobsson. 2007. Corporate globalisation, civil society and post-political regulation—whither democracy? *Development Dialogue* 49: 143–57.

Moody-Stuart, Mark. 2006. Business and NGOs in sustainable development—common cause or endless wars? *Optima* 52 (1): 22–37.

Moore, Henrietta. 2004. Global anxieties. Concept-metaphors and pre-theoretical commitments in anthropology. *Anthropological Theory* 4 (1): 71–88.

Phaswana, Fred. 2006. Africa—taking control of its destiny. *Optima* 52 (1): 60–72.

Porritt, Jonathan. 2006. Sustainability is central to survival. *Guardian*, 6 November: 15.

Sampson, Steven. 2005. Integrity warriors: Global morality and the anti-corruption movement in the Balkans. In *Corruption: Anthropological perspectives*, eds. Dieter Haller and Cris Shore, 103–131. London: Pluto Press.

Shamir, Ronen. 2008. The age of responsibilization: On market-embedded morality. *Economy and Society* 37 (1): 1–19.

Shever, Elana. 2010. Engendering the company: Corporate personhood and the "face" of an oil company in metropolitan Buenos Aires. *PoLAR* 33 (1): 26–46.

Waddell, Steve. 2004. NGO strategies to engage business: Trends, critical issues, and next steps. Oxfam America, Civicus, and Global Action Net, March.

Wilson, Craig, and Peter Wilson. 2006. *Make poverty business. Increase profits and reduce risks by engaging with the poor.* Sheffield: Greenleaf Publishing.

Zadek, Simon. 2001. *The civil corporation. The new economy of corporate citizenship.* London: Earthscan.

Dinah Rajak is a senior lecturer in Anthropology and International Development at the University of Sussex. She is the author of *In good company: An anatomy of corporate social responsibility* (Stanford University Press, 2011) and the co-founder of the Centre for New Economies of Development (www.responsiblebop.com).

– Chapter 2 –

VIRTUOUS LANGUAGE IN INDUSTRY AND THE ACADEMY

Stuart Kirsch

Several years ago I attended a symposium at my university on how to integrate sustainability into the curriculum, a topic of interest to me as an anthropologist who works with indigenous peoples affected by mining (Kirsch 2006, 2014). We were told that the university and the corporate world are now aligned in their shared commitment to sustainability. But I wondered why no one mentioned the BP oil spill in the Gulf of Mexico, which was making headlines at the time. British Petroleum's confident assertion that "we will make this right" seemed to contradict scientific uncertainty about the long-term environmental consequences of the spill. I also wanted to know what it meant that the business community and the academy were suddenly using the same vocabulary. I was not the only one in the audience with these concerns, but the presentation left us tongue-tied. It is difficult to criticize sustainability, as the environmental values it promotes are widely shared. Yet it is possible to acknowledge the need for sustainability while contesting some of the claims made in its name.

This experience leads me to question the discursive convergence of industry and the academy, which might be taken to imply mutual understanding and commitment. But the recourse to shared language can conceal all manner of difference. Sustainability and corporate social responsibility are examples of what linguistic anthropologists call strategically deployable shifters (Urciuoli 2003, 2008, 2010). Ordinary shifters are words or phrases that lack standardized lexical meanings because their referential value depends on the context in which they are employed. Shifters are therefore simultaneously symbolic and indexical (Silverstein 1976: 29). The adverbs *here* and *now* are examples of shifters, as are pronouns. Consider, for example, what have been called the "slippery pronouns" of nationalism, the third person plural that alternatively incorporates or excludes particular categories of persons (Rutherford 2012).

Strategically deployable shifters allow people to communicate across social boundaries and political vantage points (Urciuoli 2010: 55). The participants in these conversations understand themselves to be "'talking about the same thing,' when, pragmatically they are not, or are doing so only up to a point" (Urciuoli 2010: 55). This can be seen in the different ways that people mobilize the concept of sustainability. Contemporary use of the concept can be traced back to the UN Conference on the Human Environment held in Stockholm in 1972, which defined sustainability as the need to "maintain the earth as a place suitable for human life not only now but for future generations" (Ward and Dubos 1972: xviii). Sustainability was subsequently integrated into discussions about economic growth, including the argument that "for development to be sustainable, it must take account of social and ecological factors, as well as economic ones" (IUCN 1980: 1). For the mining industry, however, sustainability and sustainable development have come to mean something quite different. Thus the website of BHP Billiton (2010), one of the world's largest mining companies, asserts that "sustainable development is about ensuring that our business remains viable and contributes lasting benefits to society." Similarly, despite a historical legacy of destructive environmental impacts, the mining industry now claims to practice what it calls "sustainable mining." Such corporate oxymorons are "intended to ease the mind of an otherwise critical" public by pairing a harmful or destructive practice or commodity with a positive cover term (Benson and Kirsch 2010: 47). In the discourse of the mining industry, the relationship between sustainability and the environment has been completely elided, "emptying out" the original meaning of the term (see Negri 1999: 9).

The differences in how environmentalists and the mining industry define sustainability are more than simply rhetorical. Its status as a strategically deployable shifter allows BHP Billiton (2010) to claim that its public commitment to sustainability is its "first value" despite the negative impacts of its operations on the environment. This includes its responsibility for catastrophic damage downstream from the Ok Tedi copper and gold mine in Papua New Guinea, where I have conducted research since the mid-1980s (Kirsch 2006, 2014). BHP Billiton's environmental record did not prevent the university where I teach from appointing the company to the external board of advisers of its new institute on sustainability (Blumenstyk 2007). Nor did it prevent the university's school of engineering from displaying the company's logo on its solar car, a prominent symbol of its commitment to the environment. These examples illustrate how sustainability operates as a strategically deployable shifter that provides mining companies with symbolic capital.

The recognition that sustainability is a strategically deployable shifter leads me to ask what is being accomplished socially, politically, and discursively when such terms are invoked to describe, categorize, reform, valorize or criticize corporate practices. This question is part of a larger study of the dialectical relationship between corporations and their critics (Kirsch 2014). Sustainability is one of a series of concepts that corporations deploy under the general rubric of corporate social responsibility. The virtuous language of responsibility, sustainability, and transparency has become an important resource for corporations in their responses to criticism. That these discourses enhance corporate reputations is not simply a corollary of their use, but central to their invocation. Despite their appearance of political neutrality, these discourses promote market-based solutions to social and environmental problems as an alternative to government regulation. As strategically deployable shifters, the discourses of corporate social responsibility and sustainability facilitate conversations across a range of perspectives while concealing significant political differences (Urciuoli 2010: 49).

The discourse of corporate social responsibility has also become the subject of academic research in programs on business and management. This literature plays an essential role in "consolidating, validating, and even celebrating" claims about corporate social responsibility (Shamir 2010: 545). Academic research on CSR is "not external to its object of study," but central to its formulation and legitimation (Shamir 2010: 545). The promotion of the discourses of corporate social responsibility and sustainability within the academy enhances their credibility and complicates efforts to analyze these terms by conveying the impression that their definitions are well established and widely recognized rather than contested. However, my research on the relationship between the mining industry and its critics provides a productive vantage point from which to ascertain whether the discourse of corporate social responsibility reflects changes in how corporations and markets operate, as its proponents suggest, rather than changes in how corporations market themselves.

These preliminary observations lead to the four questions that I address in this chapter. First, why did the discourse of corporate social responsibility emerge at this particular historical moment? I answer this question with reference to the relationship between the mining industry and its critics since the 1990s. This follows the anthropological inclination to study language within specific social contexts. Second, what are the intended audiences of the discourse of corporate social responsibility? Attention to reception helps to identify the goals of the speaker. Third, which actions are identified as demonstrating corporate social responsibility and how might we distinguish between them? Here I contrast philanthropy and reform, both of which are represented as examples of corporate social responsibility. My final question has to do with academic discussion about corporate social responsibility and sustainability. How does the identification of these discourses as strategically deployable shifters help us to understand their promotion and reception within the academy?

The origins of CSR in the mining industry

Why do corporations and industries seek to enhance their reputations by invoking claims to social responsibility? Research on the relationship between the mining industry and its critics since the 1990s offers a historical perspective on the two dominant narratives invoked to explain the emergence of the discourse of corporate social responsibility. The first argument refers to corporate recognition of the need to raise industry standards. For example, one of the goals of the International Council of Mining and Metals is "to act as a catalyst for performance improvement in the mining and metals industry" (ICMM 2013). The alternative "business case" for social responsibility emphasizes the economic rationale or competitive advantage that can be gained by enhancing corporate reputations. The mining company Rio Tinto (2009) expresses this view in very specific terms: "Our contribution to sustainable development is not just the right thing to do. We also understand that it gives our business reputational benefits that result in greater access to land, human, and financial resources." In both cases, policy changes are presented as a response to internal concerns. In contrast, historical evidence suggests that pressure from external critics was responsible for the mining industry's adoption of the discourse of corporate social responsibility and sustainability in the late 1990s.

For decades, the mining industry managed to maintain a low profile. The industry's lack of visibility is related to the remote locations in which most mines operate, affording them considerable freedom from oversight or interference. In many cases, opposition to mining is suppressed by state or private security forces (Leith 2003; Ferguson 2006), reducing the need to respond to their critics. The relative anonymity of most mining companies is also a consequence of the way metals are sold to other business rather than directly to consumers. This can be contrasted with branding in the petroleum industry, in which consumers engage directly with corporations at the pump.

The spread of neoliberal economic policies during the 1990s, including the promotion of foreign direct investment, opened up new regions of the world to mineral extraction. Many of these projects are located in marginal areas in which indigenous peoples retained control over lands not previously seen to have economic value and where development has historically been limited or absent. Neoliberal reforms also dismantled state regulatory regimes designed to protect labor, the environment, and the rights of persons displaced or otherwise negatively affected by mining. Consequently, much of the responsibility for monitoring international capital has shifted from the state to NGOs and social movements (Kirsch 2002, 2014; Sawyer 2004; Szablowski 2007). Critics of the mining industry increasingly deploy new technologies ranging from the Internet and mobile phones to satellite imaging, enabling them to monitor and report on corporate activity in approximately real time wherever it occurs. They also participate in transnational action networks that forge horizontal ties to their counterparts in other regions of the world and partner with NGOs concerned with social justice, the environment, and financial accountability (Keck and Sikkink 1998; Appadurai 2000; Kirsch 2007).

One of the iconic mining conflicts of the 1990s was the political campaign and international litigation against the Ok Tedi copper and gold mine in Papua New Guinea. Since 1986, the mine has discharged more than one billion metric tons of finely ground tailings and waste rock into local rivers (Kirsch 2002, 2006, 2014). Although the people living downstream from the mine initially faced a steep learning curve, they eventually forged strategic alliances with international NGOs, who helped them call attention to the environmental problems caused by the mine. In 1994, thirty thousand indigenous people affected by pollution filed a lawsuit against Broken Hill Proprietary, Ltd. (BHP), the managing shareholder and operating partner of the Ok Tedi mine, in the Australian courts (Gordon 1997). The case was settled in 1996 for an estimated $500 million in compensation and commitments to tailings containment (Tait 1996: 19). When the

Ok Tedi mine continued to discharge tailings into the river system, the plaintiffs returned to court in 2000. Pressure from the second case forced BHP to transfer its 52 percent share in the project to a development trust that has already accumulated $1.4 billion in reserves, although only a small fraction of these funds reaches the communities affected by the mine.

The Ok Tedi campaign was an example of the politics of space, which links together a variety of actors in different locations. The resulting networks are comprised of individuals, communities, non-governmental organizations, experts, lawyers, and others. They benefit from the complementary mobilization of resources, discourses of persuasion, access to power, and forms of leverage deployed by their members (Keck and Sikkink 1998; Tsing 2004; Kirsch 2007). The ability to enroll participants in multiple locations makes these networks especially effective in challenging transnational corporations wherever they operate. The decade-long campaign against the Ok Tedi mine helped to usher in a new era in which mining companies acknowledge the need to negotiate with the communities affected by their projects in contrast to the prevailing assumption that the state has the sole authority to represent their interests (Ballard and Banks 2003). It also served notice to the industry that it could no longer afford to ignore its critics, prompting a "crisis of confidence" (Danielson 2006: 7) among mining executives, which led to unprecedented collaboration among companies that previously viewed each other as fierce competitors.

However, the politics of space has a critical shortcoming: the length of time required to diagnose the problem, mobilize a network of supporters, and mount an effective intervention. In the Ok Tedi case, the response to the environmental problems downstream from the mine came too late to save the river. More recent protests against the mining industry have shifted their attention to earlier in the production cycle before the onset of mining. These social movements seek to limit the environmental impact of mining by opposing the development of new projects. I refer to this strategy as the politics of time. Relatively small mining projects may require investments of several hundred million dollars and the budget for a large mine may be as much as ten or twelve billion dollars. Investments on this scale generate substantial political and economic inertia, especially after they begin to earn revenue for the state. Consequently, political opposition to mining is more likely to be successful when it addresses proposals for new projects, jeopardizing the ability of the mining company to raise the capital required for construction.

An important example of the politics of time is the burgeoning social movement across Latin America in which communities undertake popular votes—known as *consulta* or referenda—that express support or opposition to proposed development projects, especially new mines (McGee 2009; Kirsch 2014). These votes contest the authority of the state to grant mining licenses. The participants generally view these referenda as expressing their democratic rights and sovereignty over land and territory rather than their involvement in a larger social movement based on the politics of time. However, the organizers of these actions are familiar with their history in the region. A recent survey identifies sixty-eight consultas on mining projects in Latin America, including Argentina, Colombia, Ecuador, Guatemala, Mexico, and Peru over the last decade (Fultz 2011).

The first consulta to vote on a major mining project was held in the town of Tambogrande in north-west Peru in 2002 (McGee 2009: 604–610); 98 percent of the eligible voters opposed the mine. Three years later in Esquel, Argentina, the members of the largely middle class community voted overwhelmingly against a proposed open pit gold mine located seven kilometers upstream from the town, blocking its development (McGee 2009: 615–618). The first referendum against a mining project in Guatemala was held in Sipacapa in 2005; since then, there have been votes on mining projects in fifty-four municipalities, almost all of which were negative (McGee 2009: 618–626). These referenda demonstrate widespread opposition to mining, although they also seek to limit state interference in local affairs. In addition, they express the rights of individuals and communities to make important decisions concerning their land, territories, and access to water, as well as local livelihoods and health. Although earlier social movements based on the politics of space influenced debates about mining and indigenous peoples, new strategies based on the politics of time represent a more hopeful turn given their potential to prevent other environmental disasters from occurring.

The promotion of indigenous rights to free, prior, and informed consent, or FPIC, is a key resource in the politics of time. FPIC was first established in binding international treaty law by the International Labor Organization (ILO) convention 169 in 1989 (McGee 2009: 585). The World Bank initially refused to recognize the principle of indigenous consent, arguing that it was too difficult to operationalize and ran counter to established principles of eminent domain (Downing 2001: 3). Employing the same acronym, but representing a much weaker standard, the World Bank adopted a policy of free, prior, and informed consultation. Many other international financial institutions followed suit (Bridge and Wong 2011).

Some of the participants in the mining industry prefer the alternative concept of a "social license to operate," which refers to the existence of broad-based community support. The expression was previously used by the American pulp and paper industry to indicate its need to gain the trust of the public and thereby avoid "costly new regulations" (Moore 1996: 23). It first entered conversations about the mining industry in 1997 (Filer, Banks and Burton 2008; Thomson and Boutilier 2011: 1179), at a time when the mining industry was under pressure from the legal action against the Ok Tedi mine. It is treated as a kind of shorthand for those aspects of relationships between mines and communities that are not directly addressed by government contracts and permits (Colin Filer, pers. comm., 2012). A key difference between a social license to operate and free, prior, and informed consent is that the purpose of the former is to reassure potential investors that a project meets certain baseline criteria, reducing their exposure to risk, whereas the latter is based on the recognition of indigenous rights and addresses the interests of those communities. The acquisition of a social license to operate is also a voluntary practice rather than a legal requirement.

Lobbying by NGOs and indigenous peoples at the United Nations led to the passage of the Declaration on the Rights of Indigenous Peoples in 2007, which mandates the principle of free, prior, and informed consent. Such "soft law" standards, while not legally binding, may give rise to new international norms. Even the World Bank has begun to take heed; in May 2011, it announced a new policy recognizing the higher standard of consent for certain projects affecting the rights of indigenous peoples (Bridge and Wong 2011: 15). BHP Billiton's (2010: 9) most recent statement of operating principles stakes out a position in the middle ground: "New operations or projects must have broad-based community support before proceeding with development. Free Prior and Informed Consent (FPIC) is only required where it is mandated by law. Evidence demonstrating support or opposition to the project must be documented." According to industry observers, although "the debate over FPIC will continue ... the realization that the game has changed is sinking in. The goal posts are shifting" (Bridge and Wong 2011: 15). Paradoxically, however, there is a risk that the protocols for implementing the new standard may result in the transfer of political authority from communities recently empowered to speak on their own behalf to private sector consultants who implement assessments on behalf of corporate sponsors, potentially turning free, prior, and informed consent into the check-box compliance of audit culture.

Thus in contrast to corporate narratives about internal recognition of the need to improve performance and the business case for responsibility, evidence from the study of social movements critical of the mining industry suggests that changes in corporate practice are hard won. Reform should be seen as the achievement of indigenous and NGO critics rather than a consequence of the spontaneous enlightenment of industry executives. Nor is there evidence to support the mining industry's assertion that it has internalized important lessons from its past mistakes and incorporated them into their decision-making (see Hoffman 1997). Instead, corporate claims to practice sustainable mining should be seen as attempts to reassure critics that their efforts and interventions are no longer necessary.

The audiences for CSR discourse

The next question is concerned with potential audiences for the discourse of corporate social responsibility. In recent decades, reputational risks have become increasingly important to the corporate bottom line. This is related to the rise of shareholder capitalism, which emphasizes share value at the expense of corporate relationships to labor, consumers, and communities (Ho 2009). Shareholder capitalism is closely associated with the financial collapse of the last decade, during which attention to share value took precedence over economic performance. It is also driven by increased participation in the stock market by individual investors, which has been spurred by the dismantling and privatization of pensions and retirement plans (Welker and Wood 2011: S59). Managing shareholder confidence has become an essential component of doing business for publically traded companies. Corporations seek to reassure both shareholders and potential investors by adopting policies on corporate social responsibility.

Another potential audience for the discourse of corporate social responsibility is the consumer. One of the ways corporations seek to reassure consumers is through certification programs that provide commodities with the stamp of public approval (Szablowski 2007). Certification consists of a set of rules or guidelines and a mechanism for monitoring or self-reporting that indicates compliance (Szablowski 2007: 63). But participation is voluntary, compliance is not enforceable, and the sanctions that do exist tend to be informal, including dialogue, peer pressure, and the threat of expulsion (Szablowski 2007: 63–64). An example of a certification regime in the mining industry emerged in response to concern about the trade in "blood diamonds" from conflict zones in Africa. Corporations may also envision the possibility of competitive advantage in addition to the achievement of a new kind of legitimacy through participation in these initiatives; for example, support for the Kimberly Process that imposed restrictions on diamond trading had strategic value for De Beers, which controls the bulk of the world's diamond trade and benefited from the resulting reduction in supply, which keeps diamond prices high. The Kimberly Process has gradually been weakened as various parties find ways to circumvent its restrictions. But the anonymity of most metals — as it is impossible to identify the source of the copper wire in our computers or the gold in our jewelry, for example — means that the mining industry is largely immune to consumer politics.

As the history of mining conflicts suggests, another potential audience for the discourse of corporate social responsibility is non-governmental organizations. The language of CSR helps corporations persuade many NGOs to move from confrontation to collaboration in what the mining industry likes to call "win-win" relationships (Rajak this volume). NGOs are increasingly likely to join arm in arm with CEOs in the boardroom rather than subaltern peasants manning the barricades. This has led to the fragmentation of the NGO community according to their willingness to collaborate with industry. One example of these new collaborations is the way conservation organizations increasingly align themselves with mining companies, endorsing their projects in return for financial support for conservation set-asides (BBOP 2009; Seagle 2012). These partnerships have led indigenous peoples in many areas of the world to regard conservation organizations as their enemies rather than potential allies or partners in the protection of local biodiversity (Chapin 2004). The proliferation of relationships between mining companies and NGOs has also made it easier for the industry to marginalize organizations that reject corporate collaboration and are skeptical of market-based solutions to environmental problems.

Finally, the discourse of corporate social responsibility may also be addressed in part to labor. For example, Jessica Smith Rolston (2010) found that CSR messages at a gold mine in Washington State were directed primarily at its own employees, as the mining company sought to overcome stereotypes about the industry in a region in which much of the labor pool possesses strong environmental values. The multiple audiences of the discourse of corporate social responsibility illustrate how strategically deployable shifters facilitate interactions that conceal important contradictions.

The varieties of CSR work

It is possible to distinguish between two kinds of CSR work: "doing good" through corporate philanthropy and "doing better" by improving corporate practices. A distinguishing feature of CSR is the link between philanthropy and public relations. Large corporations have long made important charitable contributions: sponsoring a local sports team, for example, or participating in fundraising for nearby hospitals. These were seen as demonstrations of the corporation's role as a good neighbor (Marchand 1998). More recently, corporations have also begun to donate employee labor in charitable undertakings such as house building for Habitat for Humanity, which enhances employee loyalty while building community ties.

Even when operating overseas, local philanthropic contributions have been perceived as a demonstration of corporate responsibility. Given that these donations are not readily visible from a distance, raising corporate profiles in the international arena requires new forms of philanthropy. In particular, global public health has become a key focus for corporate donations. In the last decade, the companies that comprise the Fortune 500 have contributed to campaigns against some of the world's major health risks, most notably HIV/AIDS, malaria, and tuberculosis. These campaigns are often announced in full-page ads in the *New York Times*, such as the two-page ad from Chevron on 1 June 2011 with the caption: "Fighting Aids Should Be Corporate Policy. We Agree." A similar ad from the Global Business Coalition on HIV/AIDS, Tuberculosis, and Malaria, which lists a number of mining companies as patrons, salutes the winners of the 2007 Awards for Business Excellence with the headline: "Fighting AIDS, TB and Malaria Is Our Business." These contributions help corporations "gain access to new kinds of moral and social resources" that can be mobilized "in pursuit of their economic goals" (Rajak 2011: 18).

The mining industry's attention to malaria is of particular interest. The mining giants Anglo American and BHP Billiton are two of the key corporate funders of Africa Fighting Malaria, an NGO that seeks to overturn the ban on DDT use. Africa Fighting Malaria is also supported by the American Enterprise Institute, a conservative organization not ordinarily known for its involvement in Third World humanitarian causes. Widespread public concern about DDT can be traced to Rachel Carson's (1962) *Silent spring*, which described the threats posed to humans and the environment by the use of chemical fertilizers and pesticides in industrial agriculture. Carson's work provoked widespread criticism of the chemical industry, leading to the establishment of the US Environmental Protection Agency, which subsequently banned DDT. The recognition that DDT and other insecticides enter the food chain and accumulate within certain organisms was already well established in the scientific community prior to the publication of her work (McWilliams 2008). The toxic effect of DDT on songbirds provided Carson with the evocative image of a "silent spring" in which "no birds sing," galvanizing popular understandings of the harms caused by industrial pollution. This opened up a critical space for political intervention that facilitated the emergence of the environmental movement in the 1970s and the subsequent efflorescence of environmental NGOs during the 1980s, suggesting one reason why Carson's work remains a target for the conservative movement so long after its publication.

Criticism of the ban on DDT might also be seen as an attempt to put the genie of public participation in science back in the bottle, returning policymaking to scientists and their corporate employers. If it could be demonstrated that NGO opposition to DDT use for malaria prevention was misguided, this would discredit NGOs on the very grounds through which they claim legitimacy, their ability to protect the rights of vulnerable populations. The assertion that millions of people have needlessly died as a result of Carson's work seeks to reverse the shift toward public participation in scientific decision-making (see Oreskes and Conway 2010: 216–239). It may also help to explain why the American Enterprise Institute and the mining industry support Africa Fighting Malaria.

A second focus of the mining industry in promoting its contribution to society is poverty reduction, which is increasingly invoked by mining industry executives as a key objective. For example, the mining industry was determined to make a strong presentation at the 2002 World Summit on Sustainable Development (WSSD) in Johannesburg, South Africa, in order to preempt civil society's ability to advocate for stronger regulatory control over its operations (Reed 2002: 218). To this end, the industry commissioned a ten million dollar study of the challenges facing the mining industry (Danielson 2002). When the final report of the Mines, Minerals and Sustainable Development project was presented at the Johannesburg summit, Brian Gilbertson (2002), the CEO of BHP Billiton, invoked John F.

Kennedy's call to "abolish all forms of human poverty," and Nelson Mandela on the need to fight against "poverty and lack of human dignity" in relation to the industry's contribution to sustainable development. Gilbertson (2002) also argued that "the real challenges of Sustainable Development arise when a major project goes awry, when one stares into an environmental abyss. For BHP Billiton, that abyss was Ok Tedi." He praised BHP Billiton's "solution" to the problems downstream from the Ok Tedi mine, the transfer of the company's share in the project to a development trust, but failed to mention the alternative option of staying in Papua New Guinea to clean up the polluted river system. Gilbertson also commended the Mines, Minerals and Sustainable Development project for having "brought much self-examination throughout the industry."

In contrast to corporate philanthropy, or "doing good," are reform efforts that result in the reduction of corporate harm, which might be described as "doing better." Despite the self-congratulatory tone of Gilbertson's speech in Johannesburg, the mining industry largely failed to raise its operating standards in the decade following the 2002 summit. There are several important exceptions, such as BHP Billiton's pledge not to discharge tailings into the river system in any new project. Its chief competitors, however, refused to follow suit. Rio Tinto, for example, argues that it is counterproductive to make general policy decisions on tailings disposal and continues to address these issues on a case-by-case basis. The problem with voluntary reforms is that non-compulsory measures create free-rider problems when corporations that decline to follow the new standard gain a competitive advantage over companies operating according to the higher standards. Given the high cost of environmental mitigation in the mining industry, only the lowest cost producers can afford to operate during an economic downturn, which discourages participation in voluntary reforms.

The mining industry is also largely insulated from shareholder preferences. This is especially true for gold, which serves as an important hedge against the volatility of the stock market, because the price of gold is counter-cyclical with the market's economic performance. Mining company stocks are also relatively immune from the pressures of the "shareholder democracy" in which investors use their voting power to promote corporate reform (Foster 2008). One of the most significant innovations in shareholder activism over the last two decades was the establishment of social and green choice investment funds. These funds have generally outperformed the market average due to their popularity and the resulting supply of capital. Consequently, rather unlikely corporations and industries have lobbied for membership, often invoking industry awards for sustainability and corporate social responsibility (Rajak this volume) as their rationale. During the period between the Kyoto Accord on global climate change in 1997 and the 2011 Fukushima crisis, when nuclear power received the reluctant endorsement of mainstream conservation organizations concerned about greenhouse gases emanating from carbon-based energy sources, the uranium mining industry sought inclusion in green choice funds. These efforts were subsequently delegitimized by the tsunami that brought Japan's nuclear industry to the brink of disaster. Ironically, stock fund managers invoke green and social choice funds as a rationale for blocking shareholder resolutions by arguing that individuals who do not wish to invest in particular corporations have the option of investing in these more specialized funds. For example, a 1999 shareholder initiative to force TIAA-CREF, the major pension fund for American professors and schoolteachers, to divest its shares in Freeport-McMoRan, which owns and operates the controversial Grasberg mine in West Papua, Indonesia, was rebuffed by the management of TIAA-CREF (Social Funds 2000).

CSR in the academy

Finally, how does the discourse of corporate social responsibility affect academic debates? The issue arises at a historical moment when corporations and the market are influencing the academy in a variety of ways. Universities are increasingly adopting new business models, including the application of "audit culture" to assess research performance (Strathern 2000). Public universities are required to justify their activities in terms of contributions to local economic growth, with implications for course offerings and academic positions. This includes a shift in resources from the humanities and the social sciences to the STEM fields of science, technology, engineering, and mathematics. These changes are accompanied by the proliferation of corporate-academic partnerships in the life sciences and other fields, resulting in new research priorities and accountabilities (Bocking 2004: 37).

Even within the field of anthropology there has been a rise in demand for our skills by corporations. In the arena in which I work, anthropologists may choose to collaborate with the participants in indigenous political movements, work with NGOs and lawyers, provide expert testimony to multilateral organizations, and so forth (Kirsch 2014). But my colleagues are more likely to consult or work for mining companies than criticize or oppose them. They argue that they are better able to effect positive change by working within these organizations than addressing problems and concerns from the outside, ignoring corporate mechanisms for neutralizing internal dissent and disciplining employees (Beamish 2002). This includes the threat of legal action or the termination of their contracts, which prevents anthropologists from making the results of their research available to the public (Coumans 2011).

Neoliberal confidence in the ability of the market to solve complex problems also influences the role played by the study of business and management in universities, especially in relation to the environment. No one at my university objected when the business school established a new institute to foster sustainable business practices. But the proponents of market-based solutions to environmental problems have not been content with greening their own institutions. The establishment of a joint master's degree program between the business school and the school of natural resources prompted criticism and concern, even though this might be seen as a return to the school's original mission, which was to make more efficient, rational, and productive use of the state's natural resources in contrast to the environmental values that have influenced the school since the 1970s. Advocates of market-based reforms have also sought to promote their approach to these issues across the campus by helping to establish a new institute for sustainability. The external board of advisers appointed to this institute included a number of corporations with controversial environmental records, including Dow Chemical, Duke Energy, Shell Oil, and BHP Billiton, the mining company responsible for the Ok Tedi disaster. The acting director of the institute defended the decision to include BHP Billiton on the board to the *Chronicle of Higher Education*: "'There's no pure company out there,' he says. 'I have no reason to doubt that this company has really screwed a lot of people,' just as nearly every other company is 'unjust to people' at one point or another …'These organizations are part of the problem, and they're also part of the solution'" (Blumenstyk 2007). In these transformations of the academy, critical attention to the ways in which market forces are responsible for environmental problems risk being elided in favor of promoting the ability of the market to offer potential solutions, much like the way the environment is no longer seen as a crucial element of sustainability. Such claims are also presented as though they were politically neutral.

Conclusion

In this chapter, I argue that the discourse of corporate social responsibility is a strategically deployable shifter that claims to represent values we all support. CSR discourse extends the power of corporations to achieve their goals through the use of virtuous language. It assigns positive value to one side of political debates about the role of corporations and markets in society at the expense of a critique that calls for greater regulation or other interventions. Nonetheless, the discourse of corporate social responsibility conveys the impression that it is technocratic, professional, fair, innovative, optimistic, and open-minded, whereas the critics of CSR risk being scolded for their "low-minded sentimentality" for believing the worst about corporations and their motives (Sen 1999: 280).

It is the task of scholars in the social sciences and the humanities to analyze discursive claims, and to study how, when, why, and by whom these discourses are mobilized. But strategically deployable shifters like sustainability and corporate social responsibility have the potential to neutralize their critics, limiting their ability to question these claims. Indeed, this may be the primary objective of the discourse of corporate social responsibility. The only way to demystify such virtuous language is to examine its history, and in particular the concrete struggles through which it emerges in contrast to "just so" stories of corporate enlightenment or the economic rationalization of the business case for social responsibility, the audiences to which it is directed, what it claims to accomplish, and the consequences of its deployment in both industry and the academy.

Acknowledgments

This essay was initially published in Charlotte Walker-Said and John D. Kelly, eds, *Corporate Social Responsibility? Human Rights in the New Global Economy* (Chicago University Press, 2015, pp. 92–112). I am grateful to Dinah Rajak and Catherine Dolan for their invitation to include it here.

References

Appadurai, Arjun. 2000. Grassroots globalization and the research imagination. *Public Culture* 12(1): 1–19.

Ballard, Chris, and Glenn Banks. 2003. Resource wars: The anthropology of mining. *Annual Review of Anthropology* 32: 287–313.

BBOP (Business and Biodiversity Offsets Program). 2009. *Compensatory conservation case studies*, http://content.undp.org/go/cms-service/stream/asset/?asset_id=2469112

Beamish, Thomas D. 2002. *Silent spill: The organization of an industrial crisis*. Cambridge, MA: MIT Press.

Benson, Peter, and Stuart Kirsch. 2010. Corporate oxymorons. *Dialectical Anthropology* 34(1): 45–48.

BHP Billiton. 2010. Our sustainability framework, www.bhpbilliton.com/home/aboutus/Documents/ourSustainabilityFramework2010.pdf

Blumenstyk, Goldie. 2007. Mining company involved in environmental disaster now advises sustainability institute at U. of Michigan. *Chronicle of Higher Education* 54(15): A22.

Bocking, Stephen. 2004. *Nature's experts: Science, politics, and the environment*. New Brunswick: Rutgers University Press.

Bridge, Maurice, and Angus Wong. 2011. Consenting adults: Changes to the principle of free, prior and informed consent are changing the way in which firms engage communities. *Mining, People and the Environment* (July): 12–15.

Carson, Rachel. 1962. *Silent spring*. New York: Houghton Mifflin.

Chapin, Mac. 2004. A challenge to conservationists. *Worldwatch Magazine* (November/December): 17–31.

Coumans, Catherine. 2011. Occupying spaces created by conflict: Anthropologists, development NGOs, responsible investment, and mining. *Current Anthropology* 52(S3): S29–S43.

Danielson, Luke, ed. 2002. Breaking new ground: Mining, minerals and sustainable development. International Institute for Environment and Development. London: Earthscan, http://www.iied.org/mmsd/finalreport/index.html

Danielson, Luke. 2006. Architecture for change: An account of the mining, minerals, and sustainable development project. Berlin: Global Public Policy Institute, http://info.worldbank.org/etools/library/view_p.asp?lprogram=107&objectid=238483

Downing, Ted. 2001. Why comment on the World Bank's proposed indigenous peoples policy? *Anthropology News* 42(9): 23–24.

Ferguson, James. 2006. *Global shadows: Africa in the neoliberal world order*. Durham, NC: Duke University Press.

Filer, Colin, Glenn Banks, and John Burton. 2008. The fragmentation of responsibilities in the Melanesian mining sector. In Ciaran O'Faircheallaigh and Saleem Ali, eds., *Earth matters: Indigenous peoples, extractive industries and corporate social responsibility*, pp. 163–179. Sheffield, UK: Greenleaf.

Foster, Robert L. 2008. *Coca-globalization: Following soft drinks from New York to New Guinea*. London: Palgrave McMillan.

Fultz, Katherine. 2011. Local referendums on mining projects in Latin America. Unpublished report in the possession of the author.

Gilbertson, Brian. 2002. Speech to the World Business Council for Sustainable Development / International Institute for Economy Development, Mining, Minerals and Sustainable Development meeting. World Summit on Sustainable Development, Johannesburg, 30 August, http://www.qni.com.au/bbContentRepository/Presentations/WorldSummit.pdf

Gordon, John. 1997. The Ok Tedi lawsuit in retrospect. In G. Banks and C. Ballard, eds., *The Ok Tedi settlements: Issues, outcomes and implications*. Pacific Policy Paper 27, pp. 141–166.

Canberra: National Centre for Development Studies and Resource Management in Asia-Pacific, the Australian National University.

Ho, Karen. 2009. *Liquidated: An ethnography of Wall Street*. Durham, NC: Duke University Press.

Hoffman, Andrew J. 1997. *From heresy to dogma: An institutional history of corporate environmentalism*. San Francisco, CA: New Lexington Press.

ICMM (International Council on Mining and Metals). 2013. Homepage, www.icmm.com

IUCN (International Union for Conservation of Nature). 1980. *World conservation strategy: Living resource conservation for sustainable development*. Gland, Switzerland: IUCN, UNEP, and WWF.

Keck, Margaret E., and Kathryn Sikkink. 1998. *Activists beyond borders: Advocacy networks in international politics*. Ithaca, NY: Cornell University Press.

Kirsch, Stuart. 2002. Anthropology and advocacy: A case study of the campaign against the Ok Tedi mine. *Critique of Anthropology* 22(2): 175–200.

Kirsch, Stuart. 2006. *Reverse anthropology: Indigenous analysis of social and environmental relations in New Guinea*. Stanford, CA: Stanford University Press.

Kirsch, Stuart. 2007. Indigenous movements and the risks of counterglobalization: Tracking the campaign against Papua New Guinea's Ok Tedi mine. *American Ethnologist* 34(2): 303–321.

Kirsch, Stuart. 2010. Sustainable mining. *Dialectical Anthropology* 34(1): 87–93.

Kirsch, Stuart. 2014. *Mining capitalism: The relationship between corporations and their critics*. Berkeley: University of California Press.

Leith, Denise. 2003. *The politics of power: Freeport in Suharto's Indonesia*. Honolulu: University of Hawai'i Press.

Marchand, Roland. 1998. *Creating the corporate soul: The rise of public relations and corporate imagery in American big business*. Berkeley: University of California Press.

McGee, Brant. 2009. The community referendum: Participatory democracy and the right to free, prior and informed consent to development. *Berkeley Journal of International Law* 27(2): 570–635.

McWilliams, James E. 2008. *American pests: The losing war on insects from colonial times to DDT*. New York: Columbia University Press.

Moore, W. Henson. 1996. The social license to operate. *Paper Industry Manufacturing Association (PIMA) Magazine* 78(10): 22–23.

Negri, Antonio. 1999. The specter's smile. In M. Sprinker, ed., *Ghostly demarcations: A symposium on Jacques Derrida's specters of Marx*, pp. 5–16. New York: Verso.

Oreskes, Naomi, and Erik M. Conway. 2010. *Merchants of doubt: How a handful of scientists obscured the truth on issues from tobacco smoke to global warming*. New York: Bloomsbury Press.

Rajak, Dinah. 2011. *In good company: An anatomy of corporate social responsibility*. Stanford, CA: Stanford University Press.

Reed, Darryl. 2002. Resource extraction industries in developing countries. *Journal of Business Ethics* 39: 199–226.

Rio Tinto. 2009. Corporate website, www.riotinto.com

Rolston, Jessica Smith. 2010. What are good intentions good for? Corporate social responsibility in the mining industry. Unpublished paper. Annual Meetings of the American Anthropological Association, New Orleans, 18 November 2010.

Rutherford, Danilyn. 2012. *Laughing at leviathan: Sovereignty and audience in West Papua*. Chicago: University of Chicago Press.

Sawyer, Suzana. 2004. *Crude chronicles: Indigenous politics, multinational oil, and neoliberalism in Ecuador*. Durham, NC: Duke University Press.

Seagle, Caroline. 2012. Inverting the impacts: Mining, conservation, and sustainability claims near the Rio Tinto/QQM Ilmenite mine in southeast Madagascar. *Journal of Peasant Studies* 39(2): 447–477.

Sen, Amartya. 1999. *Development as freedom*. Cambridge, MA: Harvard University Press.

Shamir, Ronen. 2010. Capitalism, governance, and authority: The case of corporate social responsibility. *Annual Review of Law and Social Science* 6: 531–553.

Silverstein, Michael. 1976. Shifters, linguistic categories, and cultural description. In K. Basso and H. Selby, eds., *Meaning in anthropology*, pp. 11–55. Albuquerque: University of New Mexico Press.

Social Funds. 2000. Merrill Lynch fund participant pioneers divestment resolution, 27 July, http://www.socialfunds.com/news/save.cgi?sfArticleId=321

Strathern, Marilyn. 2000. Introduction: New accountabilities. In M. Strathern, ed., *Audit cultures: Anthropological studies in accountability, ethics, and the academy*, pp. 1–19. New York: Routledge.

Szablowski, David. 2007. *Transnational law and local struggles: Mining, communities and the World Bank*. Portland, OR: Hart Publishing.

Tait, Nikki. 1996. Ok Tedi copper mine damage claim settled, *Financial Times*, 12 June, 19.

Thomson, Ian, and Robert G. Boutilier. 2011. Social license to operate (Chapter 17.2). In P. Darling, ed., *SME mining engineering handbook*, pp. 1779–1796. Littleton, CO: Society for Mining, Metallurgy, and Exploration.

Tsing, Anna Lowenhaupt. 2004. *Friction: An ethnography of global connection*. Princeton University Press.

Urciuoli, Bonnie. 2003. Excellence, leadership, skills, diversity: Marketing liberal arts education, *Language and Communication* 23: 385–408.

Urciuoli, Bonnie. 2008. Skills and selves in the new workplace. *American Ethnologist* 35(2): 211–228.

Urciuoli, Bonnie. 2010. Entextualizing diversity. *Language and Communication* 30: 48–57.

Ward, Barbara, and René. J. Dubos. 1972. *Only one earth: The care and maintenance of a small planet*. New York: W.W. Norton.

Welker, Marina, and David Wood. 2011. Shareholder activism and alienation. *Current Anthropology* 52 (S3): S57–S69.

Stuart Kirsch is Professor of Anthropology at the University of Michigan. He is author of *Reverse anthropology* (Stanford, 2006) and *Mining capitalism* (California, 2014). He is currently working on a book about the politics of engaged research.

– Chapter 3 –

RE-SITING CORPORATE RESPONSIBILITY
The Making of South Africa's Avon Entrepreneurs
Catherine Dolan and Mary Johnstone-Louis

❧

Delivering poverty reduction door-to-door

"If you *tell yourself* that you *want* to do this, *you can do it.*" These words were spoken by Amanda,[1] one of Avon's door-to-door "entrepreneurs," as she stood in the garden of her home in rural Limpopo. Though the South African government provided her with the shell of her house as part of "reparations" for apartheid, Amanda's home remained sparsely furnished and structurally incomplete. Lacking a ceiling, and with a floor pocked by holes large enough to engulf her children, her home could be read as a kind of "dream deferred." But when we met Amanda, she was anything but dispirited. Since joining Avon, she said, she had reason to hope for her future.

Amanda's anticipated future is shared by millions of female "entrepreneurs" in developing countries today. Miles away in rural Bangladesh, poor women are selling Danone yogurt and Bata shoes house-to-house, while in India Unilever's *Shakti Ammas* (mothers) distribute soaps among remote villages. In the wake of C. K. Prahalad's 2004 publication, *The fortune at the bottom of the pyramid*, "bottom-of-the-pyramid" (BOP) schemes have featured prominently in the corporate-responsibility landscape. Lauded as the century's most influential model of socially responsible business (Anderson and Billou 2007), the BOP approach weds ethical practice and the pursuit of profit, maintaining that development goals can be achieved by simply extending the scope and scale of capitalism to the four billion men and women who live on less than two dollars per day (Cross and Street 2009, Prahalad 2004). It is a vision driven neither by corporate largesse nor Corporate Social Responsibility (CSR) frameworks, but by a web of entrepreneurs purported to stimulate capitalism while delivering poverty reduction and gender empowerment door-to-door.

This article explores how "the poor" are repurposed as the instruments of ethical capitalism through the progenitor of the BOP model—Avon Cosmetics. Avon has charted the course for several celebrated BOP schemes including Living Goods in Uganda and Unilever's Project *Shakti* in India, and has long stylized its entrepreneurial opportunity as a channel to a transcendent realm of self-actualization and social transformation. As Avon CEO Andrea Jung has described, "our success is measured by … how many lives we change, how many doors we open" (Avon 2010). In this article, we explore how Avon pursues this vision through a set of discourses and calculative practices that aim to produce industrious, self-disciplined, and "empowered" Avon representatives: "entrepreneurs" who are "beneficiaries" not of the company but of their own enterprising selves. It is a vision that appears to diffuse a familiar set of neoliberal rationalities: an emphasis on governance at a distance, calculability, and the promotion of self-activating and individuated subjects (Rose 1999). Yet while the company aims to instill a "self-driven" market discipline among a cadre of "underproductive" yet aspirant entrepreneurs, Avon's CSR ambition hinges on spheres that are conventionally anathema to a neoliberal view of a rational and asocial market economy—the affective world of family, kin, and community. It is through the social interactions of "Avon ladies," rather than the invisible hand of the market, that Avon aims to cultivate a workforce that is economically rational (Lemke 2001: 201).

Avon's capacity to draw thousands of unemployed women, as well as their attendant networks of kin and community, into productive work has rendered it an exemplar for private-sector approaches to poverty alleviation (Chu 2009). In South Africa, where unemployment, particularly among black women, is a pressing problem, such opportunities are not to be lightly dismissed. However, while BOP systems like Avon provide new avenues for income generation for some "poor" women, the practices through which women are "converted" into "empowered" entrepreneurial subjects can induce new forms of discipline and control. We suggest that while targeting the "bottom of the pyramid" may elide the distinction between the maximization of profit and the imperatives of sustainable development, devolving CSR to the "entrepreneurial poor" raises new questions on the implications of "making poverty business."

Making poverty business

BOP models are built on the premise that companies can fulfill the twin objectives of reducing global poverty and increasing corporate profits by targeting the world's poor as both consumers and "entrepreneurs." Yet in contrast to other CSR tools—protocols, compacts, and standards—BOP approaches do not simply "extend" rights, protections, or opportunities. Rather, they often work through self-regulatory modes of governance, or what Foucault (1977) terms the "technologies of the self." This "business" approach to alleviating poverty seeks to capacitate individuals, rendering the "self" rather than the global corporation the vehicle through which development aspirations can be realized. Through technologies of government widely associated with neoliberalism—a grammar of self-mastery and self-determination, practices of behavioral and bodily refinement, and rationalities of efficiency and responsibility— the individual becomes what Foucault (2004: 312) terms a "machine of competences." This human machine, "who is his own capital, his own producer, his own source of property" (ibid.: 314), is represented in the now-familiar archetype of the entrepreneur, an individual who governs him- or herself in the name of both personal empowerment and community "uplift," thus fusing entrepreneurial conduct with civic responsibility (von Schnitzler 2008). In what Rose describes as the "double movement of autonomization and responsibilization," the entrepreneur, whether a *Shakti Amma* or an Avon representative, is both a subject and an object of power, "set free to find their own destiny.... [but] made responsible for that destiny, and for the destiny of society as a whole in new ways" (Rose 1999:174).

BOP approaches advance a form of "ethical capitalism" that positions the (poor, often female) individual rather than the state or the market as ultimately responsible for generating (or not) development. They tend to promise the poor not only an income, but as Unilever claims of its much-vaunted *Project Shakti*, "self-esteem, a sense of empowerment and a place in society" (Unilever 2005). Yet through which processes are these "intangible assets" and new subjectivities produced? Which technologies of government are deployed to construct this new economy of corporate responsibility?

In the following, we explore these questions through the original BOP initiative, Avon Direct Selling.

Since its founding as the California Perfume Company in the United States in 1886, Avon has built a global workforce of more than 42,000 direct employees dedicated to recruiting, training, and motivating 5.5 million independent sales representatives to sell beauty and fashion products door-to-door. However, Avon frames the purpose of its firm, and the sales force that drives it, in terms that make no reference to the nature of the products they purvey. Rather, Avon positions itself as "the company that empowers women." As the firm's CSR report states:

> For 123 years, we have demonstrated our message of women's empowerment at every level and in every market that Avon serves.... [W]e have given tens of millions of Avon ... Representatives the opportunity to generate wealth, provide for their families and realize their personal dreams. (Avon 2010)

Avon's corporate vision seamlessly knits together its growth strategy with the moral aspirations of CSR, seeking to forge new subjectivities that are simultaneously "responsible and moral" and economically rational (Lemke 2001: 201). The company therefore provides a valuable aperture into the corporate ethics of BOP entrepreneurship—of what is meant to be transformed and how—when the everyday commodities of body lotion and perfume are heralded as keys to development.

This article is based on a qualitative and quantitative study of black South African Avon representatives and consumers conducted in three municipalities from 2007–2010: Johannesburg, Ekurhuleni Metropolitan, and Polokwane. Over the two-year period, we implemented two semistructured surveys (167 and 300 respondents respectively) and conducted approximately 75 in-depth interviews with randomly selected Avon associates (at all organizational levels) and consumers, as well as several open-ended interviews with management at the Johannesburg headquarters. We also took a closer ethnographic look at the workings of Avon through informal conversations and participant observation of Avon trainings and direct selling in a range of settings.

The moral mission of direct selling

Avon was one of the first multinationals to export female direct selling across the world, expanding into Latin America in the 1950s, Asia in the 1970s, and into Eastern Europe, China, and Russia in the 1990s (Marcial 2008). In 1996 Avon began operations in South Africa, where it has experienced phenomenal growth; there are currently 102,000 "Avon ladies" in the country, up from 35,000 in 2007 (Avon-Justine, interview 11/7/2010).

Emerging economies have propelled Avon into a position as the largest direct seller of beauty products in the world (Avon 2010), hatching millions of recruits among women who seek fortune and personal transformation through the company, and fostering what Katherine Verdery (1996: 203) has called a kind of "competition ... of the excluded." In South Africa, this competition became particularly acute in the postapartheid period, as policies associated with "free-market" capitalism spawned uneven economic opportunities and unleashed new areas of friction among the country's already poor and marginalized (Mindry 2008). In a nation that boosts Africa's highest GDP, one quarter of adults remain illiterate, and only fourteen percent of black South Africans have a high school qualification (South Africa Info 2006). While there has been an overall reduction in absolute-income poverty since the 1990s, the gap between the "haves" and the "have-nots" has widened (Turok 2008: 13), creating an asymmetry that is both racialized and gendered. This context, and its attendant backwash of "get-rich-quick" narratives, has rendered Avon's promise of economic and social mobility a magnet for thousands of black women (Comaroff and Comaroff 2000).

Crafting the entrepreneurial self

For Avon, the "promise" of empowerment is not a corporate "gift" (Rajak 2008), but one that is attained through fidelity to the principles of self-mastery and individual responsibility. This ethos of "productive citizenry" gained traction in the late 1990s, as South Africa embraced a welfare strategy founded on "neoliberal motifs of 'empowerment'", 'self-sufficiency' and "independence" (Ferguson 2007: 74; see also ANC 1997), promoting an entrepreneurial citizen who would supplant the inefficient state-led development (Colvin, Leavens, and Robins 2009: 9). Government programs such as Black Economic Empowerment (BEE) aimed to galvanize the participation of black South Africans in the "productive" economy, conceptualizing the market not as a *natural* system of relations but a realm to be cultivated through the development of entrepreneurial dispositions (Lemke 2001: 196). By recasting the unemployed as "micro-entrepreneurs" (Ferguson ibid.: 74), the government provided fertile ground for Avon's "empowerment" approach, mapping a national discourse of economic self-sufficiency onto the bodies of newly enterprising individuals.

The notion of the "self-maximizing entrepreneur" is a well documented feature of neoliberalism's "cultural and political lexicon" (Koelble 2008:166). Scholars of development have drawn attention to the way "informal," "subsistence," or otherwise underproductive workers are repurposed as entrepreneurial "clients" and "partners," as development practice in a neoliberal context shifted from state- to market-led approaches such as microcredit (Elyachar 2005; Rankin 2001; Sharma 2006), while anthropologists have described how neoliberal economic policies have instrumentalized the citizenry of states through entrepreneurial narratives that valorize individual success (Ferguson and Gupta 2002; Jeffery 2001:20; Ong 2006). Such conceptions of enterprise also form the crux of Avon's transnational management practices, as we observed when attending a training session in a Johannesburg township. Representatives there were told: "You have to *try and be ambitious* so that *you can succeed*," "You *can make it*, you just need to *have faith* in yourself," and "It is you that *decides what you want to do* with your team *in order for them to be successful*." We listened as the trainer described a bedridden Avon representative who was, because of her ambition, the highest earner in the area. Managing her sales using "a phone and a laptop on her stomach," this "amazing" woman was touted as an example to the trainees, who were chided for being outperformed by a woman confined to her bed. The pervasive emphasis on the link between positive attitude, hard work, and material success can have a quixotic appeal, speaking to the latent capacity of each person to succeed, if they simply "'develop,' 'exercise,' or 'give rein to'" their inherent potential (Jeffery 2001: 32). Yet in a socioeconomic and political context with palpable constraints on personal achievement—for black South Africans in general and for black South African women in particular—the championing of individual agency can be both liberating and oppressive. Because one can never have "enough" motivation, drive, or commitment, the insistence that poor women "are in charge of [their] own success," means that any failure can be equated with individual deficiency. As Bröckling (2005:9) summarizes in his analysis of the enterprising self: "In every incentive to do 'more,' the verdict of 'not enough' is hiding."

The Avon structure: Affect and value creation

Scholars influenced by Foucault (Dean 1999; Rose 1999; Rose and Miller 1992) have described how governance has shifted from control exercised by the centralized state to forms that facilitate management "at a distance" (Rose and Miller ibid.). Within Avon, the technology that makes this distance possible is the "upline/downline" system, a relational management system through which Avon produces and reproduces a workforce with the requisite dispositions of individual accountability, efficiency, and motivation (Rose ibid.).

Like other BOP schemes, Avon harnesses a large, flexible, and self-regulating work force without incurring the cost of managing employment relations or reproducing labor (Biggart 1989). Representatives are independent contractors onto whom Avon outsources key business functions including employee management, marketing, and distribution. Each representative is a current or previous customer of their "upline" and each person they recruit into the organization (who is him- or herself a customer) becomes a "downline" (Lan 2002). "Uplines" and "downlines" form the DNA of Avon's two corporate objectives: sales and recruitment. Income can be earned by selling products or by selling and recruiting others to sell and recruit, thus accumulating profit from those laboring "underneath" (Jeffery 2001) and galvanizing a continual process of upward mobility and generational reproduction.

The success of the upline/downline system lies in its capacity to orchestrate relationships within the network. Whereas the separation of affective ties from the workings of capitalism was once deemed necessary for managerial control, "affective labor" is central to many BOP initiatives (Hardt 1999: 90). Rather than relegating social relations to the unproductive, private sphere, door-to-door selling internalizes them into a core business practice, employing narratives and practices of communal care to create affective (and effective) labor relations. Avon encourages representatives to graft their incipient businesses onto existing social networks by recruiting and selling to people they know, a strategy that both colonizes and commodifies social relations by reframing them as objects of economic calculation (Jeffery 2001; Lan 2002). Avon also familiarizes the impersonal, parlaying business ties into fictive family structures that create affective bonds between representatives and analogizing the organizational structure to the intimate space of the family (see also Lan ibid.). Barbara, describing how she creates moral imaginaries of family among her downlines said: "I make sure that I introduce them to one another. It's like you are all my children, meet your sisters.... [T]hese are all your sisters and I am your mother. Get to know each other, exchange numbers." This "affective labor" serves calculative ends by inducing a "collective disposition" of emotional obligation across the horizontal and vertical axes of the company, blending the "instrumental action of economic production" with the "communicative action of human interaction" (Foucault 1977: 143; Hardt ibid.: 96). But as Lan (ibid.) has shown, metaphorical genealogies also act as mechanisms of network control, through which a language of affect veils a culture of mutual monitoring.

Preaching the gospel of Avon

In their analysis of contemporary capitalism in South Africa, Jean and John Comaroff (2000: 292) describe the rise of a "messianic, millennial capitalism," one that "presents itself as a gospel of salvation ... that, if rightly harnessed, is invested with the capacity to wholly transform the universe of the marginalized and disempowered." This gospel forms the crux of Avon's vision, which through a range of discursive strategies promotes the mundane practices of direct selling as a channel to a transcendent realm of self-actualization. For example, the "testimonial"—a confessional of self-transformation—is central to Avon's operations, simultaneously legitimizing and evangelizing the ethical script of the company. Sitting in a Soweto café one afternoon, we heard several Avon representatives recount journeys from homelessness, squatter camps, and AIDS-ravaged families to the community of hope and possibility afforded through Avon. Among them was Lindiwe, a young HIV-positive woman who had recently relocated to the outskirts of Johannesburg after her uncle had raped her, and her father, two sisters, and brother had died. She was living in government housing with her elderly mother, disabled brother, and a small child when we met, and she described to us her deliverance through Avon:

> In the past, I didn't do anything, I didn't care.... I was just waiting for my dying day because I didn't have the guts to kill myself. I just don't want to die anymore.... I don't think that there is another way I can survive except to stick [with Avon]. To put all my dedication to this because now I can feed and clothe my kid.... At least when I die I [will] know I left my baby something.

Similar accounts featured in many of our conversations with Avon representatives. Like the vignettes displayed on the Web sites of many a BOP scheme, women drew on a shared register of transformational narratives related to the tangible and intangible benefits of their newfound income stream. For example, the saying that representatives "can buy a loaf of bread with one lotion commission; if they sell five body lotions, their kids will have bread for the whole week; if they sell ten, they'll buy sugar and tea bags" is recited repeatedly, as are descriptions of life-affirming "blessings" of confidence and self-esteem. Florence, a Johannesburg upline, explained "I could have not achieved things that I have achieved ... without Avon. It developed me.... I didn't see that I had potential.... I did not realize that I can be a leader."

Representatives' testimonials mirror the ethical vision propagated by the company, and circulate in similar form from Bangkok (Wilson 1999) to Mexico City (Cahn 2006). Through repetition and routinization, these transformation stories become what Giddens (1991) would term "structurated" into a consistent set of discourses across the organization. But the transformational narrative is also localized, textured by the nation's fractious racial history and the transition to a "New South Africa." Several women cast Avon as a calling; an invocation to empower the black community through economic uplift. This ethic of moral responsibility became apparent when we escorted "long-time" representative Louise on her rounds to pick up orders. As we drove through the poorly serviced but vibrant world of informal settlements, Louise pointed out homes that had been transformed by Avon and described the personal anguish she felt about the ones that had not. "It makes me so sad," she said, "because ... I know how much they need this. That's why ... I have to push them, [and say] you can't do this [quit]! ... [W]hen a person like that fails what's going to happen ... Maybe she is going to start robbing houses and pickpocketing people's bags." The implications of a wayward downline not only represented a potential financial loss for Louise, but was interpreted as a setback for her society, one that frustrated Avon's promise to "change the world" (Avon 2010).

It is through the production and reproduction of such empowerment narratives that new subjectivities and collectivities are produced, even if they are, as we will discuss, directly exploited to produce capital (cf. Hardt 1999). But how is it that representatives come to view work not as economic calculus, but as a social duty, an economy of moral as well as financial cultivation (Mahmood 2003)? It is to this question that we now turn.

The calculative practices of empowerment

Avon operates not through the "managerial gaze" of shop-floor supervision, but through what Callon (2009) terms "calculative devices" that transform the "unproductive self" into a "productive" one (Hanser 2005), by extending calculative rationalities into the hitherto noneconomic sphere of social relations. Described by Callon (ibid.: 270), "entities to be calculated are first 'detached' or moved and ordered into a single space whether a … spreadsheet or an invoice, then some manipulations or transformations are performed upon the entities before, finally, a result, a sum or a choice, is extracted." In the case of Avon, women are deliberately detached from a perceived torpid world of dependency and enfolded into the enterprising "community" of Avon, remade as "entrepreneurs" through practices that seek to banish idleness in any form. Unstructured "free" time can and should be "redeemed," interpersonal relationships can and should become sources of income, and a representative's body can and should be transformed into a business asset. In the following, we will examine how Avon employs several calculative practices—targets and tracking, time management, and fashioning the imagined future— to construct the subjectivity of the "empowered" entrepreneur. It is in understanding the disciplinary effects of these strategies that a friction between Avon's vision of gender empowerment and the dilemma of the enterprising self becomes apparent.

Targets and tracking

Avon representatives are christened into the company through a personal orientation process with their uplines, who are then responsible for managing their performance with the organization. Dubbed "Training for Success," this orientation presents Avon as a "relationship business" that can generate "personal empowerment and amazing earning potential" by capitalizing on everyday social interactions (Avon 2008). Uplines are responsible for indoctrinating new representatives into the habits, dispositions, and modes of conduct required to succeed and "reproduce" in the Avon family. This process aims to impart inspiration as much as information, converting hearts and minds to the Avon vision in order to transform "the act of 'selling' into an act of 'believing'" (Lan 2002: 172). It also involves creating "spaces of calculability," contexts that facilitate "the capacity for economic calculation" (Callon 2009: 270) through a range of devices such as performance targets, pedagogical tools ("Weekly

Goals" worksheets), monitoring regimes ("Progress to Date" check-in calls), and performance reviews ("Let's Talk" chats[2]). Through these devices uplines exercise control, facilitating the productivity of "active" members and pulling wayward downlines back into the fold "whenever they become idle" (Lan ibid.: 176).

Avon establishes specific targets governing the levels of recruitment and sales necessary for representatives to earn commission. These goals are fixed and clearly remunerated. They can also be exacting. For example, in order to quality for commission, a mid-level representative must reach a personal sales target, recruit a given number of new representatives, and, through relational supervision, ensure that her downlines' sales meet specific levels. If not, as Louise explained, even those who "really go an extra mile" on personal sales lose their commissions. At a training session, Louise emphasized to the uplines gathered in her small sitting room the importance of meeting institutional targets. Describing the process of recruitment, she said, "This is a numbers game.... Don't just go out and say that you are going to see what happens.... You set yourself a target.... You say 'I am going out prospecting and I won't come back until I have ten names.'" Callon's "binaries" are thus created as representatives are confronted with the choice between success or failure and enterprise or idleness infinite times a day, and become accountable to their Avon "family" for their choices.

These targets do not craft self-directed workers alone; rather, their achievement is closely observed and assessed through upline/downline relationships, replacing, as Lan notes (2002: 181), the "iron cage of bureaucratic management" with the practices of "network surveillance." At one training, Louise cautioned her downlines to "focus" hard on their recruits so that they wouldn't "miss anything." They would not, she advised, want to repeat the same mistake as Caroline, a "friend" who lost her commission because two of her downlines sold 0.5 percent under their target. Louise offered a palliative to such fates: a set of tools to monitor, and hence render downlines governable, including "Development Call Observation Forms" (used to assess downlines during "informal appointments") and "Training Logs" (to track the "development" of a downline to "make sure they are successful"). Results, she noted, were to be continually measured, and success (and failure) tracked. Similarly, representative Barbara described how assiduously she tracks her downlines' performance to ensure that their sales keep "going up, because if it goes down there is going to be trouble ... I am going to be on the phone. The one thing that they [downlines] hate about me is when I am really, really mad, I will SMS them at midnight and they just hate it." Indeed, while such strategies are cast as the ticket to market success, they may be counterproductive. As one representative noted, "Reporting everything, how many recruits you have made or how many orders, immediately demotivates you."

The strategies of calculability, however, are often more subtle. Stephen, a representative in the city of Polokwane, described how he plays the roles of "good cop" and "bad cop" with his downlines, explaining that he had to be "strict" and "tough" to reach his team's performance targets, but once they were achieved he would "laugh and joke" with his team "so that they can feel more at home." Other times, uplines cultivate discipline by tapping into cultural sentiments that venerate obligation to kin and community. Louise, for instance, reminded her downlines of their maternal responsibility to help their recruits, saying "You are mothers now. You need to help your babies." This familial metaphor, however, obscures the web of calculation that upholds it: Avon mothers are not only "watching" their "babies" but are also being "watched" themselves, positioned in the center of a generational hierarchy with ties of responsibility to members above and below them.

Such strategies aim to produce the "empowered" and high-performing women that are central to Avon's mission. But they also render representatives subjects of, and subject to, the discipline of ongoing monitoring, the effects of which are sanitized by the company's informal vernacular of "chats" and "check-ins." Monitoring and surveillance are recoded as "Let's talk"; prospecting for a sale or a new recruit becomes "striking up a conversation with a friend"; and achievement and performance evaluation are euphemized as "being a good example for your downlines." As in Benson and Kirsch's (2010) study of corporate oxymorons, the deployment of benign idioms serves to confound the distinction between discipline and empowerment, while at the same time effecting what might be considered a "strategic ignorance" among representatives (Carrillo and Mariotti 2000).

Time management

Uplines are encouraged to "show, share, and observe" their subordinates, vigilant, above all, for underperformance. Diaries are provided to new representatives so that they can banish "unproductive" time through careful planning and "time management." This imperative to partition time is, on one level, a symbolic and material

"boundary" between an aimless past and a modern future (Rose 1999).
Yet it is also a technology of discipline that inscribes the efficiency of
the clock into the comportment of representatives, by normalizing a
system of time management that is "all Avon, all the time." Uplines
drill their downlines on the "Four A's" of Avon, a motto that urges
representatives to "anytime, anywhere, always ask"[3] if they can share
an Avon brochure, thus fusing representatives' public and private
worlds and recasting each and every human interaction as a business
opportunity. As we waited for colleagues at a petrol station in
Limpopo, a senior representative traveling with us took advantage of
our "spare" ten minutes, "redeeming her time" by leaving our vehicle
and introducing the Avon opportunity to women at and around the
station. Representatives thus inhabit a universe that troubles easy
binaries, where the economic bleeds into the social, the public into
the private, and the sacred into the profane, effectively diffusing the
"entrepreneurial form to all forms of conduct" (Burchell 1996: 275).
Louise, for example, describes the need to prevent her downlines
from resting "too much" over the Christmas holiday, while Stephen
explained that he would have little sympathy for a downline who
missed a target because she had to attend a funeral, claiming that "it's
not an excuse … you meet people there at the funerals." A funeral, he
reasoned, provides a good opportunity to show off a new fragrance,
and by engaging in conversations with other funeral attendees, one
might have as many as five new customers at the end of the event.
Every moment and interaction thus become expectant, as all spheres
of social life—sustenance, worship, grief, and leisure—can and should
be appropriated for commercial ends.

Fashioning the imagined future

As Nikolas Rose (1990: 103) argues, the figure of the productive subject
corresponded to a reframing of the nature of work as an activity
through which individuals "produce, discover, and experience"
themselves. It became the process, rather than outcome of work, that
engendered an actualized self, an observation borne out in Avon's
techniques of dream-building and body-fashioning. Indeed, one of
the most visible ways in which representatives internalize Avon's
vision of empowered entrepreneurs is through what Lan (2003) terms
"bodily labor": a set of "productive" practices centered on physical
deportment and bodily refinement (see also Mauss [1935] 1973). These
practices are personified in the iconic figure of the Avon lady—a
professional, "modern" woman whose dress, makeup, and manner

reflect the global beauty aesthetic and transnational cosmopolitanism purveyed by the company. This display and circulation of gender norms is not simply a mechanism of labor control through which the company "disciplines" the docile subjects required by transnational capital (see, e.g., Salzinger 2003). Rather, gender and sexuality are what workers are expected to produce. The South African "Training for Success" brochure, for instance, asks: "What does Avon expect from you?" and informs representatives that they are to dress appropriately, wear Avon fragrances, and most importantly "Smile!" (Avon 2008: 10). Through a process that Ann Anagnost (2006) describes as "value coding," deportment not only marks success but qualifies women "as this or that type of person (i.e. enterprising, unenterprising)" (McCabe 2008: 372). As a group sales leader from Pietermaritzburg explained, "there's a difference" between the deportment of "Avon ladies" and others, a difference that is reified by the glossy catalogues and free samples women carry—the symbolic capital that stylizes Avon representatives as upwardly mobile in the "New South Africa." The groomed body thus acts as a dual "placing strategy" (Jeffery 2001), anchoring representatives within the organizational hierarchy as successful (or not) entrepreneurs while transporting them to an imagined geography of global sophistication.

Techniques of self-fashioning are also diffused through Avon's "Build Your Dream Campaign," a planning device that helps individuals to envision a future born from their self-initiative and promises that "this is the year when your dreams come to fruition … when your visions of achievement … are transferred from the realm of possibility into your everyday reality" (cited by Dolan and Scott 2009: 212). Upline Priscilla emphasized that her downlines should begin the "dream-building" process in their new recruits' homes in order to take stock of the material possessions that are "missing" and steer the conversation toward their acquisition. Standing with her recruit in a sparsely furnished bedroom with a mattress on the floor, Priscilla might describe the representative's bringing home a bed frame purchased with Avon earnings, installing a matching bedroom set, and decorating the room for her children. Similarly, Polokwane representative Penelope begins the "dream-building" process by asking her downlines to strategically position magazine images of desired objects around their homes. Illustrating how the dream-building process is both disciplining and aestheticizing, she explained that goals must be visual and measurable, stating "you're committing to yourself, you're only going to hurt yourself if you break that promise. So you commit with the picture."

The possibilities unleashed through the process of dream-building frequently associate the Avon opportunity with access to lavish consumer goods. Yet in a country where unemployment and racialized poverty remain pervasive, a considerable gap often exists between women's life-worlds and the objects of their desire. Representative Prudence, who lived with her children in a one-room rented dwelling without plumbing, told us: "I'm dreaming ... I want a four room or maybe five rooms [house] and a car with my Avon money...," while others told us they dreamt Avon could make them a millionaire. By fanning dreams of consumption, dream-building "detaches" women like Prudence from the bounded world of the present, enabling them to envisage a self that is entirely dissociated from the reality of current circumstance using the currency of clear intention and self-belief. But while such practices aim to instill a belief in the "democratization" of opportunity, they can also mask the genuine barriers women face to realizing their imagined futures amidst the inequalities and hardships that continue to mark life for many in South African townships.

Conclusion

"Market-based" approaches to poverty reduction have gained considerable purchase in recent decades, endowing transnational business with both the moral authority and the obligation to tackle global development challenges. Within this context, the BOP proposition, which claims to stimulate corporate profits while drawing the "under-productive" poor into new forms of commercial activity, has emerged as a "paragon" of ethical capitalism, admired by corporations and NGOs alike (Cross and Street 2009). Yet despite these accolades, how the entrepreneurial developmentalism of the BOP approach is practiced and experienced in everyday lives at the bottom of the pyramid has been little explored.

This article has considered how a BOP-driven "ethical economy" is produced in South Africa, through an examination of Avon Cosmetics, a prototype for a range of BOP initiatives that mark the landscape of corporate responsibility today. Since its beginnings, Avon has sought to combine corporate growth with a moral imperative to uplift women, aspiring to open entrepreneurial possibilities to those excluded from the commercial mainstream. Yet the entrepreneurial "Avon lady" is not an "always-already" figure. Rather, she is purposively engineered, whetted through corporate practices that aim to graft market rationality onto all spheres of life.

Indeed, becoming one of Avon's "empowered" entrepreneurs requires not only a shift in women's work lives, but a redrafting of their physical, spiritual, and social worlds for instrumental ends.

Avon seeks to blend the seemingly discordant spheres of moral value and market rationality through a range of calculative practices, from time management and tracking targets to life planning and bodily fashioning, in order to craft entrepreneurial subjects with the requisite traits of self-discipline, industry, and enterprise. These subjectivities, however, are not produced through direct corporate supervision. Rather, Avon choreographs this process of self-renewal from a distance, enrolling women in their futures through corporate idioms of competence, preparedness, and self-reliance and a script of self-invention. Indeed, corporate aspirations come to fruition precisely because the company inculcates market discipline among "underutilized" entrepreneurs by engineering a governance of the self. Avon representatives thus serve as their own Panopticons, "exercising" as Foucault wrote (1980: 155), "surveillance over, and against" themselves, while engineering and assuming "responsibility" for their own "empowerment."

In fact, while it is glossed as *corporate* responsibility, the locus of Avon's moral obligation lies far from the company's Manhattan headquarters. Rather, it sits with its South African "entrepreneurs," who must generate the subjectivities required to transform their "realm of possibility" (in Avon vernacular) into their "everyday reality." Yet while outsourcing "empowerment" to the BOP allows transnational firms like Avon to enjoy new markets as well as considerable reputational currency, and provides some women with a viable opportunity for generating income, the economic and social benefits this form of corporate responsibility promises will remain elusive to those women who lack the resources, "discipline" or "enterprise" to reinvent themselves.

Acknowledgments

We thank Dinah Rajak, Luisa Steur, and two anonymous reviewers for their constructive comments on this paper. We also thank the ESRC/DFID and the Oxford University Press John Fell Research Fund for their generous support of the research, and the management, staff and representatives of Avon-Justine (Pty) in South Africa for sharing their time and experiences with us. The views expressed in the article are those of the authors alone.

Notes

1. All names are pseudonyms.
2. "Getting Started in Sales Leadership" presentation, Johannesburg, South Africa, 15 March 2010.
3. See: http://www.avon.co.za/PRSuite/selling/benefits.jsp.

References

Anagnost, Ann. 2006. Strange circulations: The blood economy in rural China. *Economy and Society* 35 (4): 509–529.

ANC. 1997. Social welfare white paper marks major shift in welfare strategy. *Parliamentary Bulletin*, 19 February, http://www.anc.org.za/show.php?doc=ancdocs/pubs/whip/whip09.html.

Anderson, Jamie, and Niels Billou. 2007. Serving the world's poor: Innovation at the base of the economic pyramid. *Journal of Business Strategy* 28 (2): 14–21.

Avon. 2008. *Training for success*. Johannesburg: Avon Justine (Pty).

Avon. 2010. *Corporate responsibility: Making the world more beautiful.* New York: Avon Company.

Benson, Peter, and Stuart Kirsch. 2010. Corporate oxymorons. *Dialectical Anthropology* 24 (1): 45–48.

Biggart, Nicole. 1989. *Charismatic capitalism: Direct selling organizations in America*. Chicago: University of Chicago Press.

Bröckling, Ulrich. 2005. Gendering the enterprising self: Subjectification programs and gender differences in guides to success. *Distinktion* 11: 7–23.

Burchell, Graham. 1996. Liberal government and techniques of the self. In *Foucault and political reason*, eds. A. Barry, T. Osborne, and N. Rose, 19–36. London: University College London Press.

Cahn, Peter. 2006. Building down and dreaming up: Finding faith in a Mexican multilevel marketer. *American Ethnologist* 33 (1): 126–42.

Callon, Michel. 2009. Devices and desires: How useful is the "new" new economic sociology for understanding market attachment? *Sociology Compass* 3/2: 267–82.

Carrillo, Juan, and Thomas Mariotti. 2000. Strategic ignorance as a self-disciplining device. *Review of Economic Studies* 67: 529–44.

Colvin, Christopher, Joan Leavens, and Steven Robins. 2009. Seeing like a "PWA": A study of therapeutic citizens and welfare subjects in Cape Town, South Africa. CPRC Working Paper 144. Manchester, UK: CPRC.

Comaroff, Jean, and John Comaroff. 2000. Millennial capitalism: First thoughts on a second coming. *Public Culture* 12 (2): 291–343.

Chu, Jeff. 2009. Avon calling: Could beauty be a path out of poverty? *Fast Company*, Wednesday, 25 Mar 2009.

Cross, Jamie, and Alice Street. 2009. Anthropology at the bottom of the pyramid. *Anthropology Today* 25 (4): 4–9.

Dean, Mitchell. 1999. *Governmentality: Power and rule in modern society*. London: Sage.

Dolan, Catherine, and Linda Scott. 2009. Lipstick evangelism: Avon trading circles and gender empowerment in South Africa. *Gender and Development* 17 (2): 203–218.

Elyachar, Julia. 2005. *Markets of dispossession: NGOs, economic development, and the state in Cairo*. Durham: Duke University Press.

Ferguson, James. 2007. Formalities of poverty: Thinking about social assistance in neoliberal South Africa. *African Studies Review* 50 (2): 71–86.

Ferguson, James, and Akhil Gupta. 2002. Spatializing states: Toward an ethnography of neoliberal governmentality. *American Ethnologist* 29 (4): 981–1002.

Foucault, Michel. 1977. *Discipline and punish.* Harmondsworth: Penguin.

Foucault, Michel. 1980. The eye of power. In *Power/knowledge: Selected interviews and other writings 1972–1977 by Michel Foucault*, ed. C. Gordon, 146–65. Sussex: Harvester Press.

Foucault, Michel. 2004. Naissance de la biopolitique: Cours au Collège de France (1978–1979). Paris: Seul.

Giddens, Anthony. 1991. *Modernity and selfidentity: Self and society in the late modern age.* Cambridge: Polity.

Hanser, Amy. 2005. The gendered rice bowl: The sexual politics of service work in urban China. *Gender and Society* 19 (5): 581–600.

Hardt, Michael. 1999. Affective labor. *Boundary 2* 26 (2): 89–100.

Jeffery, Lyn. 2001. Placing practices: Transnational network marketing. In *China urban: Ethnographies of contemporary culture*, eds. N. Chen, C. Clark, S. Gottschang, and L. Jeffery, 23–66. Durham: Duke University Press.

Koelble, Thomas. 2008. Market and economy. In *New South African keywords*, eds. N. Shepherd and S. Robins, 157–68. Johannesburg: Jacana.

Lan, Pei-Chia. 2002. Networking capitalism: Network construction and control effects in direct selling. *The Sociological Quarterly* 43 (2): 165–84.

Lan, Pei-Chia. 2003. Working in a neon cage: "Bodily labor" of cosmetics saleswomen in Taiwan. *Feminist Studies* 29 (1): 1–25.

Lemke, Thomas. 2001. The birth of bio-politics: Michel Foucault's lecture at the Collège de France on neo-liberal governmentality. *Economy and Society* 30: 190–207.

Mahmood, Saba. 2003. Ethical formation and politics of individual autonomy in contemporary Egypt. *Social Research* 70 (3): 1501–1530.

Marcial, Gene. 2008. Gene Marcial's stock picks. *Business Week.* 27 October 2008.

Mauss, Marcel. (1935) 1973. Techniques of the body. *Economy and Society* 2: 70–88.

McCabe, Darren. 2008. Who's afraid of enterprise?: Producing and repressing the enterprise self in a UK bank. *Organization* 15 (3): 371–87.

Mindry, Deborah. 2008. Neoliberalism, activism, and HIV/AIDS in postapartheid South Africa. *Social Text* 26 (194): 75–93.

Ong, Aiwah. 2006. *Neoliberalism as exception.* Durham: Duke University Press.

Prahalad, C. K. 2004. *The fortune at the bottom of the pyramid: Eradicating poverty through profits.* State College, Penna.: Wharton School Publishing.

Rajak, Dinah. 2008. Uplift and empower: The market, the gift and corporate social responsibility on South Africa's platinum belt. *Research in Economic Anthropology* 28: 297–324.

Rankin, Katherine. 2001. Governing development: Neoliberalism, microcredit, and rational economic woman. *Economy and Society* 30 (1): 18–37.

Rose, Nikolas. 1990. *Governing the soul: The shaping of the private self.* London: Routledge.

Rose, Nikolas. 1999. *Powers of freedom: Reframing political thought.* Cambridge: Cambridge University Press.

Rose, Nikolas, and Peter Miller. 1992. Political power beyond the state: Problematics of government. *British Journal of Sociology* 43 (2): 173–205.

Salzinger, Leslie. 2003. *Genders in production: Making workers in Mexico's global factories.* Berkeley and Los Angeles: University of California Press.

Sharma, Aradhana. 2006. Crossbreeding institutions, breeding struggle: Women's empowerment, neoliberal governmentality, and state (re)formation in India, *Cultural Anthropology* 21 (1): 60–95.

South Africa Info. 2006. *Education in South Africa*, http://www.southafrica.info/about/ education/education.htm.

Turok, Ben. 2008. *From the freedom charter to Polokwane: The evolution of ANC economic policy.* Cape Town: New Agenda.

Unilever. 2005. Project *Shakti*. Creating rural entrepreneurs in India, www.unilever.co.uk/ Images/es_Project_Shakti_tcm28-13297.pdf.

Verdery, Katherine. 1996. *What was socialism, and what comes next?* Princeton: Princeton University Press.

von Schnitzler, Antina. 2008. Citizenship prepaid: Water, calculability, and techno-politics in South Africa. *Journal of Southern African Studies* 34 (4): 899–917.

Wilson, Ara. 1999. The empire of direct sales and the making of Thai entrepreneurs. *Critique of Anthropology* 19 (4): 401–422.

Catherine Dolan is on the faculty of anthropology at SOAS, University of London, and holds fellowships at the James Martin Institute, Green Templeton College and Said Business School, all at University of Oxford. Her research centers on contemporary forms of moral capitalism, including Fairtrade, inclusive development and bottom of the pyramid business in Africa. She is a co-founder of the Centre for New Economies of Development (www.responsiblebop.com).

Mary Johnstone-Louis is a doctoral candidate in the Marketing Programme, Saïd Business School, University of Oxford. Her research focuses on the links between business and economic development. Before joining Oxford she worked in both economic development policy and in the private sector in Europe and Latin America.

– Chapter 4 –

POWER, INEQUALITY, AND CORPORATE SOCIAL RESPONSIBILITY
The Politics of Ethical Compliance in the South Indian Garment Industry

Geert De Neve

Corporate codes of conduct and voluntary labor standards have begun to affect the world of production across the globe. Such codes and standards seek to improve the conditions of employment of workers in sourcing factories, especially those located in developing countries. While the corporate social responsibility (CSR) concerns of Western companies cannot be reduced to a set of codes and standards, in sectors such as food and garment production such labor codes nevertheless form the primary tool through which western companies and chain stores seek to influence the social and environmental conditions of employment in their outsourcing networks (Nadvi and Wältring 2004: 71–73).

A burgeoning literature has emerged that concerns itself with the definition and classification of such codes and standards (Nadvi and Wältring 2004), their implementation by multinational companies and producing firms (Nadvi 2004), and their relative success in improving conditions of work for male and female workers (Barrientos, Dolan and Tallontire 2003; Barrientos and Smith 2007). However, relatively little has been written on the political changes that such social and ethical standards engender in the relationships between Western buyers, supply firms and subcontractors in non-Western parts of the world. This chapter therefore focuses on what I call the politics of ethical compliance—that is, the ways in which ethical corporate regulations are shaped by and constitutive of power relations and inequalities in the global market. It explores the ways in which ethical and social standards imposed on supply firms help to generate not only measurable and auditable changes in conditions of work, but also mold social relationships between different actors in transnational production chains. It will be argued that codes and standards are not merely technical tools to regulate labor regimes. They do not merely contribute to the manufacturing of commodities to specified standards; they also generate new social regimes of power and inequality.

In an illuminating description of the effects of European Union (EU) food processing standards imposed on Polish farmers and processing plants, Elizabeth Dunn discusses how EU food standards aimed not only at improving product quality but also transforming firms and procedures in line with EU practices (2005: 176). In this process, the justification for imposing standards was based on a discourse that casts Polish farmers and processors as unsafe and risk-bearing subjects, for which standardization was posited as the antidote (ibid.: 180). Dunn essentially argues that standards are never neutral. They are carriers of value and judgment, and hence creators of value hierarchies. Standards also produce hierarchies of subjects— be they states, regions, industries or firms—ranked according to their relative compliance with the benchmark concerned. For Polish food processors, Dunn comments:

> The hierarchy of value that standards lay out quickly transmutes *difference* into *impurity*. Standards thus act as more than technologies for organizing and regulating markets, and express fundamental social relations between groups. They set up a distinct power differential between the rule-making western European members of the EU, and Poland (ibid.: 181).

Here, I am similarly interested in the processes through which Western buyers and chain stores enforce compliance with company codes of conduct and labor standards among garment suppliers in the industrial cluster of Tiruppur, South India. I am particularly interested in the ways that the implementation of codes and standards is imposed at the local level, how supply firms react to such codes, and how the CSR policies of Western companies have become a tool for structuring the relationship between buyers and suppliers and, further down the chain, between suppliers and their subcontractors. Discourses and policies of CSR have become a central tool through which postcolonial power inequalities are being maintained and reshaped, and often even intensified by dominant players in the global market. Dolan has similarly argued, with reference to the imposition of standards in Kenya's fair-trade flower chain, that "the universalist ethos embraced by fair-trade consumers, which aims to render disparate economies and producers commensurable, is tempered, as the technologies of standards and certification reify ... distinctions within as well as across communities" (2008: 273).

At the heart of corporate ethical sourcing policies lies a set of social auditing and monitoring mechanisms through which buyers instigate a regime of control that casts Western companies and consumers as knowledgeable, caring and disciplined, and their non-Western suppliers as backward, uncaring and lacking self-control. Hence, the latter are in need of disciplining, and buyers seek to achieve this through the strict imposition of codes and standards, and through frequent inspections and careful auditing processes that enforce compliance. Dolan writes that such auditing and verification exercises operate as "a technology of governance, one that identifies, manages and packages information about Southern producers in the name of ethical accountability" (ibid.: 288).

Hence, along with the regulation and standardization of production processes, ethical codes and standards also spread values and create persons and selves. They form an explicitly classificatory device that ranks people according to the extent to which they have internalized the values that standards embody. This is not to argue that supply firms in South India, their owners, managers and workers have all internalized the values promoted by standards, nor is it to suggest that they blindly oblige, for, as we shall see, there are various expressions of resistance to this imposition. Rather, I argue that producers are forced to engage with a set of values about how to produce and how to deal with labor that are not of their own making and that they frequently see as an external—Western—intervention that both ignores and devalues their own ways of organizing production.

The Indian context in all of this is relevant too. In many ways, contemporary disciplining projects by Western companies can be considered a neocolonial practice, mirroring earlier colonial interventions that similarly sought to regulate, educate, and classify (Cohn 1996; Dirks 2001; Dolan 2008). Under the current neoliberal regime in India, the corporate imposition of new "regulatory mechanisms" is facilitated by both state and general political support for liberalization policies. In a context where the state strongly supports neoliberalism (Chopra 2003; De Neve 2008), it is relatively easy for Western corporate labor codes and international standards to enter the country and shape labor regimes across export industries. It could be argued that the very openness of its economic policies makes

India vulnerable to new and external forms of corporate governance that have already begun to shape its industrial landscape.

The Tiruppur garment industry

Tiruppur, located in Tamil Nadu, South India, is one of the largest garment manufacturing clusters in South Asia. It has boomed almost without interruption since the early 1970s when manufacturers began to export to Europe, and today it is a leading center of garment export for the world market. The Tiruppur industrial cluster constitutes one of India's most important foreign exchange earners, with a total export value of around Rs 11,000 crore or $2 billion in 2007. Tiruppur is primarily a garment cluster, producing T-shirts, sportswear, underwear and nightwear for niche markets in Europe and increasingly in northern America. Production is organized across different types of firms. Some large export firms are fully integrated, from spinning mills to garment production units, and may employ a few thousand workers. The majority of firms, however, are small or medium-size, specialize in only one or two stages of the production process, and employ between five and fifty workers. Some firms specialize in knitting, others in dyeing and processing, and others again in garment production or quality checking. Estimates suggest that there are about 10,000 production units in Tiruppur, employing more than 400,000 workers, but real numbers may well be higher than this. Much of the labor force consists of commuters from the region, long-distance migrants (mainly recruited from the southern districts of Tamil Nadu), and increasingly migrant workers coming from as far as Manipur and Nagaland in the north-east (De Neve 2003). The important point to make is that the success of the Tiruppur cluster rests on its dense subcontracting network, in which garments move through a series of production units—often as many as twenty or thirty—before being sent off to their overseas destinations (Chari 2004).

Labor practices within the cluster vary widely. Whereas in large export firms working conditions are on the whole more favorable than in the factories of subcontractors, a number of labor issues remain a matter of concern across the industry. Overtime is hard to control, with a twelve-hour working day being the norm; pensions and social insurance provisions are absent in all but the largest companies; freedom of association is severely curtailed across firms; and gender inequality shapes the feminization of major sections of the industry. I hasten to add, though, that few of these conditions can be easily addressed by international codes and standards, and universal labor standards may poorly meet the specific requirements of Tiruppur's diverse workforce (De Neve 2008). Many migrant workers, for example, prefer to work twelve-hour shifts in town in order to make a living and send money home, while some actively avoid working in firms where an eight-hour shift is imposed or where ESI (employees' state insurance) and PF (provident fund) contributions are deducted from their daily wages.[1]

Following the opening of the market in the 1980s and the phasing out of the Multi-Fibre Arrangement (MFA) between 1995 and 2005, textile and garment industries across the globe have been radically restructured, with subcontracting and price competition on the rise (Scott 2006; McCormick, Kamau and Ligulu 2006). Some warn of an ever-faster "race to the bottom," which they claim is unavoidable given the enormous power wielded by giant retailers and branded merchandisers (Appelbaum 2005).

At the heart of global production processes lies a rapidly deepening contradiction. Western competition for the cheapest possible products pushes down prices paid to suppliers and their workers, while at the same time retailers and chain stores claim to be increasingly concerned with working conditions at the sites of production. It is this concern that has shaped much CSR intervention in the garment sector over the last two decades. Various "regulatory interventions," developed by global buyers and Western companies, seek to regulate employment conditions in their supply networks (Dolan and Humphrey 2000; Tallontire 2007). In Tiruppur, such interventions take the form of company codes of conduct and voluntary labor standards that Western buyers increasingly require garment manufacturers and subcontractors to comply with.

The rise and rise of codes and standards

While carrying out fieldwork in Tiruppur in 1999 and 2000, company codes of conduct and labor standards were not mentioned once in conversations with manufacturers. Factory owners and exporters alike talked extensively about the need to improve the quality of their garments and to enhance production capacity in preparation of the anticipated post-2005 rise in exports. As far as product standards were concerned, an increasing number of large export companies sought to comply with ISO 9000, a widespread international product quality assurance standard. While being ISO 9000 certified might improve exporters' chances of getting better and larger orders, this certification was in no way essential to obtain orders, nor did it give producers any major advantage over local non-certified competitors.

By 2005 the picture had changed quite drastically. Interviews with exporters suggested that product quality was no longer the main issue of concern, and today it is generally agreed that Tiruppur manufacturers are able to produce whatever quality Western consumers want and to meet whatever lead time is required. Today, it is the "codes of conduct"—as they are commonly referred to—that are the recurrent topic of conversation and concern. With "codes of conduct" manufacturers refer to the buyer-imposed codes of conduct and certified labor standards as well as to the ever more intrusive inspections and audits that their firms are now subjected to. It is with these social standards that this chapter is concerned.

The most popular form of private standard initiative in the Tiruppur garment industry is the company codes of conduct, first introduced around 2000. Company codes seek to regulate the social conditions of employment in garment firms. They are usually made up of a fairly fixed list of regulations, set by the buying company, which supply firms are asked to comply with (see Table 4.1). They are a private standard initiative that allows buyers to select supply firms on the basis of their relative compliance with a series of regulations.[2] Most company codes of conduct refer in the first instance to the implementation of the labor laws of the concerned countries and in addition list a set of minimum labor standards stipulated by the company itself.

Given that such standards are set internally by the buying company and monitored by its own inspectors, a great deal of suspicion surrounds their implementation and hence their effectiveness in

Table 4.1. Generic ethical code of conduct

1. Compliance with local labor laws and workplace regulations.
2. Prohibition of child labor.
3. Regulation of contract labor.
4. Non-discrimination.
5. Prohibition of forced labor.
6. Freedom of association and the right to collective bargaining.
7. Humane treatment.
8. Minimum wages, living wage and other benefits.
9. Regulation of working hours.
10. Working conditions (health and safety).

improving conditions of work (Nadvi and Wältring 2004; Barrientos and Smith 2007). While such codes of conduct are rapidly spreading in Tiruppur and while the pressure to comply increases by the day, I encountered a great deal of skepticism among manufacturers, unions and non-governmental organizations (NGOs) about their real impact on the shop floor and about compliance among smaller firms and subcontractors, as we shall see below.

In addition to company codes of conduct, several international voluntary labor standards have made their inroads into Tiruppur too, the most prevalent of which are the Social Accountability 8000 Standard (SA8000) and the Worldwide Responsible Apparel Production certification (WRAP). These are generic standards that seek to harmonize social minimum standards across industries. They incorporate the core International Labor Organization (ILO) labor standards, refer to national legislation, and aim to streamline independent company codes (Nadvi and Wältring 2004: 81–84). SA8000 was developed by Social Accountability International (SAI) and is primarily used by Europe-based chain stores and buyers. WRAP is an independent non-profit organization based in the US and its certification is mainly used by US-based companies.

Tiruppur exporters can obtain certification for their garment factories by putting the required social management systems in place and having their units audited by an independent auditing company. Unlike the case of company codes, compliance with certified standards is checked through a "third-party" auditing process, which is said to enhance the standard's credibility and hence the value of certification itself. In Tiruppur, a local branch of the Swiss international certification company Société Générale de Surveillance (SGS) was opened in 1996. Though initially they only undertook product testing and inspection, since 2000 they have also been carrying out social audits, and they are now one of Tiruppur's leading accredited auditors for SA8000, WRAP and other certifications such as Environmental Management Systems (EMS).

Certification and audit procedures are available, but who uses them and what are their implications for supply firms and subcontractors in Tiruppur? The implications of adopting codes and certifications are substantial. At a material level, they necessitate significant investments in factory buildings, canteens, workers' hostels and so on, to comply with regulations pertaining to working conditions, occupational health, safety and the environment. For larger export firms, these usually require a number of one-off adjustments to buildings and equipment, albeit often at a considerable financial outlay. For smaller manufacturers, this amounts to prohibitive investments, making compliance with any codes and certifications largely impossible, especially as buyers rarely contribute to the cost of compliance. At the level of management, the implementation of codes and standards requires a much more pervasive overhaul of existing labor regimes, in which eight-hour shifts have to be put in place, overtime has to be rewarded at much higher rates, and regular contracts with social provisions have to be made available for the entire workforce. For all but the largest export houses—who rely on regular orders from established buyers—this is simply impracticable. The majority of manufacturers, and especially subcontractors, work with unpredictable and fluctuating orders, making the recruitment of a regular labor force highly problematic and the provision of social benefits largely unaffordable. Most garment manufacturers are thus "trapped" in a situation where they are unable to comply with regulations that are increasingly pressed for by Western buyers.

Who, then, goes for certification? Venkatesh,[3] a senior social auditor at SGS in Tiruppur, explained that company codes and certified standards only really began to spread in 2004, but that even today codes, rather than certified standards, remain a much more popular means through which buyers seek to influence supplier behavior. Venkatesh estimated in early 2006 that barely thirty export companies in Tiruppur were accredited with SA8000 or WRAP, which amounts to less than 5 percent of the export firms.[4] By early 2009, this number had hardly changed. "No firm can get these certifications at once," he explained, "manufacturers are slowly preparing their units and then they get the certification." It is to these processes of learning to comply and to the discourses that surround these processes that I now turn.

"Until the pain overcomes the fear"

Today, Tiruppur's largest and most successful exporters agree that compliance with codes and standards is a requirement for business and that the social audits that accompany this process are unavoidable. Many leading manufacturers have not only resigned to this fact, but they seem to have internalized an explicitly Western discourse about the need for "corporate care" for labor. Anand, the managing director and owner of one of Tiruppur's fastest growing high-tech garment firms, is representative of this top layer of exporters. His units are ISO, SA8000 and WRAP certified, and a WRAP audit was being carried out while I visited his company in late 2005. Anand explained to me in great detail what his personal CSR consists of and how he interprets what workers need. He daily asks one of his 3,000 workers to fill in a feedback sheet to find out what they expect from the company, contribute to the company, learn from the company, and what they hope to achieve in life. Every day this sheet is displayed in the offices, and Anand explained that more than money it is good health and a good education that his workers consistently write about. He was also proud to be running the company with two shifts rather than one long shift, even though this substantially increases his production costs. He negotiated with the banks to get ATM bank cards for all his workers so that wages can be paid directly into their own accounts. He has given loans to workers for the purchase of bicycles, and was in the process of arranging housing loans as well. While I do not doubt that Anand is sincere in wanting to "care" for his workers, I am less convinced that this is a project entirely of his own making. Underlying Anand's acts of philanthropy is a fear of buyers' constant surveillance, and Anand is well aware of buyers' critical gaze monitoring his corporate behavior.

Like most exporters, Anand identifies the new interventions through standards and codes as an external requirement, imposed by foreign buyers who increasingly refuse to do business with companies that are unable or unwilling to comply with their social standards. His comments are critical of Tiruppur manufacturers too:

> In Tiruppur we say that people won't change until the pain overcomes the fear. More and more companies try to get SA8000 and WRAP certified because they realize that otherwise they can't get any orders anymore. Here no one will try to implement regular pay and working hours on their own initiative … CSR slowly becomes important for the consumer as they want to know what is happening to the Third World workers. … But most Tiruppur manufacturers and exporters have no corporate social responsibility consciousness.

While the largest exporters may present their care for worker welfare and employment standards as a matter of personal consciousness and commitment, the majority of manufacturers openly admit that codes and standards have been externally imposed and that the associated inspections and audits are key to how compliance is enforced by buyers. Fear, as Anand mentions, is indeed central to the interactions between buyers and suppliers, and the fear of losing business is the main drive behind supplier compliance.

Yet, resignation does not mean unconditional acceptance or complete internalization of the values that the codes and standards stand for. Most manufacturers are quite critical of the labor standards imposed on them. Mr Rajendran, who built up the human resources (HR) department of one of Tiruppur's leading export companies between 1999 and 2006, points a finger at the Western consumer:

> Look, there are two methods of production: a clean method and a short-cut method. The consumer wants cheaper and cheaper clothes and at the same time better produced goods. In the past we produced a T-shirt for £2–3 and it was sold for £15. Today the same T-shirt is sold for £5. The consumer is too powerful … you can't produce in a clean manner for free.

Rajendran, like several others, blames the consumer for wanting to have their cake and eat it. But there is an underlying critique of Western buying companies and chain stores, whose competition for the cheapest prices pushes down the rates they are negotiating with suppliers, at a time that they expect the latter to produce to tight schedules and in a socially responsible manner. The managing director of a large SA8000 accredited export house put it this way in January 2009: "Suddenly, the buyers will place an order that they want us to deliver very quickly, and they won't care how many hours we work to finish it off … at that point the whole SA8000 goes out of the window!" But there are other inconsistencies that they are keen to comment on. Mr Logan, who runs a buying house in Tiruppur, critiques what he perceives to be the randomness of social audits:

> I work with a chain store in Paris and I asked my buyer whether they also insist that their Chinese suppliers comply with their company code of conduct. The guy told me that they don't because social audits are not allowed over there; they are not allowed to enter the factories and inspect them. But they still source from them anyway. So I asked him: why do you demand us to comply with your code but not them? And he said that he had to show his bosses in Paris that he had done *something* in terms of CSR and that it was easier to get it done in India.

Although at first this had taken Logan by surprise, he now shrugs his shoulders, resigned to the fact that free trade does not equal fair trade. Tiruppur exporters frequently comment on the mounting power inequalities between global retail companies and themselves. While the former have the power to demand compliance with their social regulations, the latter have to comply without being able to pass on the extra cost of such compliance to their buyers or negotiate better terms of trade. Logan's awareness of these inequalities transpires from his skepticism:

> At the end of the day, if we fulfil all codes and standards and then we ask 5 percent more, the company will simply go elsewhere. The cheapest deal is

what they are ultimately after. Western buyers are not interested in Indian workers, and we should not expect them to look after our workers either ... they are only concerned about their own reputation among consumers.

The politics of social standards gives global buyers extended leverage over their suppliers as it allows them to demand compliance without necessarily having to contribute to its costs or preparation. It also provides buyers with a new tool for negotiation beyond price and quality: ethical compliance. Through the enforcement of social responsibility, the "social" itself shifts to the center of market relations and trade negotiations, and begins to shape the relationship between global buyers and their localized suppliers.

Shaping the buyer-supplier relationship: Learning to comply

While negotiations about quality and price of orders are important, particularly revealing are the exchanges that take place between buyers and suppliers around social compliance, as well as around the recurrent audits and factory inspections. These exchanges give us a unique insight into how buyers and exporters relate to each other, and into the assumptions and stereotypes that frame their interaction.

As the SGS auditor emphasized above, when buyers started asking their suppliers to comply with labor codes and standards, no companies in Tiruppur were fulfilling the required labor regulations. However, the largest export companies, supplying major Western stores and brand names, quickly realized that social compliance was to become a key business requirement, and potentially a competitive advantage not only vis-à-vis their local competitors but also vis-à-vis China and other garment-producing regions. But preparing for code implementation and certification turned out to be an onerous and convoluted process. Exporters began to develop the required social management systems and made efforts to bring the physical environment of their factory units in line with health and safety regulations. They also began to adjust production processes in order to limit overtime work, and pay minimum wages, provide statutory leave, and so on. As social compliance became a more detailed and complex issue and as factory owners themselves lacked the required legal and practical knowledge, the first human resource departments were set up in Tiruppur. The career of Nandini, a proactive HR officer, gives us an insight into the early days of social compliance in Tiruppur.

Ms Nandini, in 2005 a social complaints officer at Quantum Companies, recounted how she was one of the first HR officers to be employed in the industry. Nandini completed an MA in Human Resource Management, and in 1999 was employed by the Clean Clothes Campaign (CCC) as a social auditor to inspect export companies on their behalf. Working for CCC, Nandini audited the eight garment companies of Tiruppur's leading Viswa Group. Her audit report was sent via CCC to the Group's principal buyer in Europe. Nandini explained that although the owner and MD of the Viswa Group was initially opposed to social auditing, he very soon realized its importance. Complying with social regulations was no longer an option; it was rapidly becoming a core requirement for business. By the end of 1999, Viswa Group had established a HR department for which they employed Nandini as their first social compliance officer. By 2001, Viswa Group was one of the first groups of factories in Tiruppur to obtain the SA8000 certification, and it is one of the very few companies that has continually renewed its certification since.

While Viswa Group was greatly pressurized by its buyer to implement social policies among its workforce, the case is quite exceptional in Tiruppur, as the Group was lucky to benefit from having had a long-term and constructive collaboration with a single European buyer for over 30 years. This not only meant that the Group's firms had benefited from steady and reliable business over this period, but also that the buyer and supplier had mutual interests in joining efforts to improve their production and CSR strategies. Most suppliers, however, are less fortunate. Given the fierce competition, the majority of exporters have to accept orders from multiple buyers simultaneously and face a high turnover in clients. Each of these buyers comes with their own code of conduct, and with their own specifications of standards to comply with. Suppliers as well as social auditors in Tiruppur routinely complain about the lack of clarity about what exactly buyers expect from them, how to practically implement very generic regulations, and the endless minor variations between codes presented to them by buyers.

Mr Rajendran, one of Viswa Group's senior social compliance officers and a man with extensive experience of social audits in Tiruppur, expressed a great deal of frustration about suppliers' often desperate attempts to meet the "wishes of the clients." Social audits are becoming increasingly intrusive, yet because suppliers fear losing a "good" buyer they try as best they possibly can to meet the buyers' increasingly stringent demands. Rajendran's example is illustrative:

It's really hard for us to meet the wishes of the clients. Take age certificates, for example. One client came and asked us for certificates that confirm the age of all workers. Now, how can we get such certificates? One way is to get birth certificates, but older people may not have these. Another way is to get school-leaving certificates, but again many workers don't have these. A third way is to have a ration card, but often photos and names have been changed on such cards. A last way is to get a medical certificate. So we got documents that confirmed the age of our workers, but then one buyer came and said that they were inadequate and that they wanted medical certificates for all workers. So we had to get medical certificates for all 600 workers! That's what we have to pay to get through a social audit!

Rajendran was highly skeptical. Not only did he mock suppliers' submissive attitude toward buyers' demands, he also derided buyers' naivety in believing that medical certificates would offer them a more secure proof of a worker's age than any other document presented. After all, he said, everyone knows that even medical certificates can be bought! Yet, the point to reiterate here is that the "politics of social responsibility" are not merely reflecting inequalities between buyers and suppliers, they are constitutive of the terrains of power that shape the social relations of international outsourcing.

Complying, conforming and implementing are largely a matter of trial and error. Companies usually first implement the less stringent company codes of conduct, following instructions provided by buyers, and then gradually prepare their units for a more comprehensive SA8000 or WRAP standard certification. If they fail an inspection due to nonconformity, the audit is repeated at a later stage. For the workers on the shop floor of the larger firms, these audits are rapidly becoming a familiar encounter, given that inspections by both local and foreign auditors now take place on an almost weekly basis. In the absence of state regulation on the shop floor, it is the hand of the market that becomes evermore visible and gripping. Through a plethora of inspections, audits and checks, foreign buying companies tighten their control over suppliers and extend their governance over a widening radius of firms and workers.

The social audit: Fear and intimidation

I now turn to the audits themselves, or rather to the discourses and social interactions between suppliers and buyer representatives that surround the audits. Today, most large chain stores and retail companies send their own managers to Tiruppur to carry out regular inspections of both production processes and working conditions. Their main concerns are product quality and delivery deadlines, but buyer representatives are increasingly involved in factory inspections and social audits, often in collaboration with accredited local auditors.

Interviews with buyer representatives in Tiruppur revealed a great deal not only about the way buyers view their suppliers' productive capabilities and social consciousness, but also about how they seek to influence it. Rebecca, the merchandising manager of a leading UK retailer of baby clothes, was not atypical in her depiction of her company's engagement with Tiruppur. In our interview she first explained her company's relationship with Indian suppliers:

> We have been working with the same suppliers for the last five years ... When we started working with them five years ago, some of them were tiny. I went to one place which was like a shed, and Raj's factory was just a small room where women were sitting on mats trimming garments. But they have grown with us and have become big exporters now ... It's like a partnership and we are really proud of it!

While the image of a partnership was repeated to me by several buyers, their descriptions of how inspections are carried out in the factories revealed a different picture: one of stark inequality, in which buyers' moral superiority and social responsibility is contrasted with suppliers' lack of understanding, social consciousness, and ethical concern. The buyer takes on the role of teacher; the supplier is depicted as the apprentice, who has to be taught, disciplined, and tested. This is how Rebecca talks about the audits, and hence about her suppliers:

> We do inspections all the time ... We do random and unannounced checks, so that they cannot prepare for it. We are really tough and they know it! ... You see, when I enter a factory for inspection, I know that the last 10 days will be properly filled out in the books, but I close the books and start from the beginning and check at random places ... So when I do it this way, they are really scared! We are really tough but they have to realize that these things are important.

Rather than an image of equal partnership, it is a picture of inequality that emerges, in which fearmongering and intimidation are central to the way that compliance is enforced by buyers. While suppliers admit that it is fear that drives them to comply, it is buyers who explain how this fear operates as a technique of governance and control. Rebecca continues:

> It is at the top that they have to realize; they should not blame the workers. Needle protection, for example, is essential for us. Garments have to be 100

percent needle free; we can't risk having a needle in a baby garment. When the goods arrive in our warehouse in the UK we still perform a 10 percent needle check. Once it happened that the top of a needle was found in a garment and at that point we checked the complete delivery again. But we didn't do it ourselves, no, we made the supplier come over and sit in our warehouse in Southampton for a full week, and we made him do all the checks of the complete delivery himself! … You see, if he says that a 100 percent needle check has been done, then he is responsible for it … he has to realize this at the top!

Buyers routinely present themselves as the conscious and responsible partner in their interactions with suppliers, who they depict as needing education and guidance on "issues that matter." There is no doubt that much of their "guidance" takes the form of threats and intimidation, through which they seek to bring suppliers in line with their requests. Buyers exercise a considerable amount of power over suppliers and it is the open threat of this power that continually reminds suppliers of the need to abide with buyers' rules.

In 2005 the UK retailer for which Rebecca works opened an office in Tiruppur where a permanent representative of the company is based. Rebecca explained that this office is proof of their involvement in the locality:

The factory owners were very happy and impressed that we set up our office in Tiruppur itself and not in Bangalore or Delhi. It shows real commitment, it shows that we are committed to work with them … It shows that we want a lasting relationship, a partnership. They are our partners.

While the language of partnership has become ubiquitous among transnational corporations and indeed provides their activities with a considerable degree of legitimation, it also hides "dramatic inequalities and conflicting interests … behind the veneer of equal collaboration" (Rajak 2007: 14). Rebecca, for one, leaves no ambiguity as to who has the upper hand in this partnership, and points out that their permanent presence in town also has an important disciplining effect:

Now that we've got a local office here, they are even more afraid of us … they know now that we can pop in and inspect them at any time … Our suppliers know us … they know that we are strict. There is no kidding us [laughs]!

Disciplining and monitoring are considered essential for a number of reasons. One is that local suppliers are commonly seen by buyers to be untrustworthy and unprofessional. Amanda, who visited Tiruppur for the first time in 1993 as the then representative of a UK-based buying house, explained to me that

The problem is to find someone whom you can trust in Tiruppur. There were some real horror stories in the beginning, for example, of boxes arriving in the UK with uncut fabric in them rather than with the garments that had been ordered...

Buyer representatives in Tiruppur make it clear that they are the ones who "taught" local suppliers how to produce quality garments in a professional manner. Lin Wong, who works as a quality controller for an upmarket Italian brand, travels back and forth between Hong Kong and Tiruppur to follow up orders. He complains that he can never trust that a manufacturer will keep to what has been agreed, and that quality control is a relentless process. Lin Wong depicts Tiruppur manufacturers as reckless children who can never be left on their own:

As soon as I am away for a few weeks I come back to a lot of trouble and delays. Especially shipping deadlines are not kept. At the moment, Tiruppur exporters take on any order they can get without thinking about how they can produce it in time, and so they end up subcontracting the work ... and delaying the delivery with three or four months. That's exactly what happened to us last year ...

Suppliers are not only presented as highly unreliable and untrustworthy, but also as lacking technical know-how and unwilling to learn. Buyers consider themselves superior on at least two fronts: their technical ability and knowledge on the one hand, and their moral convictions and social responsibility on the other hand. Interviews with buyers about social responsibility routinely evoke comments about "differences" between Westerners and Indians. In such comments Western companies appear as the knowing partner and the Indian supplier as the lacking partner; the Western as the rational and the Indian as the irrational; the Western as the morally conscious and the Indian as the ethically unconcerned. When buyer representatives mention "growing together" and "forming partnerships," they are effectively talking about their one-way (and top-town) efforts to impart technical knowledge and ethical sensitivities to their Tiruppur suppliers. The language of partnership merely masks inequalities of power and voice, and allows Western companies to present their own morality as superior, altruistic, and worthy of emulation.

But there is more to it. Buyers' moral discourse also emphasizes their commitment to the locality and seeks to counter a popular image of the multinational corporation as unconcerned about its local footprint. Buyers mentioned how they take the lead in "community development" and plenty of examples were given of their involvement in the establishment of primary schools, donations to local hospitals, and general care for the welfare of the people of Tiruppur. Buyer representatives go to great lengths to show that they take their social responsibility toward the locality very seriously and that they are committed to raising the ethical consciousness in Tiruppur more generally. One of the ways in which this commitment is publicly manifested is through acts of charity and philanthropy, which are presented as powerful examples of buyers' real concern for workers and of moral high ground more generally.

Such acts of philanthropy are presented as "gifts" toward "the community" in addition to what is already "given" through codes of conduct and labor standards. Rebecca told me with pride:

> We've also set up a mothers and toddlers nursery in Tiruppur. We asked our local supplier to contribute something and we too contributed to buy the land and construct the building. And now the people can enjoy it. It is our way of giving something back to the people. We want to do something for the community. It's a way of saying 'thank you'... And we are very proud of it!

I asked her if the company was doing this under consumer pressure, to which she replied:

> No, this is just our way of working, we build up partnerships and grow together. The people here work hard, but they are happy. They are a very nice community. Whenever I come here, people are so friendly and I feel cleansed whenever I leave India. I feel that we've done something good for the people. Like now too we brought a whole stack of pens for the school ... the people wave and are happy to see us and are very grateful.

The above exchange illustrates how buyers' social responsibility is personalized and experienced as a matter of personal fulfilment by those involved in its implementation. In the context of the CSR activities of a multinational mining company in South Africa, Rajak has similarly shown that front-line CSR practitioners often find themselves "acting as local patrons and benefactors" (2007: 17) and that the social responsibility of the company tends to be personalized by front-line managers charged with the implementation of company CSR policy.

But buyers' sense of social responsibility is also presented as "natural" ("just our way of working"); as a "natural" part of doing business, thus blurring the boundaries between philanthropy and CSR. Or, as Rajak put it, the assumed dichotomy between gift and market exchange "is disrupted by the phenomenon of CSR which overtly reconnects the apparently modern and depersonalised world of commerce with the moral discourse and social politics of giving" (2007: 9–10). Indeed, Western philanthropy is not seen as lying "outside" the world of business, but as deeply embedded in market relationships. What such discourses of giving disguise, however, is that they also reify moral inequalities: they act as a means through which Western company representatives present themselves as different from and superior to their Indian counterparts, and thus justify their moral interventions. Such discourses contribute to the reproduction of inequalities of power through which global outsourcing operates.

Compliance and resistance: Who plays the game?

But where does this leave the Indian suppliers? Are there no alternatives left to them but to comply? Is the grip of buyers' moral discourse so forceful that it cannot be resisted? Have exporters fully internalized the values and morality of their buyers? It would be wrong to answer these questions positively. Tiruppur exporters do not slavishly comply with the rules set by buyers. They have various strategies to avoid codes and standards, and alternative moral discourses to justify their actions toward workers.

One way to avoid relentless regulations is to export selectively. Larger buying companies and retailers such as Gap or Wal-Mart are preferred buyers, as they usually place larger and more regular orders, but they are also known to be the most demanding customers in terms of product quality and social policies. Exporters balance the advantages of getting business from such buyers against the disadvantages of having to comply with their quality and ethical requirements. It is common knowledge among Tiruppur exporters that global retailers and major brand names are on the whole more stringent than smaller or less well-known retailers; that importers are less demanding than direct buyers; and that buyers from southern Europe are on the whole easier to deal with in terms of ethical compliance than those from northern Europe and North America. Suppliers make careful trade-offs between different foreign customers, and export selectively.

This is illustrated by the case of Yuvaraj. Having supplied a regular European buyer for many years, Yuvaraj began to search for buyers in the US and Canada from 2002 onwards, and attended trade fairs in Las Vegas to approach new customers. In 2005, he started his first exports to the US and by the end of that year he received approval from Wal-Mart in Canada to act as a supplier to them. Yet Yuvaraj commented:

Those social audits are a real disadvantage for us. I've been in contact with Wal-Mart and they came here to do a full social audit and I got their approval, but I've now said no. I don't want to supply to them, as I would be a slave to them. I would have to fulfil so many rules that I would lose all my freedom. Even though I got their approval I've decided not to go ahead with them. Some people will get the approval for one unit, but then they will produce the garments in nine other units for which approval was never given.

Yuvaraj is not exceptional. Like him, most exporters are selective in who they choose to deal with and many decide to keep supplying less demanding buyers. Moreover, exporters seek to supply several customers simultaneously to avoid becoming entirely dependent on any one of them and being at the whims of their ever-changing demands. Supplying multiple buyers gives exporters some leverage in trade negotiations and allows them to say "no" to whoever they consider unfavorable to their own business interests. It also protects them from complete bankruptcy in case an order is canceled or a buyer shifts suppliers.

A related strategy is to limit exporting altogether and to focus on the domestic market. While profit margins are known to be smaller in the domestic market, the latter has some definite advantages: regular and predictable business, faster payments, fewer risks, more personalized relationships with customers, and—at least for the time being—less demanding clients in terms of social and environmental policies. Many export firms started off producing underwear garments for the domestic market and later diversified into products for the export market. Yet a good number of them retain a foothold in the domestic market to avoid complete dependence on foreign customers.

Some manufacturers seek to evade compliance with labor standards altogether. This happens at several levels. First, subcontractors and job workers can rarely afford to fulfil the requirements of codes and standards. They continue to export, but only indirectly—that is, through larger exporters and buying agencies. But direct exporters evade regulations too, on a routine basis. One way is to produce part of the orders in units that are uncertified. Certification is factory based, and exporters have to acquire certification for each of their production units. But given that few exporters have certifications for all their units, they usually have access to factories—either their own or of subcontractors—where overtime and pay regulations are followed less strictly. Another way in which compliance is evaded, or rather devolved, by larger export firms is by passing on responsibility for compliance to subcontractors. Certified exporters are supposed to work with subcontractors who also comply with standard requirements. But here responsibility for compliance is devolved to the subcontractors themselves, who are required to carry out what effectively amounts to a self-audit. Exporters for whom they work give them a form to fill out, in which the subcontractors confirm that their units comply with the SA8000 or WRAP social standards. The crucial point about this form is that it devolves responsibility—and hence risk—for compliance down to the subcontractor. By signing the form and stating that they comply with the codes or standards, it becomes the subcontractors' own responsibility to ensure compliance. In case a subcontractor is inspected by a buyer representative or a social auditor and a violation of regulations is found, it is the subcontractor who will be held responsible and not the exporter, as the latter will be able to refer to the signed form as proof that he was dealing with a compliant subcontractor. In this way, exporters protect themselves against violations by subcontractors, to whom they pass on the blame for breach of contract.

The politics of compliance has thus not only begun to shape the relationship between global buyers and Tiruppur suppliers, but also the relationship between successful Tiruppur exporters, on the one hand, and smaller subcontractors and job workers further down the chain, on the other. The politics of compliance not only helps to protect the power of the large exporters by allowing them to devolve part of the responsibility for compliance to subcontractors, it also provides a new instrument through which such exporters can consolidate their competitive advantage over up-and-coming firms, and manage risk. It essentially provides them with a tool to devolve risk, cost and responsibility down the production chain, which in turn contributes to the intensification of self-exploitation by subcontractors. Indeed, subcontractors are increasingly forced by exporters to produce at lower rates, but with either higher costs (in case they comply with the codes and standards) or with higher risks (in case they fail to comply). This downward shift in social responsibility contributes to the concentration of power in the hands of a limited group of exporters, with whom smaller subcontractors and job workers find it increasingly impossible to compete. Like price and quality, social compliance has become yet another tool through which inequalities can be reproduced in the global market.

Finally, as explained by auditors, unions, NGOs and exporters alike, there are certain areas of compliance that remain fraught with problems and where implementation of social standards is hard to check, let alone enforce. These are the areas where non-compliance can lead to substantial rent prices and significant competitive advantages for some companies. Codes and standards may improve physical conditions of work within factories (for example, health and safety) and they may help to eradicate the worst forms of child labor. Yet other areas of workers' lives lend themselves much less to systematic regulation. These include, among other things, regulation and payment of overtime, issues of non-discrimination, gender equality, and guaranteeing political rights of workers, such as freedom of association and collective bargaining (Barrientos and Smith 2007: 720; De Neve 2008). In Tiruppur, codes and standards do not even begin to challenge the social, political and economic inequalities between buyers and suppliers, between exporters and subcontractors, and between capital and labor.

Tiruppur manufacturers clearly have their own ways of avoiding compliance or devolving responsibility and risk onto less powerful actors in the chain. In similar ways, they articulate their own and distinct discourses of morality and social consciousness. Such discourses largely draw on paternalistic patron-client relationships ("we take care of our workers") and build on industrialists' own life histories, in which their working-class and rural origins are often presented as a source of social awareness and "understanding" of workers' needs (Chari 2004). Exporters and manufacturers claim to know how to look after their workers, and loathe being told by others how to deal with labor. Yet, at the same time, this moral discourse is not simply juxtaposed to that of CSR. The generic and universal language of corporate codes of ethics is increasingly being internalized and reproduced by the leading Tiruppur exporters. As Mr Anand's discourse above illustrates, exporters' talk about moral consciousness and social responsibility combines a personalized set of ethics with the global language of CSR. It is here that the morality of codes and standards appears to have yet another pervasive impact.

Conclusions

This chapter has moved beyond a discussion of the practical impacts of CSR policies to address the more political question of how codes of conduct and labor standards are beginning to transform social relationships between Western buyers and their suppliers in Tiruppur, South India. Echoing arguments made by Dunn (2005) and Dolan (2008), it is suggested that the politics of ethical compliance lies at the heart of the ways in which new hierarchies are created between values, moralities, people, and societies. Ethical standards and degrees of compliance (or non-compliance) have become new yardsticks of modernity. It is through global standards— and the wider CSR discourses of which they are a part—that ethical and social values are defined and imposed in global production networks, and that firms, peoples and societies are classified according to their ability to comply.

Moreover, rather than improving the rights of a workforce at the sites of production, the politics of ethical compliance provides the more powerful actors in the global garment industry with a new tool to extend their control over others and to enhance "their ability to capture high economic rents" (Barrientos and Smith 2007: 717). Ethical compliance allows for a powerful politics of inequality to unfold precisely because it is wrought in the nebulous languages of CSR, philanthropy and partnership, and because it presents the market as benevolent and the actors involved as caring and compassionate. As a result, the politics of compliance contributes to the consolidation of the power of standard-setting actors by facilitating the devolution of risk, uncertainty and responsibility to the weaker "partners" in the chain. The ultimate paradox is that while CSR claims to protect the weakest and poorest from the ills of the market, it in fact allows the market to govern in its most unchecked fashion. Through the politics of CSR, powerful corporate regimes of control and governance are unleashed that construct new hierarchies of value and morality. Fear, intimidation and accusation lie at the heart of CSR's front-line operations, and they are becoming powerful market techniques shaping economic and political relationships in the era of neoliberal government.

Acknowledgments

This chapter is based on fieldwork carried out in Tiruppur in 2000, 2005–2006 and 2008–2009. The research was funded by a Leverhulme Research Fellowship (2005–2006) and an ESRC-DFID Research Grant (RES-167-25-0296). The chapter first appeared in *Economic and Political Weekly* (volume 44, issue 22, 2009). I thank K. Murali for invaluable research assistance in the field, and am particularly grateful to Grace Carswell, Judith Heyer, Jeff Pratt, Dinah Rajak, Supriya RowChowdury and the anonymous reviewer for comments on earlier drafts of this chapter. All shortcomings remain my own.

Notes

1. Codes and standards affect workers in very different ways, and workers hold a range of opinions about the pros and cons of working in certified companies. The question of how workers relate to corporate social regulations has been addressed elsewhere (see De Neve (2014)).
2. Tallontire uses the term "private standard initiatives" to refer to "all standards set outside the realms of public sector," and distinguishes between private *company* standards (set and monitored by a single firm) and private *collective* standards (that have their roots in collective, often stakeholder or industry-based initiatives) (2007: 777).
3. All names are pseudonyms.
4. This is in line with a recent study on the implementation of SA8000 in Indian garment firms that mentions that twenty-seven garment firms in Tiruppur were SA8000 certified in 2006 (Stigzelius and Fredricsdotter 2006: 3).

References

Appelbaum, Richard. 2005. The end of apparel quotas: A faster race to the bottom? *Global and International Studies Program Paper 35*. University of California: Santa Barbara.

Barrientos, Stephanie, Catherine Dolan, and Anne Tallontire. 2003. A gendered value chain approach to codes of conduct in African horticulture. *World Development* 31(9): 1511–1526.

Barrientos, Stephanie, and Sally Smith. 2007. Do workers benefit from ethical trade? Assessing codes of labour practice in global production systems. *Third World Quarterly* 28(4): 713–729.

Chari, Sharad. 2004. *Fraternal capital: Peasant-workers, self-made men and globalization in provincial India*. Stanford: Stanford University Press.

Chopra, Rohit. 2003. Neoliberalism as doxa: Bourdieu's theory of the state and the contemporary Indian discourse on globalization and liberalization. *Cultural Studies* 17(3/4): 419–444.

Cohn, Bernard. 1996. *Colonialism and its forms of knowledge: The British in India*. Princeton: Princeton University Press.

De Neve, Geert. 2003. Expectations and rewards of modernity: Commitment and mobility among rural migrants in Tiruppur, Tamil Nadu. *Contributions to Indian Sociology* 37(1&2): 251–280.

De Neve, Geert. 2008. Global garment chains, local labour activism: New challenges to trade unionism and NGO activism in the Tiruppur garment cluster, South India. In Geert De Neve, Peter Luetchford, Jeff Pratt, and Donald C. Wood, eds., *Research in economic anthropology: Hidden hands in the market: Ethnographies of fair trade, ethical consumption and corporate social responsibility*, pp. 213–240. Bingley: Emerald Group.

De Neve, Geert. 2014. Fordism, flexible specialization and CSR: How Indian garment workers critique neoliberal labour regimes. *Ethnography* 15(2): 184–207.

Dirks, Nicholas. 2001. *Castes of mind: Colonialism and the making of modern India*. Princeton: Princeton University Press.

Dolan, Catherine. 2008. Arbitrating risk through moral values: The case of Kenya fairtrade. In Geert De Neve, Peter Luetchford, Jeff Pratt, and Donald C. Wood, eds., *Research in economic anthropology: Hidden hands in the market: Ethnographies of fair trade, ethical consumption and corporate social responsibility*, pp. 271–296. Bingley: Emerald Group.

Dolan, Catherine, and John Humphrey. 2000. Governance and trade in fresh vegetables: The impact of UK supermarkets on the African horticulture industry. *Journal of Development Studies* 37(2): 147–176.

Dunn, Elizabeth. 2005. Standards and person-making in East Central Europe. In A. Ong and S. Collier, eds., *Global assemblages: Technology, politics and ethics as anthropological problems*, pp. 173–193. Oxford: Blackwell Publishing.

McCormick, Dorothy, Paul Kamau, and Peter Ligulu. 2006. Post-multifibre arrangement analysis of the textile and garment sectors in Kenya. *IDS Bulletin* 37(1): 80–88.

Nadvi, Khalid. 2004. The effect of global standards on local producers: A Pakistani case study. In H. Schmitz, ed., *Local enterprises in the global economy: Issues in governance and upgrading*, pp. 297–325. Cheltenham: Edward Elgar.

Nadvi, Khalid, and Frank Wältring. 2004. Making sense of global standards. In Hubert Schmitz, ed., *Local enterprises in the global economy: Issues in governance and upgrading*, pp. 53–95. Cheltenham: Edward Elgar.

Rajak, Dinah. 2007. "I am the conscience of the company": Responsibility and the gift in a transnational mining corporation. In K. Browne and L. Milgram, eds., *Economics and morality: Anthropological approaches*, pp. 211–231. Lanham, MD: AltaMira Press.

Scott, Allen J. 2006. The changing global geography of low-technology, labor-intensive industry: Clothing, footwear and furniture. *World Development* 34(9): 1517–1536.

Stigzelius, Ingrid, and Linda Fredricsdotter. 2006. Implementation of SA8000 in Indian garment manufacturing: A socio-economic assessment of the impacts on working conditions and business practices. MBA Dissertation. Uppsala: Swedish University of Agricultural Sciences.

Tallontire, Anne. 2007. CSR and regulation: Towards a framework for understanding private standards initiatives in the agri-food chain. *Third World Quarterly* 28(4): 775–791.

Geert De Neve is a Reader in Social Anthropology at the University of Sussex. He has carried out long-term fieldwork in various industrial regions of Tamil Nadu, South India. His research interests include industrialization, trade liberalization, corporate social responsibility, and social transformation in South India. He is the author of *Everyday politics of labour: Working lives in India's informal economy* (2005) and co-editor of various edited volumes including *Industrial work and life: An anthropological reader* (2009).

– Chapter 5 –

DETACHMENT AS A CORPORATE ETHIC
Materializing CSR in the Diamond Supply Chain
Jamie Cross

$e\!\!\!\sim\!\!\!\frown$

From hard rock to diamond ring

By the end of the twentieth century the global trade in diamond gemstones—one of the world's most iconic luxury commodities—had become an important focus for campaigns by international human- and labor-rights organizations. In 2000 the De Beers Group, whose monopolistic business practices saw it control the global supply of rough diamonds during the twentieth century, responded to these campaigns with two regulatory interventions. The first was the "Kimberly Process Certification Scheme," a UN-backed mechanism intended to certify the origin of all diamond gemstones and curtail the trade in conflict diamonds. The second intervention was the "Best Practice Principles" (BPP) program that introduced a new set of voluntary regulations into what De Beers calls its "diamond pipeline."

Rough diamonds that are dug out of the ground in mines owned by De Beers in Africa and North America are sorted, valued, and distributed by a daughter company, the Diamond Trading Company (DTC). The DTC sells rough stones to a tightly controlled number of buyers, called "Sightholders." Sightholders either process rough stones in their own facilities, or contract rough stones out to specialized manufacturers who cut and polish them into consumer-quality diamonds. De Beers' code of practice, developed without the participation of any other industry stakeholders, introduced a new set of standards into this complex global web of traders and manufacturers.

When it was launched, the BPP program was heralded as a new commitment to self-regulation at all levels of De Beers' diamond pipeline, "from hard rock to diamond ring" as publicity materials put it. Under the program, all cutting and polishing facilities fully or partially owned by De Beers and its Sightholders (as well as facilities they subcontracted work to) were required to become fully compliant with a set of minimum business standards. Their compliance would be guaranteed through what De Beers described as a "systematic assurance program" that involved a series of documentary procedures and a third-party financial, social, and environmental audit. The new initiative, it was announced, would ensure "that the De Beers Family of companies, Sightholders and applicable third parties operate to an ethical, legal professional, social and environmental standard," and that the exploration, extraction, sorting, cutting, and polishing of diamonds took place in ways that did not "endanger the health or welfare of individuals" or the environment. The BPP would, De Beers claimed, "lead to a general improvement in responsible business practices" across the diamond industry.

Detachment as a corporate ethic

De Beers' best-practices program presents anthropology with a classic example of "corporate ethicizing" at the beginning of the twenty-first century. Responding to civil society concerns, the scope of its corporate responsibility program encompassed a complex and diverse global supply chain to include the buyers of its stones and their subcontractors. Valorizing the willingness and the capacity of market actors to safeguard and guarantee business practices, De Beers deployed what is now a familiar array of tools, including a code of practice and a set of performance indicators against which a diverse chain of diamond sorting, processing, cutting and polishing facilities could be audited, evaluated, and reported.

There is now an established social scientific critique of corporate social responsibility. A growing body of literature shows how CSR advances and entrenches neoliberal capitalism by "embedding social relations in economic processes" (Shamir 2004, 2008), naturalizing the role of market actors as the stewards and arbiters of justice (Blowfield and Dolan 2008) and reproducing North-South relationships of dependency and subordination (Rajak 2008). In this critique, corporate codes of conduct and systems of inspection are agents of abstraction and virtualism (Carrier and Miller 1998; Miller 1998; Strathern 2000, 2002). They produce "decontextualized" relationships and knowledge, by collapsing the everyday politics of work and the complexity of located personal relationships, questions of procedure and norms, outcomes and indicators, and by translating complicated and messy social worlds into standardized concepts and categories (Dolan 2008).

In this article I extend the anthropology of "corporate ethicizing" by examining the introduction of De Beers' BPP program at an offshore diamond manufacturing facility in India. Like other articles in this special issue, I explore "corporate ethicizing" as a process rooted in the mundane, quotidian work of doing business. The offshore manufacturing zone is a unique space of contemporary global production, one that is marked by the near total removal of controls and regulations on corporate practices. Drawing on ethnographic fieldwork, I show how ethical accounting regimes feed into the ongoing efforts by supply-chain capitalists and factory managers within this space to separate themselves legally, morally, and socially from binding obligations and responsibility to producers. Codes of conduct and social audits are materialized in global supply chains in ways that provide executive and manager new purchase on what we might call an "ethic of detachment."

What do I mean by "detachment"? Current trends in economic sociology approach the bracketing and ending of relationships between two parties in a transaction as crucial acts in the performance of a market, and seek to grasp how the terms of this "detachment" are established and coordinated (Callon 1998; MacKenzie et al. 2007). Anthropologists have responded to this discussion by arguing that "detachment" is a fiction of economics, one that can never really be achieved in real-world transactions, and emphasize the constant, complex nature of attachments linking people in market transactions (Holm 2007; Miller 2002). One route through this debate is to see detachment as a relationship, or as relational. There is emerging interest among anthropologists in "disconnection, distance, and detachment" as meaningful frameworks for action and forms of virtue (Candea et al. 2009). In this light the bracketing, limiting, and ending of economic relationships, like those between actors in a market transaction, are always still relationships; and, to the extent that detachment is a guide to conduct, it is an ethic.

One way to think through detachment as a corporate ethic is to see it as the antithesis of an ethic of attachment or reconnection like that promulgated by the Fair Trade movement. Fair Trade initiatives construct, convey, and manage a set of ethical values through the commodity chain, inscribing the relationship between consumer and producer with notions of sociality, respect, obligation, long term attachment, and the possibility for intimacy (Dolan 2008: 274–80). This ethic of attachment is what makes Fair Trade unique, and why ethical accounting regimes are at their most prominent and vociferous in the commodity chains for Fair Trade goods.

The supply chains of many consumer goods in the Euro-American world, however, stand in direct contrast. The actions of many corporate entities and managerial subjects continue to be guided by the principle that successful, globally competitive business demands finite limits on and the possibility of closure from relationships with producers. Beyond the rhetoric of corporate social responsibility, companies and managers continue to be deeply invested in the creation of short-term, nonbinding attachments to producers. They are constantly engaged in establishing limits and endpoints to relationships in their supply chain, ensuring that contracts are time-bound and spatially defined, resisting proximity and intimacy, and framing relationships around difference and distance.

Capitalist modernity has given rise to diverse spatial formations (Thrift 1996), devices (Callon 2007) and disciplines (Rose 1999) that might be said to produce "detachment." These are brought together in a productive synthesis inside the free-trade zones that have proliferated across the global South. Ostensibly built to encourage foreign investment and promote rapid industrialization, economic zones create unique territorial, judicial, and discursive spaces (see, e.g., Cross 2010b; Ong 2006). Detachment is instantiated in the zone: built into its physical design, its legal constitution, the political economy of its investments, and the social architecture of relations between manufacturing companies that locate inside them and the people they employ. Little surprise perhaps that zones have gained such notoriety as the gray areas in global supply chains (Tsing 2009).

Detachment is different from what Anthony Giddens meant by "disembedding" (Giddens 1990). Where dissembedding described a historical dynamic of ever-increasing separation between society and the market that was symptomatic of capitalist modernity (see also Thrift 1998), detachment describes a relationship that has to be constantly made as such. It is in this sense that Nigel Thrift describes capitalism as a "practical order that is constantly in motion" (ibid.: 78). Detachment as a corporate ethic is one that must be constantly performed in the everyday operations of management. In this, I suggest, codes of practice and audit technologies emerge as unique material technologies that enable transnational corporations and individual managers to establish limits and endpoints in their relationships to producers.

Worldwide diamonds

Between 2004 and 2006 there were eighty-four companies on De Beers' list of Sightholders. Twelve of these companies subcontracted the cutting and polishing of diamonds sourced from De Beers to an offshore manufacturer based in South India. This factory, called Worldwide Diamonds, was located in a nondescript whitewashed building inside a secure and gated offshore manufacturing enclave in the state of Andhra Pradesh. Established in 1997, Worldwide Diamonds applied modern assembly-line technologies and hyper-efficient work processes to the diamond industry. Work here was casual, insecure, low-waged, and labor-intensive, and by 2005 the factory had undercut all its major competitors to emerge as one of the world's premier low-cost, high-volume producers of small-sized, medium-quality diamonds. At its peak it employed 1200 people and processed 14,000 carats of rough diamond each month, with an export value of approximately $4 million.

Between January and December 2005, I was given open access to the Worldwide Diamonds factory as part of a wider research project on industrial life and work in India's new economic zones. My research drew on a tradition of ethnographic research in which anthropologists of work "learn by doing." For twelve months I trained as a diamond polisher in the factory's cornering, blocking, and bruiting sections, and carried out repeated and extended interviews with the factory's managers, sitting in on meetings and planning sessions. The gatekeepers who made this research possible made no demands on my data and no requests that I conceal the factory's identity. The names of companies that appear in this paper are all real, but the names and identities of individuals have all been changed.

In the second half of the twentieth century diamond manufacturers were engaged in a struggle to remain globally competitive, by detaching their cutting and polishing operations from forms of state and social regulation. Since the 1970s, increased global demand had seen diamond manufacturing shift from long established cutting and polishing workshops in Belgium to international locations with cheaper labor costs and more relaxed industrial legislation. Gemstone dealers in the Indian states of Gujarat and Maharashtra captured a high proportion of this global trade. But in the 1990s India's new economic zones, which offered a raft of exemptions from tax and labor regimes, promised new opportunities for international investors.

Worldwide Diamonds was the international diamond industry's first direct investment in India's new offshore economy. The investment was a joint venture between Bettonville, a Belgian company that is the world's largest manufacturer of tools and equipment for the diamond industry, and Hennig, a British company that is the UK's largest diamond broker. Their factory was conceived of as an "in-house" processing facility that would provide access to India's low-cost labor market for De Beers' European and North American Sightholders. The social organization of production here reproduced historic relationships of power and domination, with a labor force comprised of Telugu men and women who were differentiated by caste, class, and language from the factory's Indian managers and its white European executives (Cross 2009).

Because they have been such notorious sites of labor abuse in global supply chains, free-trade zones have also emerged as political sites in which companies that aspire to be good corporate citizens must seek to limit or manage potential damage to their reputations. Economic zones have become increasingly significant as spaces in which companies seek to establish, enact or perform themselves as "ethical." Sure enough, in 2004, one of Worldwide Diamonds twelve clients decided that its offshore contractor fell within the remit of De Beers' new ethical accounting regime.

Best practices

At the end of 2004, the Millennium Group's chief financial officer travelled to London, and Worldwide Diamonds' senior managers travelled to Mumbai, for training workshops on the BPP program run by the Diamond Trading Company. The framework for implementing De Beers' BPP program created a spatial-temporal map of responsibility across a global network of traders and suppliers. The need for "action" was determined on the basis of an agent's proximity to or distance from De Beers. Companies in which De Beers or its Sightholders held a stake had to demonstrate their compliance with the BPPs within two years, while facilities like Worldwide Diamonds' that had written or oral contracts with De Beers' Sightholders were required to become compliant by June 2005.

Becoming compliant was a two-stage process. First, a manufacturer had to commission an independent on-site audit by the Société Générale de Surveillance (SGS), a Geneva-based company that offers third-party inspection, testing, certification, and verification services to a wide range of major corporate clients, and which was the certified auditor for the BPP process. This audit would take place once.

Secondly, a manufacturer had to complete a self-assessment process and provide written evidence that the factory recognized De Beers' practices and principles. This self-assessment was to be submitted for independent monitoring, verification, and peer review and was due to be repeated on an annual basis.

Worldwide Diamonds' senior executives returned to their factory largely unfazed by the implications of its new accounting regime. As they saw it, transnational corporations like De Beers had to perform a delicate balancing act. On one hand they had to make the kind of regulatory performance demanded of a good corporate citizen. On the other, they had to reaffirm their commitment to market freedoms as demanded by their own Sightholders. From their perspective, the BPP was a device that allowed the industry's dominant actor to limit its future exposure to negative publicity, while ensuring that business practices in the supply chain remained "competitive." Adam, the Millennium Group's chief financial officer, described the rationale to me:

> *Adam:* For De Beers it is essential to safeguard the industry. If there are any accusations about the diamond industry in the future ... Any accusations that the industry is doing something bad.... Well now, before any negative publicity has a chance to come out De Beers can say: 'We have our codes of conduct. We are strictly implementing them. If someone is found to have done something wrong, we will take action against them. You can't blame the diamond industry....'

At the same time, he explained, regulatory interventions had to be bracketed, confined to specific areas of business. Ambiguity was essential:

> *Adam:* Their code has to be ambiguous. It cannot control all aspects of business behavior. There are some things it can check, like whether or not we are employing child labor, if we have fire exits or if we provide drinking water. But the moment they try to control the business environment ... the moment that they try to put restrictions on salary structures or on incentive systems, well ... See: there is a line and De Beers have to ensure that they don't cross it to interfere with the business environment.

The Millennium Group hired a Hong Kong-based consultancy firm, "Best Practice Consultants," to guide them through the BPP program. Two Israeli entrepreneurs had established the consultancy firm specifically for this purpose. "Without the right navigation," the company's sales brochure states,

> the journey towards compliance with the Best Practice Principles can be frustrating and time-consuming.... Dealing with all aspects of BPP

compliance is a complex process that requires specialized knowledge. Our rich knowledge of all current BPP legislation and procedures ensures that our clients take the fastest and most cost-effective track towards complying with BPP requirements....

At the end of 2004 these two consultants travelled to Hyderabad, the state capital of Andhra Pradesh, and ran a workshop for Worldwide Diamonds' managers. The participants included two senior European executives and twelve young Indian management trainees, to whom the task of actually bringing Worldwide Diamonds into line with the BPP program was delegated.

Walking the line

Worldwide Diamonds' management trainees were aged between 22 and 26, and had graduate master's degrees in engineering or management from provincial English medium colleges in South India. With salaries of 8000 rupees (approximately USD 200) a month, their earnings were more than double that of the factory's production workers, but still represented the bottom of India's white-collar graduate labor market. These young managers all dreamt of moving upwards into the higher ranks of business professionals, or of travelling overseas to pursue further educational qualifications.

As they saw it, the biggest everyday challenge of modern factory management was to avoid becoming embroiled in a web of close, binding, personal relationships with the people they were employed to manage and control. They clamored away from relationships with the factory's workforce, afraid that any intimation of closeness, friendship, or intimacy with individuals might offer them some kind of leverage in requests for a promotion, a wage increase, extra leave, extra overtime, or a reduction in workload. Managers like Vikram, Jeet, and Chiru put these problems succinctly during interviews with me on and off the factory floor. Their anxieties stand testament to the difficulties of imposing a high-intensity production regime on people with whom you enjoy close relations, and to the constant work or effort involved in successfully achieving a degree of "distance" from workers. Detachment was seen as a precondition for the rational, market-oriented calculations and impartial decisions required of a modern professional, essential for achieving control and productivity. Achieving detachment meant purging oneself of sentiment, foreclosing any affective ties of obligation or reciprocity.

Vikram: Relations with workers can't be avoided. They're necessary, they're a must. Without them you can't get the required outputs on the shop floor. But at the same time you can't try to build good relations with workers here. You'll never be successful like that. If you want them to meet targets and to keep the quality up then you have to be strict, you have to be disciplined. You can't go with your sentiments. You can't get production with sentiments.

Understanding, finding, and maintaining this fine line was a preeminent day-to-day concern and was a repeated motif in my conversational interviews.

Jeet: You can't be friends or enemies with the workers here.... There will be some situations when I have to compel workers to do certain things. And if I am maintaining a friendship with them I just won't be able to do that. But you also just can't get things done by being authoritative! I'm talking about being on the shop floor where you spend eight hours a day. When you're there you have to get personal with workers so that you can create a good atmosphere for work. But there are always some limitations. Because when there is a managerial gap between you and them—and there should be a gap—you must not show it. You should not show the gap physically or allow others to feel it. But you have to maintain it. You have to maintain it for yourselves. How to maintain the line, though ... well that varies from time to time ... I can't draw the line straight away. If I immediately and stubbornly draw a line then it's sure that I'll lose the workers, and I don't want to lose them. These are the things that show our competencies.

Reciprocal social ties are sometimes described in Telugu as *tapana*: actions that provoke a sense of compulsion in the recipient to do something in return. The accounts of young managers describe a keen aversion to *tapana* relations with workers, and to the obligations and responsibilities they bring. Chiru explained how these bonds worked in the context of his family.

Chiru: Say I am at my house, with my two brothers. If I help my brother in one situation, he will help in another. If I do something for him then he will think to do something for me too. He will get some sense that he should help me. He will be feeling *tapana*. And some delay will be there. And that delay is useful. If I support someone at one time, later they will feel that they can come to me.

In the context of a manufacturing unit in which there was pressure to increase the quantity and quality of production, *tapana* relations and their expectations of delayed reciprocity were precisely what managers like Chiru sought to avoid.

Chiru: I have not been touching the personal aspects up til now. No. I've just been going to a superficial level. If we go into the deep personal aspects it means touching a deep sensitive part of them. Am I right? If you go twenty to thirty percent deep into personal aspects it won't affect them much. If I go deep it increases my responsibility also. I feel there would be some responsibility on my shoulders …

Such strategies of avoidance were tightly bound up with the creation and performance of a professional managerial self, a stable normative identity that was frequently associated with the figure of the engineer.

Vikram: When I came here, I learned from the workers. I used to be friendly with them so that I could manage problems that came up. But I maintained those relations in a smooth and cool manner. I behaved as an engineer.

So while managers observed and profiled workers, they resisted any efforts by workers to collect information about them. They worked to maintain a distance from workers.

Jeet: The workers should not know me. I should only know them. They should not be able to guess me, because they can use that. But I should be able to guess them. I should be able to know their strong points and their weak points. From the first, I didn't bring personal relations into the job. According to me, the job is entirely different and personal is entirely different. Managers are not interested in personal matters. So I won't allow people to ask me about myself. That is my way of living style. My father used to say 'don't bring personals into job profile' because if you bring any one of the personal reasons into the job people will start to ask you: 'Sir will you help me in this manner or that manner.'

It was against the backdrop of these managerial struggles to establish and maintain limits and boundaries on relationships with workers that De Beers' BPP program was introduced to Worldwide Diamonds. For the factory's management trainees, this was to be their first exposure to the language of CSR, to codes of conduct and social audits. What is today an important feature of graduate education at business schools in Europe and North America has yet to enter the curricula of provincial colleges in South India. As I will show, their efforts to bring the factory into compliance with De Beers' BPP program become inseparable from their efforts to become management professionals. The specific form in which the program was materialized on the factory floor presented new tools with which to further their detachment from workplace relationships.

Materializing CSR

At their workshop in Hyderabad, Worldwide Diamonds' management trainees were presented with a large, glossy lever-arch folder. Inside were three documents: 1) a "BPP Requirements Book," an annotated bibliography of the international laws, covenants, regulations, and agreements that were used as the basis for the BPP's performance indicators; 2) a BPP manual, which provided a detailed description of the program, including a timetable for its implementation; and 3) a workbook, a series of tables with the specific BPP performance indicators against which a company's compliance would be audited. The folder was carried back into the factory, where it was dumped on a shelf in a rickety steel cabinet in a corner of the laser cutting room. It was the sheer physicality of the BPP program and the written tasks that these documents created that presented managers with their most immediate problems. "This thing is really a big headache," said Vikram. "Don't get me wrong. But I just don't like very clumsy, very bureaucratic things. I had so many other things to do and now, on top of everything, I've got that huge, great clunky folder and all that paper."

Like all ethical accounting regimes, De Beers' BPP program is primarily constituted not as a process or a practice but as a material object: a set of written documents. Since 2004 these documents have been distributed, downloaded, and emailed along De Beers' diamond pipeline, gradually finding their way to contractors.

Documents are central to the performance of corporate social responsibility. Yet the material significance of documents and the work involved in their production, circulation, and dissemination has been overlooked by recent anthropology. As the work of Annelise Riles (1998, 2006a, 2006b) reminds us, the document is the "paradigmatic material artefact of modern knowledge practices," the artifact that materializes them all. Ethical accounting regimes hinge on the performance and enactment of proper bureaucratic rituals, procedures, and practices, all of which require an engagement with the document as a material technology. Indeed codes of practice and auditing, monitoring, and verification mechanisms can all be described as "calls to documentation" (Riles 2006a: 6). De Beers' BPP program is a case in point. The successful implementation of the program required documents to beget more documents.

In 2005, each facility being submitted for auditing and verification under De Beers' new ethical accounting regime was required to complete an audit workbook and write separate, substantive replies to each question. In addition, they were required to maintain an up-to-date series of policy statements. These documents were collated and uploaded via an electronic submission system to a central database run by the BPP team. The BPP database sent out an automatic email notification that the documents had been received, and sent an email alerting De Beers' external auditor, SGS, that they were ready for inspection. At one of SGS's regional offices in India, the documents would be downloaded and proofread: checked for any missing answers or missing policies. The documents would then be passed on to SGS's head office in Geneva, where they were "monitored for global consistency." Any infringements, what are called major or minor breaches of the BPP, would be made visible in the database. A factory that was in breach of the code was notified in writing, and its response was made in the same way.

The problem facing anthropologists is how, as Annelise Riles puts it (1998), to bring into view the creative work involved in this work of documentation, and in the production of "convincing, effective documents" — that is, to reveal the material significance of documents rather than just their discursive power. Attention to the materiality of CSR and the work of creating or using documents is a different point of entry into current debates than that taken by anthropologists writing in the Foucauldian tradition. In this tradition, the key instruments used to implement an ethical accounting regime (like the codes of practice and the audit checklist) are discursive technologies that encode different levels, genres, and expressions of governmentality. The focus here is on the "hidden politics of meaning" contained within a burgeoning library of international codes, protocols, guidelines, and standards, and their power as "instruments of political or ideological control" that produce selves, persons, and society (Riles 1998, 2006). In this vein, accounting tools can appear to install, as Dolan evocatively puts it, "new metrics of governance" (Dolan 2010: 34).

A document like De Beers' BPP Workbook is particularly conducive to this kind of analysis. The workbook was effectively a checklist that translated the key clauses of internationally recognized protocols into a series of standardized and verifiable questions about financial and business procedures, employment and working conditions (including health and safety), and environmental practices. Among those on "employment," for example, was question number 23: "Are all workers aware of and clearly understand the terms and conditions of their employment including working hours, wage structure and standing orders?" And under "health and safety" was question number 30: "Are all workers advised of their duties, responsibilities and rights with regard to health and safety and are they made aware of the entity's health and safety procedures?" By erasing the ways that power and political economy are transcribed on the working body, such questions and categories made individual workers the sole bearers of responsibility for health and well-being. Like other attempts to codify health and safety risks in the modern industrial workplace, they removed from consideration all other factors that affected the individual's well-being at work, and they produced the worker as an autonomous and flexible laboring subject (Cross 2010a; Martin 1994).

Yet in this Foucauldian tradition of analysis, as Riles argues (2006a), texts and categories can come to exert an unduly hegemonic and overdetermining influence. Documents, she writes, both "anticipate and enable certain actions," "they are both open and closed." While this BPP Workbook may demand certain kinds of responses form Worldwide Diamonds' managers, it could not complete itself, and the work of completing it, of producing appropriate documentary responses, was also a pathway for action. To think about codes and checklists as material artifacts is to ask how they are being used, and what actors may be doing with them (ibid.: 10–12). As I will show, the power of De Beers' BPP program was not simply that it crafted new managerial subjects, but rather that it offered people new purchase in their ongoing struggles to extricate themselves from ties and obligations.

Technologies of detachment

Vikram, Jeet, and Chiru threw themselves into the task of completing the BPP documents with considerable zeal. They organized meetings with each other to discuss the precise wording of the workbook questions, and they drafted multiple replies. As they formulated these responses, Vikram, Jeet, and Chiru turned to the original texts, borrowing sentences, phrases, and categories for quotation and repetition. The BPP documents were a vital resource and appear to have been designed precisely for this purpose. The BPP Manual, for example, gives detailed instructions on what company policies should look like, even offering generic sentences or statements that can be cut and pasted into a company's written responses. A section on employment, for example, states that: "Key elements in a policy on freedom of association and collective bargaining might include: a statement that worker representatives must have access to their members in the workplace, and that the employer does not interfere with the activities of worker organizations." Making Worldwide Diamonds' documents convincing was, as Riles argues (1998: 386), "less about transparent meaning than about the aesthetics of logic and language," and Vikram, Jeet, and Chiru's job was to make the documents look right.

In their own accounts, the practical task of implementing De Beers' new accounting regime begins to emerge as a creative rather than a subjectifying task: a task through which they could perform themselves as modern professionals and derive a reflexive satisfaction.

> *Jeet:* I've learnt a lot from working in this factory, especially the qualities of a professional leader, a manager. He should be smart, professional, very formal. He should know the rules and regulations systems, like ISO and BPP. All of it.

> *Vikram:* Some factories are like football. They're rough, they don't have many rules, you push and you shove. But our company is like cricket, it's full of rules and regulations. And being here, you have to come to how to play the game. You have to know how to handle the rules, how to deal with the paperwork, and like that you move from being amateur to going pro.

As they reflected on what they had learned over the first year of their management training, their understanding of how to organize, manage, and control the factory's labor force was inextricably bound up with the bureaucratic systems and procedures associated with the BPP program. The task of creating effective BPP documents seemed to have helped them legitimize or formalize the fine line between what they called the personal and the professional, and extricate themselves from binding ties or obligations to workers. As Jeet told me after the BPP documents had been submitted in 2005:

> *Jeet:* These systematic procedures are necessary if we want to make this company professional. What is written has to be done.

Similarly, Vikram described the BPP documents as "step by step guides, so there would be no confusion about what to do." Chiru put the efficacy of the documents most bluntly:

> *Chiru:* No one can complain now. What we do here, what happens here is the company's will. The will of the company. Not of any one person.

As they filled out the audit workbook and finalized their written responses, the work of documentation permeated their everyday interactions on the factory floor. Confronted with small requests for personal favors or special treatment by workers, they used the documents to justify or explain a refusal to enter into what they understood as close or personal relationships.

> *Chiru:* I've learnt a different management style in this factory.... Now I know the predetermined parameters that you should keep in mind. I learnt how a professional manager should go.... There is no partiality in him. That's the philosophy that a professional manager should follow. People should not

create disparity by liking one person more than another. The rule for one is the rule for all.

> *Vikram:* A professional manager should not spend time listening to the words of workers. A professional person is never sentimental. They're experts. If they are to be professional then they have to think about quality and production, and not get distracted by conditions and salaries. If we have all these systems in place, we don't have to get distracted by workers complaining to us that the conditions are not good, that the toilet facilities are bad, that the production is too heavy, that the seats are uncomfortable, that the dust is there, that the salaries are not good.

The same effect was visible higher up the management hierarchy. Worldwide Diamonds' senior management executives used the code to define and delineate what was meant by terms and conditions of work, bracketing or separating from them the actual costs of labor. "I think we mostly comply with the BPP," Adam concluded, after the company had submitted the audit workbook.

> *Adam:* There are a few problems with fire escapes and things like that here but codes like this are basically for diamond workshops where there are really bad working conditions, like those on the other side of India, in Surat and Mumbai. The real problem is with sweatshops. Not factories like this where people work in humanitarian conditions.

The power of audit documents in a low-waged, hyper-efficient manufacturing unit comes in the combination of their discursive and material qualities. Inside Worldwide Diamonds, De Beers' code of conduct and audit workbook were never just ideologically loaded texts that abstracted and decontexualized relationships between transnational capital, managerial subjects, and a global labor force. Instead it was precisely the discursive power of these texts—the power to abstract and decontextualize, to extract relationships from local contexts of interaction, to codify and standardize relationships—that resonated most with managers. The work of filling out and completing the documentation opened up new paths of action that extended, deepened, and entrenched an ethic of "detachment." They delineated specific terms to the relationships between employer and employee, manager and worker. They limited these relationships both temporally (to the period of the working day) and spatially (to the borders of the workplace). And they ensured that any commitments or obligations that might have arisen out of everyday relationships with workers were "encompassed" by global institutions and accountability regimes that aggregated moral authority (Strathern 2005).

Conclusion

Since 2005 and my original fieldwork for this paper, the scope of De Beers' BPP program has been significantly adjusted, as a result of what industry insiders call "pushback" from Sightholders. Confronted with the implications and costs of monitoring their diverse trading, mining, and manufacturing facilities, Sightholders have lobbied De Beers to limit the scope of the BPP program. Some time between 2007 and 2008, a significant clause was introduced into the small print. Today only a Sightholder's "significant contractors"—those to whom it provides seventy-five percent or more of their annual turnover—are required to comply with the terms of De Beers' BPP program. A major diamond manufacturing company like Worldwide Diamonds that offers services to a number of Sightholders—none of whom individually accounted for seventy-five percent or more of its business—is no longer required to submit itself for inspection. Indeed, after the events described in this article, Worldwide Diamonds ended its participation in the BPP program.

Empirical accounts of corporate social responsibility at sites of offshore manufacturing have often chosen to emphasize the deliberate efforts of corporations or factory managers to subvert or bend an inspection process. In such cases "an imperative for transparency and accountability can produce instead opacity and deception" (Dolan 2008: 287). In this article I have taken a different tack, showing how codes of conduct and social audits can segue perfectly into the efforts of companies and managers to organize complex global supply chains, and of offshore manufacturers to organize cost-efficient and competitive systems of mass production. My argument rests on a paradox, that ethical accounting regimes which are premised on the creation of closer ties, attachments, or relationships between global corporations and producers actually allow companies and managers new tools with which to delineate the ends and limits to these relationships, fostering what I have called an ethic of detachment.

The real success of corporate social responsibility in a global supply chain is that it redistributes responsibility and obligation across a network of actors, rather than concentrating and focusing it upon one (Crook 2000; Strathern 1996). This would appear to hold true both for large corporate entities as well as for individuals. In the diamond industry, De Beers' attempt to manage its relationships with Sightholders and subcontractors through a corporate social responsibility program is folded into managerial relationships with labor. The BPP program enabled De Beers to distribute responsibilities through a global network of Sightholders and subcontractors, allowing particular kinds of risks to be isolated and quarantined before they can spread. Meanwhile, on the factory floor of a global subcontracting company, De Beers' BPP initiative presents managerial subjects with new tools to bracket themselves from personal obligations and ties to workers. The language of CSR and the array of auditing, monitoring, and verification tools present transnational corporations and managerial subjects alike with new ways to manage, define, control, and limit their attachments to producers.

Much current anthropology has chosen to follow the kinds of attachments that are being created by discourses of corporate social responsibility. Yet much strategic and personal decision-making in today's global supply chains appears to be underpinned by an ethic of detachment. If anthropology is to examine how ethical accounting regimes are grounded in the everyday work of doing business, then perhaps we need to think about the material technologies that facilitate this work.

References

Blowfield, Michael E., and Catherine S. Dolan. 2008. Stewards of virtue? The ethical dilemma of CSR in African agriculture. *Development and Change* 39 (1): 1–23.

Callon, Michel. 1998. An essay on framing and overflowing: economic externalities revisited by sociology. In *Laws of the markets*, ed. Michel Callon, 244–69. London: Blackwell.

Callon, Michel. 2007. *Market devices*. London: Blackwell.

Candea, Matei, Joanna Cook, Catherine Trundle, and Tom Yarrow. 2009. Reconsidering detachment, *http://detachmentcollaboratory.org/?page_id=528* (last accessed December 2010).

Carrier, James G., and Daniel Miller, eds. 1998. *Virtualism: A new political economy*. London: Berg.

Crook, Tony. 2000. Length matters: A note on the GM debate. *Anthropology Today* 16 (1): 8–11.

Cross, Jamie. 2009. From dreams to discontent: Educated men and the everyday politics of labour in a Special Economic Zone in South India. *Contributions to Indian Sociology* 43 (3): 351–79.

Cross, Jamie. 2010a. Occupational health, risk and science in India's global factories. *South Asian History and Culture* 1 (2): 224–38.

Cross, Jamie. 2010b. Neoliberalism as unexceptional: Economic zones and the everyday precariousness of working lives in South India. *Critique of Anthropology* 30 (4): 355–73.

Dolan, Catherine. 2008. Arbitrating risk through moral values: The case of Kenyan fairtrade. *Research in Economic Anthropology* 28: 1–30.

Dolan, Catherine. 2010. Virtual moralities: The mainstreaming of fairtrade in Kenyan tea fields. *Geoforum* 41: 33–43.

Giddens, Anthony. 1990. *The consequences of modernity*. Cambridge: Polity Press.

Holm, Peter. 2007. Which way is up on Callon? In MacKenzie, Muniesa, and Siu 2007: 225–43.

MacKenzie, Donald. A., Muniesa, Fabian., & Siu, L. 2007. Introduction. In *Do economists make markets? On the performativity of economics,* eds. D. A. MacKenzie, F. Muniesa, and L. Siu, 1–19. Princeton, N. J.: Princeton University Press.

Martin, Emily. 1994. *Flexible bodies: Tracking immunity in American culture from the days of polio to the age of AIDS.* London: Beacon Press.

Miller, Daniel. 1998. Conclusion: A theory of virtualism. In *Virtualism: A new political economy,* eds. James G. Carrier and Daniel Miller, 187–217. London: Berg.

Miller, Daniel. 2002. Turning Callon the right way up. *Economy and Society* 31 (2): 218–33.

Ong, Aihwa. 2006. *Neoliberalism as exception.* Durham: Duke University Press.

Rajak, Dinah. 2008. "Uplift and empower": The market, the gift and corporate social responsibility on South Africa's platinum belt. *Research in Economic Anthropology* 28: 297–324.

Riles, Annelise. 1998. Infinity within the brackets. *American Ethnologist* 25 (3): 378–98.

Riles, Annelise. 2006a. Introduction: In response. In *Documents: Artifacts of modern knowledge,* ed. Annelise Riles, 1–39. Ann Arbor: University of Michigan Press.

Riles, Annelise. 2006b. [Deadlines]: Removing the brackets on politics in bureaucratic and anthropological analysis. In *Documents: Artifacts of modern knowledge,* 71–94. Ann Arbor: University of Michigan Press.

Rose, Nikolas. 1999. *Governing the soul.* London: Free Association Books.

Shamir, Ronen. 2004. The de-radicalization of corporate social responsibility. *Critical Sociology* 30 (3): 669–89

Shamir, Ronen. 2008. The age of responsibilization: On market-embedded morality. *Economy and Society* 37 (1): 1–19.

Strathern, Marilyn. 1996. Cutting the network. *Journal of the Royal Anthropological Institute* (N.S.) 2: 517–35.

Strathern, Marilyn. 2002. Abstraction and decontextualization: An anthropological comment. In *Virtual society?: Technology, cyberbole, reality,* ed. Steve Woolgar, 302–313. Oxford: Oxford University Press.

Strathern, Marilyn. 2005. Robust knowledge and fragile futures. In *Global assemblages: Technology, politics, and ethics as anthropological problems,* eds. Aihwa Ong and Stephen Collier, 464–82. London: Blackwell.

Strathern, Marilyn, ed. 2000. *Audit cultures: Anthropological studies in accountability, ethics and the academy.* London: Routledge.

Thrift, Nigel. 1996. *Spatial formations.* London: Sage Publications.

Thrift, Nigel. 1998. Virtual capitalism: The globalisation of reflexive business knowledge. In *Virtualism: A new political economy,* eds. James G. Carrier and Daniel Miller, 161–86. Oxford: Berg.

Tsing, Anna. 2009. Supply chains and the human condition. *Rethinking Marxism* 21 (2): 148–76.

Jamie Cross is a Senior Lecturer in Social Anthropology at the University of Edinburgh, UK.

– Chapter 6 –

DISCONNECT DEVELOPMENT

Imagining Partnership and Experiencing Detachment in Chevron's Borderlands

Katy Gardner

$\mathcal{C}\sim$

Partnership is a serious business for Chevron, an integral element to "The Chevron Way," much touted in their promotional literature:

Partnership
We have an unwavering commitment to being a good partner focused on building productive, collaborative, trusting and beneficial relationships with governments, other companies, our customers, our communities and each other.[1]

How are anthropologists of corporate social responsibility to treat such statements? Perhaps the best starting point is to ask what the language of "partnership" does for Chevron. Cornwall, Eade and others have pointed out how in "Development Speak" terms such as partnership allow a fuzzy, feel-good factor; these are "words that admit no negatives, words that evoke Good Things that no-one could possibly disagree with" (Cornwall 2010: 2). More generally, in the world of development concepts, which may have originally carried one set of (often radical) meanings, meanings are apt to lose their way, becoming flattened, or suggesting an array of different things to different people (Cornwall and Eade 2010). But whilst the lexicon is slippery, this does not mean that "Development Speak is to be dismissed or disregarded, for it does important work. Indeed, using the right language is 'an essential qualification for entry into the Industry'" (Cornwall and Eade 2010: ix).

In what follows I shall show how by using the language of partnership in their CSR programs in the villages that surround the company's gas plant at Bibiyana, Bangladesh, Chevron simultaneously aspire to create particular relationships ("partnerships") with "local communities" whilst maintaining a set of practices and meanings central to their operations: the corporate ethic of detachment (Cross 2011). As we shall see, fluency in the lingo, with a liberal use of terms such as "partnership," "participation," "empowerment" and "community" allows Chevron a pass into Development World, whilst other practices allow it to remain firmly grounded in Corporation Land.

Why bother? In the extractive industries, in which security considerations are often paramount, anthropologists have pointed out how CSR and the relationships it involves, be these of patronage, "partnership" or both, are designed in part to gain a "social license to operate," particularly in locations where there has been a history of resistance against operations and violent confrontation such as Nigeria (Zalik 2004) or Indonesia (Welker 2009). In these cases "partnership" does not merely look good for global shareholders, it creates compliance. Indeed, in the postcolonial world, CSR and its attendant discourse of partnership may be core to the creation of "secured enclaves" in which extractive industries can successfully operate (Ferguson 2005). And whilst global capital is usually highly mobile, moving on to more peaceful sites of production if one becomes too tricky, the extraction of natural resources such as oil, coal or gas is necessarily fixed. It is in these contexts that "partnership development" comes in handy (Zalik 2004).

Yet although "partnership"[2] implies an ongoing relationship, based on equality, trust and a common orientation toward what needs to be done (Pickard 2010), in Bibiyana countervailing forces push in the opposite direction. Alongside the rhetoric of connection, corporations need to disconnect, for whilst a degree of territorial fixity is necessary for natural resource extraction, geopolitical as well as environmental and geological uncertainty mean that if conditions change they must quickly disinvest and move on to pastures or gas fields new. These contradictory pressures mean that they need to create and celebrate partnership whilst simultaneously remaining detached.

In what follows I shall argue that whilst apparently building partnerships in the villages that surround one of their largest operations in Bangladesh (the Bibiyana gas field in Sylhet), Chevron successfully remain detached from the local population not in spite of but via their community development programs and employment policies. This contradiction is submerged by ideas and practices within global development discourse that celebrate the disconnection and disengagement of donors via the rhetoric of sustainability. Chiming with development praxis and the neoliberal values that underscore it, by stressing self-reliance, entrepreneurship and "helping people to help themselves," the corporation's Community Engagement Program does little to meet the demands of local people, who hope for employment and long-term investment; a form of connection that is discordant to discourses of self-reliance and sustainability, but might equally be described as "development" (Gardner 2012). The result is that as the company dreams up and celebrates imagined partnerships, local people experience and imagine disconnections of nightmarish proportions.

This chapter is based upon research conducted by myself and a small team of Bangladeshi researchers on the relationship between the gas field, social networks and poverty in the locale, which was funded by the ESRC/DFID.[3] This work involved detailed interviews, household surveys, and participant observation over a year, in both Bibiyana's borderland villages and their transnational outposts in the UK and in Chevron's offices in Dhaka. More generally, it arises from my long-term research in one of the villages adjacent to the installation, where I have been conducting fieldwork and visiting since the late 1980s (Gardner 1995, 2012).

The Bibiyana gas field: A short history

That Chevron's flagship Bangladeshi operation is about a quarter of a mile from the site of my 1980s doctoral fieldwork is a coincidence, but serves as a powerful reminder of how people's lives in apparently remote and rural places are bound up with global processes in multifaceted ways, drawing to our attention the complex interactions between global and local scales, or "the grips of worldly encounters," which Anna Tsing calls *"friction"* (Tsing 2005:4). These "grips of worldly encounters" have been taking place in Sylhet for centuries; rather than the story of Bibiyana involving the discovery of natural gas and the subsequent dragging of otherwise isolated rural communities into the global arena via resistance to and eventual compliance with multinational companies, it is one of ongoing connectedness. Bibiyana has, for example, had a long and intimate relationship with the global economy, via the lascars who worked on British ships from the beginning of the twentieth century, the men who left for Britain in their thousands from the 1960s onwards, and their families who have settled with them in the UK since the 1980s. As I have described in my other work (e.g., 1995, 1993, 2008), three of the villages surrounding the gas field are what is known locally as "Londoni" villages, meaning that a high proportion of people have either settled in the UK or have close relatives there. Whilst most families are increasingly orientated toward Britain, with children and grandchildren growing up who only visit Bangladesh for holidays and may not be fluent in Bengali (Gardner and Mand 2012), the original migrants remained orientated to the *desh* (homeland), spending most of their earnings on land, building houses and on transforming their status. By the 1980s access to the local means of production (land on which to grow rice) was almost wholly based on one's access to foreign places: Londoni families owned almost all the local land, whilst those families who had not migrated but were once large landowners had slipped down the scale to become landless or land poor. Local economic and political hierarchies were therefore dominated by relative access to the UK and other destinations in Europe, the US, or the Middle East.

These inequalities took on a distinctive local pattern, adhering to kinship networks. Whilst large and dominant lineages capitalized on the opportunities of movement to Britain and have built substantial power bases in their villages, in Kakura, which was originally settled by in-migrant laborers, no one had the economic or social capital necessary for migration. Today the village is over 80 percent landless, far higher than the national average of 56 percent (Toufique and Turton 2002); a high preponderance of people live in mud and thatch dwellings and have no access to electricity: the power line that leads from Karimpur to Nadampur passes Kakura by. In 2008 our research found many people in Kakura, as well as in landless households in Karimpur (which for historical reasons has a high proportion of Hindus) who did not eat more than two meals a day, and/or who did not know where their next meal was coming from (Gardner 2012).

When natural gas was discovered, the area was therefore already unusual in the Bangladeshi context for its relative wealth and strong connections to *bidesh* (foreign countries). Yet whilst remittances and "help" from British relatives were central to the local economy, so too was agriculture. If the owners of the land lived in East London or Newcastle or Oldham it did not mean that a large number of people were not dependent upon that land for their livelihoods, either by sharecropping or renting it, or because they worked as agricultural laborers. Access to land as well as to jobs on the land also come through social connections: sharecroppers are often related to landowners, or have long-standing relationships with them. Patron-clientage certainly involved gross inequality and exploitation, but it was also a prime source of support for the very poor—a relationship shaded by both light and dark.

The discovery of natural gas in the area by Occidental took place in the mid-1990s. By 2000 Unocal had taken over in the development of the resources; a smaller installation a few kilometers north at Dikhalbagh was to be joined by a second development, in between the villages of Nadampur, Karimpur, Kakura and Firizpur, using around sixty acres of prime agricultural land. The land was to be forcibly acquired by the Bangladeshi government and rented to Unocal, who were contracted to develop the site. Once gas was being produced it would be sold back to the government at a rate to be fixed in a "production share contract." In 2005 Unocal merged with Chevron and by 2007 the gas field went into production, joining other gas fields operated by Chevron in Moulvi Bazaar and Jalalbaad. Today Chevron produce nearly 50 percent of Bangladesh's gas.[4] Whilst executives told me that the company were hoping to stay in Bibiyana for at least thirty years, whether this happens is a moot point. Not only is the extent of reserves continually disputed but the difficulties of working with the government and attendant "risk to reputation" may make their game far more short term; in 2010 I heard rumors that they may pull out sooner rather than later.

Given the forcible loss of land, it is hardly surprising that the development of the gas plant met with consternation in the villages surrounding the site. As soon as people heard of the plans, "Demand Resistance Committees" were set up and a series of demands put to Unocal: the rate of land compensation was top of the list, followed by connection to the gas supply (the villages do not have piped gas). A school, a hospital, a fertilizer factory and improved roads were also included in the "demands." Today, people claim that Unocal agreed to these stipulations. If this was the case they were making promises they could never keep: rates of compensation, the piping of gas to the communities and the development of power plants and factories were not in their gift but determined by the government. The negotiations took place in a context of passionate agitation. In the perspectives of the landowners who led the protests, they were about to lose a resource that sustained not only their households but those of many people around them and that was irreplaceable; for some it seemed almost like a loss of self. As one of the biggest land losers told us: "The day they grabbed my land, I lost my words. If I remember that day I have to stop myself from going mad."

In 2005 the road was blocked by local people in an attempt to stop construction. The police were called, threats made by the District

Commissioner, arrests made, and writs issued. Yet whilst some local leaders tried to hold out against the inevitable others started to negotiate: the seeds of "community engagement" were sown. By this time Chevron had taken over Unocal, and the compensation process was underway: this was for land and property taken in the building of the plant and the roads that surrounded it. Today Chevron say that 95 percent of landowners were compensated at the highest rate they could negotiate with the government.[5]

Local grievances dovetailed the national resistance campaign against the extraction of Bangladesh's natural resources by foreign companies. Indeed, the role of multinationals has caused serious political unrest in the country in the last decade. In 2006, protests against a proposed open cast mine in Phulbari, in the north-east, to be operated by Asia Energy, led to the death of three and injury of around a hundred when police shot into a crowd of 50,000. More recently, national agitation has centered on the content of production share contracts with foreign companies, with the activists arguing that these grossly exploit the country's natural resources, involving large profits for the multinationals, generous backhanders for corrupt government officials, and nothing for Bangladesh. In September 2009, for example, a rally called to protest against the leasing of rights to extract offshore gas resources to multinationals led to police violence and the injury of thirty people. Rumor, counter-rumor, civil unrest, accusations and arrests are the order of the day in a fragile democracy marked by high levels of government corruption, secret deals, and little accountability. Although Chevron is a signatory to the Extractive Industries Transparency Initiative, at the time of writing the details of its deals in Bangladesh have not been made public.

Within Bibiyana many people were highly ambivalent about the gas field: angry at the loss of their land, certainly, and with a strong sense that the gas was a local resource that should benefit local people. Yet they were also hopeful that the plant would bring substantial economic development in the form of jobs, industry, improved infrastructure, and so on. At first these hopes seemed to be well founded; when the site was being built hundreds of local people gained employment as laborers, their safety training and company registration cards signaling that the plant would provide a future of secure employment and connection to modernity.

In these early days the Demand Realization Committees were optimistic that their requests would be met. Alongside the rate of compensation, connection to the gas supply was seen as hugely important, symbolizing the area's inclusion in the benefits of economic development as well involving a cleaner and less dangerous form of energy: then, as now, women cook over firewood, causing chronic respiratory problems. As the claims of the Committees imply, local understandings of the relationship between Chevron and the villages surrounding the gas field were based more on a model of compensation than partnership.

One man describes the early negotiations in the following terms:

> We were given good hopes, dreams for the future. They promised us: 'if the road goes past your village you will get transport facilities, industries will be built, you will get jobs.'

Imagining partnership

In their accounts of this period, Chevron Bangladesh's External Affairs team are keen to describe how much time and effort was devoted to developing positive relationships with the villages surrounding the gas field, transforming hostility and confrontation into partnership and support. After the rate of land compensation had been agreed, the design of community development programs became key to the company's community engagement strategy, replacing what were seen by them as impossible demands. Both a hospital and gas connection, for instance, can only be provided by the government, whilst "sustainable development," funded via non-governmental organizations (NGOs), seemed to be a realizable objective. As their publicity material states:

> Chevron Bangladesh will always consider itself a partner of the local people of Bibiyana in the community's effort to improve their socio-economic condition. The company would like to strengthen this partnership with a view to achieving sustainable development in the locality. (Chevron Publications 2008: 11)

To have a "partnership," one has to have communities with which to partner, and, indeed, "local leaders" to help facilitate that partnership. In their narratives of the early days of community engagement, Chevron executives describe how developing friendships with these "leaders" was central. In one account, for example, a top official was at pains to describe the efforts he took in building relationships with particular individuals who he assumed to be "leaders," who represented "the community." Our discussions revealed that he had no idea of internal village dynamics, coping strategies or indeed levels of poverty in the area. That the "leaders" only represented certain interests or did not have automatic lines of communication with the poorest or particular groups (e.g., Hindus) did not seem to have occurred to him. Another official told us in self-congratulatory tones how before Chevron funded its programs in the area "there was nothing there."

Whilst forging positive relationships is key to the merit-making of community engagement officers, the schemes also carry neoliberal moralities and can be seen as a way of imposing social order on what could potentially be chaotic and dangerous to the gas plant. In her ethnography of colonial, state and donor improvement schemes in Indonesia, Tanya Li argues that such schemes must be understood in Foucauldian terms as a form of governance that operates by educating desires, aspirations, and beliefs (Li 2007: 5). By rendering what are essentially political problems (such as extreme poverty or the loss of livelihoods to industrial development) as "technical" issues with a range of technical solutions, projects of "improvement" govern by the back door.

A key element of the process of control is "problematization," whereby a problem is identified and a solution offered. Another element is the role of experts, who "focus more on the capacities of the poor than on the practices through which one group impoverishes the other" (Li 2007: 7). As Li continues: "To govern through community requires that community be rendered technical. It must be investigated, mapped, classified, documented, interpreted" (2007: 234).

In their accounts, officials describe how the first stage of Chevron's community development program involved the hiring of consultants and experts to "map" the area that was soon to be referred to as "Bibiyana":

> We told them that we were more interested to know about where their strength lay, what their capacities were, before we set out to address their needs. Our goal was always to forge a partnership with the local community to play a part in the overall development of the community. Therefore we felt the need for a strategic approach to our development plan. We conducted several studies with the help of local research organizations. We first carried out a survey to assess people's perception of the company. And then we went for a baseline study to assess the socio-economic condition of the locality. The latter gave us indications of the critical needs and capacity of the community. (Chevron Publications 2008: 11)

Later came the inevitable PRA (Participatory Rural Appraisal) exercises in which problems were diagnosed and the field of action delineated (Li 2007: 246). The knowledge gained from these exercises was written up in more reports, and the "problem" (the loss of livelihoods to the gas field/ poverty) transformed into "project goals."[6] Like all development projects, the solutions offered by the reports were by definition technical in nature; once speaking the language of development it is virtually impossible to break free of its vernacular. As a result of these "scoping exercises" project objectives began to materialize, all of which found solutions in strengthening community and individual capacity. After participatory assessment and planning, community groups were to be formed, with organizational capacity-building taking place; training in literacy and other "productive" skills would be offered, alongside technical, supervisory and marketing support. According to an early report, the main project objectives were:

> to develop productive skills through training and education for economic emancipation of the vulnerable groups in Bibiyana and provide input support to enable effective utilization of the acquired skills.

Key to these objectives was the setting up of Village Development Organizations (VDOs) that would involve committees of "local leaders," who would choose beneficiaries for the credit and training. Through this mechanism, actual relationships between the donor and the eventual recipients are avoided: it is the "local leaders" and not Chevron who actually have to deal with the poor. The VDOs are modelled on a notion of natural communities, in which leaders speak for, and know, "the people," and in which the role of development is to strengthen and modernize these structures, provide training, and improve access. A second key element to the program was its implementation by a local NGO who would have an office in the area and run the actual programs in conjunction with the VDOs.

Alongside the mapping exercises, with their technical language and objectives, the area (referred to by the Head of External Affairs as "our community") is physically demarcated via Chevron's Road Safety Awareness Program. Part of this involves large billboards, which have been erected along the Sherpur-Bibiyana road to advocate road traffic safety. Picturing smiling children or students sporting hard hats and tee shirts emblazoned with the Chevron logo, these billboards create an image of a contented population, happy to be part of Chevron's "Vision."

Similar imaginings of successful partnership are created by ceremonies and visits carried out by high level Chevron executives to the area, which are publicized in the company's publicity material and reports. As David Mosse argues, in order to enroll a range of supportive actors, projects need interpretive communities, with managers frequently spending more time disseminating evidence of success than dealing with the tricky everyday problems of implementation, for: "development success is not objectively verifiable but socially produced" (2005: 172). VIP visits, project literature, brochures and videos are all part of the performance. Such performances of success are central to Chevron's Community Engagement Program in Bibiyana, and are aimed primarily at the "interpretive community," comprising Bangladeshi state officials, Chevron's international executives, competing corporations, and the company's shareholders.

A key event in the performance of success is the "handing over ceremony." School rooms or NGO offices are prepared, banners erected, and local, national and international dignitaries invited. The community is represented by a selection of "local leaders" and grateful recipients who company officials do not have any personal knowledge of (for example, when told by me that the recipients of school scholarships were actually from wealthy Londoni families, an official said: "I thought they didn't look very poor"). Once assembled, speeches are made and photographs are taken, usually at the moment of "hand over": the computer, sewing machine or stipend physically changing hands.[7]

Performances need an audience if they are to be meaningful. Whilst the assembled locals and dignitaries are important participants, handing-over ceremonies require a global audience if they are to have their full impact on "reputation." Why else would a small bridge, recently built in Karimpur, sport a brass plate with the words: "Bibiyana Friendship Bridge," when no one in the village (besides visiting transnational Londonis) reads English? Local performances of success are thus turned seamlessly into heart-warming stories of partnership and community and disseminated via Chevron's PR machinery; the reports and newsletters to be downloaded at a click, received through the post for shareholders, or handed in hard copies to visitors and colleagues. For example:

> Buffie Wilson, wife of Chevron Bangladesh President Steve Wilson, recently made a visit to the village of Karimpur, located next to the Bibiyana gas field in Habiganj. Her visit heralded a brand new beginning for the families of Champa Begum and Jotsna Dev. Both women lost their homes during the devastating flood of 2007 and in standing by the community, Chevron gave them the chance to restart their lives afresh by rebuilding their homesteads. Their homes were officially presented to the proud new owners in a simple, heart-warming ceremony and Ms Wilson was accorded a rousing reception. Champa Begum and Jotsna Dev finally found a reason to smile after last year's floods wreaked havoc, chaos and devastation in their lives.[8]

In another example, a satisfied recipient of training and credit gives testimony to how the alternative livelihoods program has turned his life around:

> I just feel exhilarated when I go to my vegetable farm. I have learned how to plant and grow vegetables and I have made sure that there will be no insect or pest attacks on my vegetables, as I have learned to apply appropriate insecticide at the appropriate time. The villagers who also received training along with me are also successfully applying the scientific method of farming and getting good results ... All my efforts are being directed to the one and only goal, which is farming ... By fulfilling this dream I will drive away poverty from my family.[9]

Let us now shift focus from the ways in which Chevron have created and represented relationships with the villages surrounding the gas field within the idiom of "partnership" to other aspects of their program, all of which involve ideologies of self-reliance and sustainability, geared toward the eventual disconnection of the donor rather than close, ongoing connection.

Disconnect development

Whilst in Unocal's days gifts such as tee shirts (with the company logo) were distributed at random, the Chevron program became increasingly aimed at "community development" and poverty alleviation. Some gifts were aimed specifically at the poorest. Slab latrines were distributed to households without hygienic sanitation.[10] Tin roofs and concrete pillars for low-income housing were also supplied, again, sporting the Chevron logo. The company could not provide piped gas, but it distributed smoke-free *chulas* (stoves).[11] These, like other donations came with a price tag: the "community" should contribute to their upkeep. In the case of the stoves, for instance, an NGO worker explained that when it appeared that people were not caring for them properly, the decision was taken that they should be "sold" to recipients at a cost of two hundred taka (production costs were eight hundred taka), in order to instill a sense of ownership.[12] In terms of development discourse, such initiatives encourage responsibility and sustainability.

It is worth noting that by being the intermediaries between Chevron's donations and its recipients it is the NGO fieldworkers who have relationships with poorer people within the villages and who receive the most flak for failing to give enough or being too dictatorial about how gifts should be used. For example, we heard frequent complaints that so and so from FIVDB had not allowed so and so from Kakura to join the savings group. Meanwhile, Chevron's community liaison officers were rarely seen around the place. Centrally too, existing relationships of patronage are maintained via the VDOs, which are composed of "local leaders," who chose which households should become beneficiaries of the programs. Unsurprisingly, these local leaders are also local patrons, from wealthier and more powerful lineages, invariably with strong transnational links. The poorest households—the sharecroppers and laborers, who use local land but do not own it—are not represented on the VDOs. One of the complaints we heard was that elections for positions on VDOs were not anonymous; poorer people therefore had to vote for existing patrons in order to maintain favor with them.

Other donations came with similar conditions, again aimed at producing a sense of ownership. Two "Smiling Sun" medical clinics were built, run by a national health NGO and partly funded by the donations of transnational villagers. These provide diagnostic services but not medicine, with a further program of outreach health workers, and an ambulance that could take patients to the nearest hospital in Sylhet, though at a cost. Our research in 2008 showed that the poorest households in the area did not use these services, since in their view there was little point in having a diagnosis if they could not afford the prescribed medicines, and if in dire need the fare of a CNG[13] was lower than that of the ambulance. Whilst not actually building a school, the company has provided support for four high schools in the area, via the funding of teachers and teaching materials, the distribution of school uniforms, and the provision of several hundred scholarships for pupils each year (Chevron Publications 2008: 39).

The clinics and scholarships are part of Chevron's explicit objective of creating "sustainable" development and community partnership in Bibiyana. In the perspectives of many local people, however, the company has not fulfilled what they believed was originally promised.[14] Moreover, the ideal of sustainability is not necessarily shared by the poorest, who subscribe to a more straightforward model of assistance (*shahajo*), which has traditionally been provided to them by land-owning patrons and visiting transnational villagers. Within this logic, that Chevron, a corporation with vast wealth, should be offering donations with price tags attached is hard to countenance. In the following analysis, made by a member of a VDO, Chevron are placed at the center of the "big disease" of poverty and disenfranchisement and are responsible for its cure. They are not "partners," but are placed almost in the role of the state, with their responsibility for the well-being of their "communities" taken for granted.

> Say you have a big disease and Chevron is giving us a Paracetamol. If the disease is big the treatment should be big too. You need a big doctor, diagnosis, operations, expensive medicine, good care, and so on. But Chevron want to satisfy us by providing Paracetamol?

Others are even more straightforward: Chevron should be providing compensation to all land users. As one man put it:

> This company has been looting our gas whilst providing nothing to us villagers. (Focus Group Discussion, 2008)

Whilst there are many who say they have benefited from the Alternative Livelihoods Programs and other program benefits, most accounts of what has transpired since the heady days of the Demand Realization Committees belie disappointment. This is conveyed as much by the leaders of the VDOs (or Chevron's "local partners") as the project's beneficiaries. Worse, some of the leaders who the company were to develop the strongest "partnerships" with were now accused by other groups of using the relationship to benefit themselves at the expense of their communities. As one such leader explains, the expectations were so high that they could never be met:

> Of all the demands we made to Chevron, we achieved about 5 percent. Our fellow villagers started insulting us because we hadn't achieved their demands. They became very suspicious, saying that we'd been 'bought' by Chevron and were no longer looking out for their interests. I suppose the reason for these suspicions is that I'm working as a contractor for Chevron, so people think I'm their man, not a man of the people. Through my tree planting project I can hire a few women laborers, but not much more, so everyone's dissatisfied with me. Their demands are so high, but I can't recruit 100 people, only 15.[15]

Another man, who lost almost all his land to the gas field, and who was at the forefront of the campaign against Unocal/Chevron in 2005, had this to say:

> They gave us some promises, but now we can see that these were just bullshit. They promised that gas would be provided to the houses, young men would get jobs; electricity would be available: no more darkness. As it turned out, we didn't get anything. Rather, we've been turned into criminals ... I have no words to say about Chevron.

Let us turn to one of the biggest disappointments for local people: the employment prospects of the gas field.

An easy flow of labor

Back in 2005 not everyone opposed the construction of the gas field. Indeed, for the many hundreds of landless people living in the villages that surrounded the installation it was seen as a huge opportunity. The early days of construction bore out these hopes. Many hundreds of people were employed as daily wage laborers, helping to build the plant and surrounding infrastructure. This included a small group of women, who worked on the roads. Whilst wage levels varied, most people recall receiving around 4,500 taka a month, or 200 taka a day (average daily rates for agricultural laborers were 150 taka). In contrast to the skilled workers at the plant, who are recruited directly by Chevron at national and international levels, none of these laborers were employed by Chevron but via contractors, who tendered for the work at the plant's inception. Once given the contracts, Chevron enlisted them as private "companies" or enterprises.

As soon as the work was finished, the majority of laborers were laid off. In the present, the men we spoke to who had been made redundant claim that the reason for losing their jobs was they did not pay bribes to the labor contractors, or were not connected to the locally powerful leaders who gained contracts with Chevron. As Parry has pointed out in his work at the Bilhai Steel Plant in India, the point of such rumors is not necessarily that they reflect the objective truth (which in Bibiyana's case was that the laborers were no longer needed) but rather that they reveal a model of how the world should be (Parry 2001). In Bibiyana, the rumors reflect a belief that local people should be compensated for the damage to their livelihoods with secure employment at the gas field that is equitably distributed in a transparent way, not doled out via the social networks of labor contractors. The complaints we heard are thus as much about the informal nature of employer-employee relations and local politics as they are about people's failure to gain employment, which as one man put it "is our right."[16]

> The leaders appropriated all the benefits. Chevron offered a high salary but the leaders [who were also labor contractors] didn't pay us much. Since the leaders controlled the jobs they became really powerful and had the authority to replace anyone who objected. At the beginning, lots of villagers worked for Chevron ... now only fifty or a hundred people are working. People were sacked for a simple reason: they weren't recruited by Chevron but by the local leaders. These local leaders' followers and relatives got the jobs ...When I worked for the gas field I got 7,500 taka a month in cash. Now I don't have a fixed income. (Ex Chevron laborer, Karimpur, 2009)

> I worked for a year and a half in the gas field, then I was sacked. I worked as a mason; I used to get 4,800 taka a month. One day I was working and the next I was told I wouldn't be needed again. When I asked why I was told I had to speak to Mr X of X Enterprise [i.e., the labor contractor]. Since then I've been passing my time doing nothing. I expected to get another job, but I didn't… I hoped to get a job as a rickshaw puller, but they said you're a mason, you don't know how to pull a rickshaw. Since then I've had a loan from the Grameen Bank and am trying to do some small business things. (Ex Chevron laborer, Kakura, 2009)

Many people have a similar story. Safety training was given and identity cards issued but suddenly the work stopped. One man told me how it had cost him 500 taka to get his photograph taken for his card in Sylhet Town; a week later he was laid off. The situation has caused deep resentment; for the widespread perception is that since Chevron are using local resources they should provide work. In an early focus group discussion that we held in Kakura in 2008, one man put it like this: "The gas field roads go straight over our hearts, so we should be given priority for work."

Whilst some local leaders were given contracts to supply labor to the gas field, our research showed that of fifteen enterprises contracting labor in 2009, only about half were "local" (i.e., from the immediate vicinity) whilst the rest came from outside the immediate area, with some bringing laborers from many hundreds of miles away. These laborers, who are all men, are housed either in purpose-built accommodation close to the gas field, or in houses owned by Londonis in the surrounding villages. Each enterprise has different areas of work. One company is contracted to supply security guards; another supplies drivers, whilst others provide catering. The wages and contracts of these men vary according to their jobs.

The advantages to Chevron of hiring labor in this way are easy to appreciate. Since the contractors recruit and pay the workers the company does not need to have any direct dealings with them. They are thus a reserve army par excellence, un-unionized and with no form of redress from the company, which offers none of the ethically irreproachable standards of employment that it reserves for its own staff, who come from outside the area or are foreign. As the community liaison officer based at the gas field explained to me, the use of labor contractors ensures "an easy flow of labor." Interestingly, rather than having a background in community relations, this man had previously worked as a manager on a tea estate, a sector not known for its promotion of human rights.

The use of contractors also means that laborers can be controlled, since they are hired informally by their patrons and are therefore unlikely to challenge the authority of their *malik* (owners, or boss), due to their "loyalty," as one contractor put it. As a contractor from distant Pabna explained:

> My own people are unemployed during the rainy season, as we have only one crop a year in our part of the world. So I bring them to the gas field ... the whole thing is based on trust. We all have to trust each other. Say, for example, if I bring people who aren't good, or who are impudent, then Chevron won't give me another contract. If I recruit people from my own village then I don't need to worry, because my villagers won't be rude to me. They'll do as I say. Also, they'll go to me with whatever they need, like for wages, borrowing money, or sending it back to the village or whatever. So that's why I recruit my own people. If you want to be a contractor you have to have repute and trust, which I do my best to maintain.

To summarize: a gas field is a capital and not a labor-intensive industrial site. This means that at Bibiyana there are few jobs for local people, who do not have the training for the highly skilled technical jobs that are available. Whilst a few men are employed as security guards, our research showed that most of these had gained their employment via their close connections to the local patrons or "local leaders," who the company had developed working relationships with. Others are employed by labor contractors, some of whom are the very same patrons/"local leaders" on the VDOs. It is with these men, not Chevron, that landless or land-poor people must have relationships with to gain the benefits of either employment at the gas field or the community engagement programs that the corporation fund.

Partnership as disconnection

We therefore come to an interesting paradox. Whilst Chevron must claim partnership to gain a "social license to operate" and enhance their reputation as an ethical and socially responsible global player, the relationships that they describe as partnerships and the development practices of their "partner" NGOs ultimately contribute to the company's disconnection from the villages that surround their Bibiyana gas field. NGOs are funded as intermediaries, carrying out programs that bring repute to Chevron but enable them to have no direct contact with the landless poor. VDOs have a similar function. Whilst working with a handful of local patrons or "leaders," the company is able to neatly sidestep the role of corporate patron in which it would be connected to the locality in the way that many local people expected but which would do nothing to gain merit in the world of development CSR, where programs are supposed to "empower" people, involving participation, self-reliance, and so on. Sustainability, the holy grail of much contemporary development work, is, after all, a process of disconnection: the donor withdraws and the good works continue.

Crucially, the company's employment regime at Bibiyana means that it does not hire local people directly but via labor contractors, who are "partners." The lucky few who find work associated with the gas field and its environs are thus not included in the strict employment standards that the company adhere to—the pensions, sick leave, and so on—but are subject to the employment procedures of contractors, and hired on the basis of patron-client relations. Once again, partnership with the few is associated with the disconnection and exclusion of the majority.

Combined with this, company staff are notably absent from the villages that surround the gas field. During our fieldwork, people frequently complained that there was no one they could contact to express their concerns over safety issues or environmental damage, and no grievance procedures. Whilst in the early days of developing the site Unocal's people visited the surrounding villages, holding "community consultation" meetings and distributing their business cards, today the general perception is that the community engagement staff have largely retreated behind the high security perimeter fence. To speak to these officials one needs to know the right people. As one man put it:

> Chevron came to see me several times, requesting that they could take my land. Now all that is over. They don't come to see me. They have my land so they don't need to come. Whenever we want to say something against them they file cases against us. That's why no one says a word against them.[17]

What local people want is connection: not just to officials who might act as patrons, but to the long-term benefits of global capitalism and the modernity it is supposed to bring, which the gas field materializes. The possibilities are tangible, almost within grasp. The roadside billboards with their explicit messages of road safety and implicit signals of corporate governance say it all: this is Chevron Country, a place where the standards of the modern world are adhered to. Salaried employment, satellite industry, roads, maybe even a hospital: all seemed possible with the arrival of the corporation. Whilst the gas field is by no means the only form of connectivity to modernity that can take place (for the history and impact of transnational migration in the area is far more profound), it is almost tantalizing in its material reality: located so close to the villages, spread across the land of the *desh* yet for the vast majority who lack the connections that are necessary to get the contracts or the jobs, impossibly distant.

This detachment from local realities was brought home to me one night as I lay awake in the late spring heat. Nights in Bibiyana are rarely quiet: barking dogs compete with cicadas and the howl of jackals, whilst the distant chanting of *milad* prayer or the beat of Hindu *puja* drums frequently drift across the fields. On that night though, what I could hear was the unmistakable boom of Western rock music. "Sevron" were having a party, I was told the next day, to celebrate the first year of the operation of the plant. Did people from the surrounding villages attend? I asked anxiously, berating myself for missing what might have been an interesting event. The answer was categorical: no, the party was not for local people, only Chevron's salaried employees.

Imagining disconnection: Nightmares of rupture in the borderland

To summarize: whilst people living in the gas field's borderlands desire connection to global capitalism whether via transnational migration, employment by Chevron or by a more generalized connection to the benefits of modernity, with its promises of a responsible state, meaningful citizenship and attendant rights, what many face is an ongoing process of disconnection. These disconnections are various and contradictory but include the ongoing movement away from land-based livelihoods and the monetarization of the local economy, and the diminishment of relations of patronage and "helping," due in part to the absence of patrons in the UK, and also the emotional and physical ruptures of migration.

The gas field, has, however, brought the threat of ultimate disconnection: a "blowout," or explosion, in which the physical connection to the gas supply is violently severed and the villages that surround the plant are ripped apart by fire and destruction. Stories and imaginings of such blowouts—which have taken place at two other gas fields in Sylhet within the last ten years—are an important aspect of how people think and talk about the gas field. Indeed, the fear of an industrial accident was vividly materialized in 2008 when a standard technical procedure in which excess gas is burnt off in a controlled flare led to widespread panic. This was described to us by almost everyone in the area as an example of the dangers of the gas field, a terrifying night when they awoke to find the sky "filled with fire" and ran, in terror, from their homes.

The incident illustrates disconnection in a number of ways. Firstly, Chevron executives blatantly failed to communicate the planned flaring to the local population, because they were not sufficiently in touch with local social realities. They HAD warned "local leaders," who they imagined would pass the message on to "their people," but this did not happen, for whilst the "leaders" told their close families, they were not connected to the poor in the ways that the Community Relations staff had imagined. Secondly, the incident, and the fear it has invoked, reflects the history of Bangladesh's relationship to multinationals in the gas sector. The government is still seeking compensation for a blowout at Magurchhara in 1997, which happened while Occidental was drilling for gas and caused considerable ecological damage to the forested area, costing the country an estimated 9 crore taka (i.e., 9 million taka). In 2005 a series of accidents occurred at the Tengratila gas field, operated by the Canadian company Niko in Surnamganj, Sylhet. In the second blowout within six months at Tengratila, flames leapt up to a height of 150 feet after a loud explosion, leading to widespread panic in surrounding villages. Luckily no one was injured in these incidents, though the environmental damage was considerable. Clearly, people have a well-founded fear of an industrial accident.

At a more profound level, however, I suggest that within local narratives blowouts can be read as metaphors for violent disconnection and rupture, whether from the transformative energy of the gas, with its contradictory possibilities of enrichment and destruction, from the land on which livelihoods depend, or the richly woven web of social connections so vital for everyday survival. Indeed, stories of industrial disaster and the fear that they express reveal the profound risks that engagement with neoliberal capitalism has involved. Within this analysis, a blowout is merely the most dramatic materialization of the uncertain world in which people struggle for survival. As old forms of connection fall away there seems little to replace them for those without formal connections to land or foreign countries. The accounts that follow are thus narratives borne from terror; they are ways of making sense of the chaos, panic and speechlessness caused by Chevron's unexpected flaring.

The gas field has had a severe impact on our life. We are scared about the flame, when it comes. Since the gas field has been operating there have been a number of incidents. When the flames grew large we had to leave our house. Recently it happened again. The villagers had to leave because of the heat, the earth walls of our house started to crack; the earth was cracking up too. Me, my children and their mother were literally running around, looking for shelter. It was midnight. Everyone was running around, the children were shouting, looking for somewhere to hide. Some people jumped into the ponds, whilst others sheltered on the banks. Listen, the day I saw that fire, oh my God, it was like the last day on earth, when everything is destroyed! (Sharecropper, Karimpur, interview notes, 2009)

Because of the gas field we live under the threat of fire. Like an earthquake, everything moves and there's a roaring sound. When the fire goes up we have to go to a safe place; we fear that the fire will engulf us. The flame is so bright that it illuminates everything even though it's night. If you dropped a piece of sewing on the ground you could find it. We run around madly. Last year Harun's wife was so scared that she fled the house, leaving her children behind. People leave their valuables. Everyone is scared for their life! Whenever Chevron ups the fire our relatives call us to see if we've survived and they live 15 miles away! Some villages fled by rickshaw.

They do this when we go to bed at night. They don't let us know they're going to up the fire. If we had known before, we would have been prepared. (Laborer, Kakura, interview notes, 2009)

In an early focus-group discussion with men in Kakura (in 2008) we heard the following statements:

We are always scared about the fire—when it comes it will spread over the whole village and kill everyone.

We have gained nothing from the gas field, apart from the threat of setting our village on fire.

Whether or not the flaring is "safe" is beside the point,[18] for the question is based upon the technical knowledge of those operating the plant, which is not shared with the local population. Within the analysis of people living in the villages close to the plant, the flames are dangerous and terrifying. How can they be seen as benign, when they rear up from this site of global capitalism, which rather than offering inclusion and connection has excluded them from its profits and operations, not to say its epistemological orders? Within the localized knowledge of people in Kakura and Karimpur, the flames are a terrifying reminder of their powerlessness and dispossession.

Conclusion:
Disconnect development and development as connection

The irony of disconnect development is striking. Whilst local people are physically, culturally and economically disconnected from the gas field, Chevron must claim connection in order to promote their global reputation for "partnership," so core to their "Vision." Moreover, a particular sort of praxis helps the company achieve the appearance of attachment via the language of partnership whilst following the corporate ethic of detachment (Cross 2011). I have termed this "disconnect development" because of the way that discourses of sustainability and "helping people to help themselves" mitigate against the long-term provision of services or assistance by donors. Instead, they promote an ideal in which, via income generation, micro credit and other globally fashionable activities, the poor are able to make enough of a living to afford the health services, education and other forms of social protection that in countries such as Bangladesh the state is generally unable to provide. Whilst originally rooted in radical leftist theories of power and political change, terms such as "empowerment," used liberally by Chevron executives mask the neoliberal tenets of contemporary disconnect development: the market is the answer to poverty; the poor must "be helped to help themselves," since the state obviously is not going to help them.

To return to Development Speak, Cornwall et al. show that the ambiguous and slippery nature of buzzwords allows them to do important "boundary work," allowing ideas and agendas to cross domains and for diverse interest groups to buy into a particular policy and differences to be fuzzed: "buzz words shelter multiple agendas, providing room for manoeuvre and space for contestation" (Cornwall 2010: 5). A vital task for anthropologists of CSR is to chart these processes, showing how however appealing they may seem, the fuzziness of terms such as "partnership" masks different agendas and realities. In Bibiyana, for example, Development Speak has enabled Chevron to promote their practices as morally irreproachable (who could take umbrage at The Chevron Way and its partnerships?), whilst the realities of connection and disconnection in the gas field's borderlands are far darker.

Notes

1. http://www.chevron.com/about/chevronway/ (accessed 2 September 2011)
2. Partnership is "the relationship between two or more people or organizations that are involved in the same activity," according to the Encarta Dictionary.
3. I am extremely grateful to ESRC/DFID for this grant. My co-researchers were Zahir Ahmed, Fatema Bashir and Masud Rana at Jahangirnagar University, Bangladesh.
4. Their Bangladesh CEO in 2008, Steve Wilson, told me that the production share contract was 60:40—that is, the government would take 60 percent of profits and Chevron 40 percent. For 100 units of gas, the company have to give 60 to the government free of charge; the remaining 40 are sold to them. This figure is disputed by activists, who claim that Chevron take 80 percent of the profits.
5. We heard of various ongoing "cases," often involving land that was already under dispute or had once been classified as "enemy property:" Hindu land that had been passed to Muslims.
6. The project goal was: "to assist the Bibiyana Gas field, affected households and disadvantaged people to enhance their productive potential, improving their asset base and make sustainable use of them to overcome poverty through alternative livelihood" (Alternative Livelihood Program for Vulnerable Families of Bibiyana Annual Report, 2006–2007).
7. The Chevron Bangladesh Newsletter of July 2008 contains nine such photographs, in twenty-four pages.
8. Chevron Bangladesh Newsletter, Year Y, Issue 2, July 2008.
9. Matin Khan, cited in Chevron 2008: 40.
10. According to literature produced by Chevron, they distributed 1,300 sanitary latrines among poorer households living near the field in the first year of operations, plus another 1,400 by March 2007 (*Bibiana gas field first anniversary report*).
11. I never saw these stoves being used; I was told when I asked about a disused Chevron chula in someone's yard that they were unsuitable for the *lakri* (firewood) used for cooking.
12. Personal communication from FIVDB field officer.
13. Scooter rickshaw, run on natural gas.
14. Note that I have no proof of what was or was not promised by Unocal /Chevron during the negotiations in 2005.
15. Interview notes, 2009.
16. Focus-group discussion, Kakura, 2009.
17. Field notes, p. 48.
18. See: http://www.corpwatch.org/article.php?id=13727.

References

Blowfield, M., and J. G Frynas. 2005. Setting new agendas: Critical perspectives on CSR in the developing world. *International Affairs* 81(3): 499–513.
Burton, T. 2002. When corporations want to cuddle. In G. Evans, J. Goodman and N. Lansbury, eds., *Moving mountains: Communities confront mining and globalisation*, pp. 109–125. London: Zed Press.
Chevron Publications. 2008. *Bibiyana gas field first anniversary report*. Dhaka: Chevron.

Cornwall, A. 2010. Introductory overview – Buzzwords and fuzzwords deconstructing development discourse. In A. Cornwall and D. Eade, eds., *Deconstructing development discourse: Buzzwords and fuzzwords*, pp. 1–19. Oxford: Oxfam Practical Action Publishing.

Cornwall, A., and D. Eade eds. 2010. *Deconstructing development discourse: Buzzwords and fuzzwords*. Oxford: Oxfam Practical Action Publishing.

Cross, J. 2011. Detachment as corporate ethic: Materialising CSR in the diamond supply chain. *Focaal – Journal of Global and Historical Anthropology* 60: 34–46.

Doane, D. 2005. The myth of CSR: The problem with assuming that companies can do well whilst also "doing good" is that markets don't really work in that way. *Stanford Social Innovation Review* fall: 23–9.

Ferguson, J. 2005. Seeing it like an oil company: Space, security and global capital in neo-liberal Africa. *American Anthropologist* 107(3): 377–382.

Gardner, K. 1993. *Desh–Bidesh*: Sylheti images of home and away. *Man* 28(9): 1–15.

Gardner, K. 1995. *Global migrants, local lives: Migration and transformation in rural Bangladesh*. Oxford: Oxford University Press.

Gardner, K. 2008. Keeping connected: Security, place and social capital in a Londoni village in Sylhet. *Journal of the Royal Anthropological Institute* NS 14: 447–495.

Gardner, K. 2012. *Discordant developments: Global capitalism and the struggle for connection in Bangladesh*. London: Pluto Press.

Gardner, K., and K. Mand. 2012. My away is here: Place, empowerment and mobility among British Bengali children. In K. Gardner and K. Mand, eds., *Through children's eyes: Transnational migration revisited*. Special issue. *Journal of Ethnic and Migration Studies*.

Jenkins, R. 2005. Globalisation, CSR and poverty. *International Affairs* 81(3): 525–540.

Kapelus, P. 2002. Mining, CSR and "the community": The case of Rio Tinto, Richards Bay Minerals and the Mbonambi. *Journal of Business Ethics* 39: 275–296.

Li, Tania Murray. 2007. *The will to improve: Governmentality, development and the practice of politics*. Durham, NC: Duke University Press.

Mosse, D. 2005. *Cultivating development: An ethnography of aid policy and practice*. London: Pluto Press.

Pickard, M. 2010. Reflections on relationships: The nature of partnership according to five NGOs in southern Mexico. In A. Cornwall and D. Eade, eds., *Deconstructing development discourse*, pp. 135–143. Oxford: Oxfam Practical Action Publishing.

Rajak, D. 2011. *In good company: An anatomy of corporate social responsibility*. Stanford, CA: Stanford University Press.

Toufique, K., and C. Turton. 2002. *Hands not land: How livelihoods are changing in rural Bangladesh*. Bangladesh Institute of Development Studies.

Tsing, A. L. 2005. *Friction: An ethnography of global connection*. Princeton, NJ: Princeton University Press.

Welker, M. 2009. "Corporate security begins in the community": Mining, the CSR industry and environmental advocacy in Indonesia. *Cultural Anthropology* 24(1): 142–179.

Zalik, A. 2004. The Niger delta: "Petro violence" and "partnership development." *Review of African Political Economy* 31(101): 401–424.

Katy Gardner is Professor of Anthropology at the London School of Economics. Her research has examined the cultural and social changes associated with international migration and globalization in Bangladesh. She has researched age, the life course and childhood amongst British Bangladeshis in London, and the relationship between anthropology and development. She has recently become interested in natural resources and industrialization in Bangladesh, and the effects of land loss, corporatization and CSR on poverty and inequality. She is the author of *Discordant development: Global capitalism and the struggle for connection in Bangladesh* (Pluto Press, 2012), and co-author (with David Lewis) of *Anthropology and development: Challenges for the twenty-first century.*

– Chapter 7 –

SUBCONTRACTING AS CORPORATE SOCIAL RESPONSIBILITY IN THE CHAD-CAMEROON PIPELINE PROJECT

José-María Muñoz and Philip Burnham

e⁓

Some have called the Chad project the new model. I see it as applying ExxonMobil's basic business model, which includes our high standards of safety, health, and environmental management, along with the high standards of business conduct and ethics to the unique issues Chad presents … We have approached the project with a focus on detailed and rigorous planning, and in cases where existing laws do not govern what we do, we bring international standards into play. As we invest to meet the world's energy needs, we are mindful of our responsibility to be a corporate citizen.

Tom Walters, ExxonMobil's Vice-President for Development in Africa, provided this statement in a hearing before the Subcommittee on Africa of the US House of Representatives' Committee on International Relations on 22 April 2002 (US Congress 2002). By then, the Chad-Cameroon Petroleum Development and Pipeline Project was well underway. ExxonMobil led the consortium, undertaking a project that had attracted considerable international attention and controversy, not least because it was presented as "a new model for natural resource development" (the title of choice for the congressional hearing).

Largely as a result of the World Bank's participation, which the oil companies involved saw as essential to manage the risks inherent in such a substantial investment in politically unstable Chad, the project took on a broad set of goals ranging from environmental and labor safeguards to the protection of indigenous livelihoods, the creation of natural reserves, an HIV/AIDS awareness campaign, and a rollback malaria initiative. From the early planning stages of the project to the aftermath of the World Bank's withdrawal in 2008, the Bank's role has captured most of the attention that the project has received (Gary and Reisch 2005; Gould and Winters 2007; Grovogui and Leonard 2007; Hernandez Uriz 2002; Hoinathy and Behrends 2014; Leibold 2011). In this chapter, we shift the analytical emphasis onto how ExxonMobil conceived and enacted its obligations as a corporate citizen.

Project procedures and rules informed by risk assessment and management tools feature prominently in the operation of oil multinationals across the world. The Chad-Cameroon project is no exception. Tom Walters's excerpted words make apparent how central the respect of laws and standards of business conduct was in ExxonMobil's vision of its corporate responsibility. In the aftermath of the Exxon Valdez accident in 1989, the corporation began to measure its practices with the yardstick of an "operations integrity management system" (OIMS), which with time acquired the status of a sacrosanct text.[1] Given the prevalence that outsourcing has acquired in the oil and gas sector in recent decades, a key element of ExxonMobil's OIMS spells out ways to ensure that its contractors meet the corporation's standards. Yet, as Jane Guyer (2011) has reminded us recently in a characteristically subtle reflection on her role as member of the Chad-Cameroon pipeline project's International Advisory Group, contracting procedures and arrangements such as these are inherently ambivalent. They are informed by the dual aims of ensuring that contractors abide by ExxonMobil's standards while also insulating the corporation from liability for contractors' departures from such standards. This chapter approaches subcontracting as a significant dimension of corporate social responsibility (CSR) strategies, one that has been identified by specialists in this field (Frynas 2009: 57) as not having received sufficient attention.

In her research on the oil industry in Equatorial Guinea, Hannah Appel (2012a: 442) has analyzed how multinationals structure responsibility in such a way that "the industry can remove itself from social, legal, political and environmental entanglements in which it is so deeply enmeshed." To capture the tools used in the industry's efforts of disentanglement, Appel (2012b: 693) proposes the notion of modularity, which she sees as "the use of mobile, compliant and self-contained infrastructures, labour set-ups, forms of expertise, and legal guidelines" that enable offshore work in one place to function just like offshore work anywhere else. Along somewhat similar lines, Jamie Cross (this volume) has argued that diamond multinationals subscribe to an "ethics of detachment" and are "constantly engaged in establishing the limits and endpoints to relationships in their supply chain, ensuring that contracts are time-bound and spatially defined, resisting proximity and intimacy, and framing relationships around difference and distance."

Appel's as well as Cross's work makes apparent that subcontracting offers fertile ground for processes of corporate disentanglement and detachment (see also Gardner 2012: 129–134). Moreover, the operations that these authors are grappling with and that result in disentanglement and detachment are ostensibly informed by principles of social responsibility. This is the paradox that our analysis of subcontracting in the Chad-Cameroon pipeline project wants to explore further. Since the 1980s, the promotion of the private sector has become a development goal in its own right and one that multinational corporations increasingly take on. Pursuit of this goal has created an additional sphere of intersection between CSR and subcontracting. The pipeline project made this explicit by including a contractual commitment to gear contractual decisions and provisions toward enhancing the capacity, skills and services of Chadian and Cameroonian businesses. "In a project that had fostering of the private sector as a development goal" (Guyer 2011: 22), relationships with host country contractors offered a privileged domain to showcase rigorous procedures and exemplary practices. The pages of ExxonMobil's periodic project reports have indeed often featured the numbers and narratives that highlighted its "local business development" actions. Building on our long-standing ethnographic engagement with two dozen enterprises that worked for the oil consortium and for its foreign partners during the pipeline construction phase in three of the provinces (Adamaoua and East and North Provinces) crossed by the pipeline in Cameroon, this chapter considers the implications of ExxonMobil's commitment, as a good corporate citizen, to the promotion of local business.[2]

The Chad-Cameroon pipeline project as a development project

The Chad-Cameroon Petroleum Development and Pipeline Project is one of the largest infrastructural projects undertaken in recent decades in West and Central Africa. Carried out by a consortium formed by ExxonMobil, Chevron, Petronas, and the Chadian and Cameroonian states, this US$3.7 billion project has developed more than 360 oil wells in southern Chad and constructed a 1,070 km pipeline to offshore oil-shipment facilities on Cameroon's coast.

Funding for this project also included a World Bank loan to enlarge the equity participation of Chad and Cameroon. From the outset, the oil companies had a fundamental interest in involving the World Bank. This was not significantly linked to financial considerations, since ExxonMobil, as the world's oil giant, was easily capable of financing the project on its own. Rather, the companies considered that World Bank involvement was crucial in managing the risks of working in a politically uncertain environment such as Chad.

The final terms of the World Bank's participation, which evolved over eight years, had a decisive impact on defining the project goals. Its presence meant that the pipeline consortium took on the task of promoting "development" in two African countries (Guyer 2002). As a result of its involvement, the project could no longer focus only on the commercial benefits to ExxonMobil and its commercial partners or on state revenue generation in Chad and Cameroon. This loan attracted much critical comment, especially from international environmentalist NGOs such as the Environmental Defense Fund. The World Bank justified its involvement as an example of the type of sustainable and participatory development it attempts to foster, and as a model case for effective public-private partnership in the development process. But as a result of these external political pressures and internal disputes within the Bank, the project was substantially delayed in taking off.[3]

Final approval of the loan bound the consortium to a strict set of World Bank-imposed procedural norms and development goals. These conditions ranged from numerous environmental management standards to a requirement to incorporate an indigenous peoples' plan relating to the treatment of the Bagyieli Pygmies living near the pipeline's right of way. Thus the Cameroon Oil Transportation Company (COTCO), the Cameroonian subsidiary of the consortium, took up a set of not fully specified socioeconomic development goals. Just how numerous and extensive these goals should be became a contentious issue among the World Bank, the consortium, and the Cameroonian government throughout the project. It must also be remembered that COTCO was subject to scrutiny by the External Compliance Monitoring Group (ECMG) consultants and the International Advisory Group (IAG), established in response to pressures exerted by international and local NGOs.[4]

World Bank hesitation concerning its involvement delayed the start of the construction works. Meanwhile, the pipeline consortium was experiencing strong commercial pressures to move ahead as quickly as possible. It had suffered substantial additional costs because it had to suspend the road improvement work of its major French subcontractor, SOGEA-SATOM, due to the delay in World Bank funding approval. This tension between the time requirements for efficient completion of the pipeline's construction and the fulfillment of the project's environmental and developmental commitments became a recurrent feature. As early as 2001 the IAG referred to a "two-speed project" in its reports: "There is an increasing disequilibrium between the pace at which the consortium operations are taking place, which follows its proposed timetable, and the pace at which governments, the public institutions, the World Bank and civil society are able to act" (IAG 2001). The final approval by the World Bank board of directors of the terms of its involvement did not take place until June 2000.

Only after World Bank approval did ExxonMobil seriously address the question of negotiating the details of the environmental and socioeconomic compliance procedures with its major contractors. These negotiations were done hastily and, subsequently, it was not surprising that there were continual disagreements and cases of noncompliance by the contractors, most of whom never fully accepted the project's development goals. Indeed, ExxonMobil itself was not entirely in tune with these goals. Project staff repeatedly emphasized the commercial aims of the project and made it clear that the company would do the minimum to satisfy the World Bank agreement.

Thus the Chad-Cameroon pipeline project was formally transformed into a development project with the consequent impact on its corporate social responsibility components only a few months before the construction phase started in October 2000. Moreover, different parties did not sign some of the legal instruments until as late as July 2001 (Guyer 2002: 112). Foremost among the documents that detailed the consortium's development commitments was an ambitious and somewhat equivocally named Environmental Management Plan (EMP) (Chad-Cameroon Development Project [hereafter CCDP] 1997 and CCDP 1999), which evolved over the several years leading up to the start of the pipeline's construction. An explicit goal of the EMP as it applied to Cameroon was the promotion of "Cameroonian business participation in the economic benefits of the project." The plan established a series of principles for work in this domain, including the creation of enabling conditions to allow Cameroonian businesses to successfully bid for pipeline contracts. Since the bulk of the construction works had been contracted with foreign companies, this in turn required the commitment of these contractors to respect such principles. The so-called socioeconomic action plans signed by each of the contractors thus contained provisions that fell under the rubric of "local business development." Given the scale of investment involved, it is hardly surprising that the pipeline project created high expectations of profitable opportunities in Cameroonian business circles in many parts of the country.

Our research covered three of the country's provinces crossed by the pipeline that have experienced the direct effects of the project. Not only were many temporary and permanent project facilities constructed in Adamaoua and East and North Provinces—including pump stations, storage yards, airfields, construction camps, communication systems, rail freight facilities, and the pipeline itself—but the project also upgraded large portions of the road and rail networks to transport its equipment. In gross financial terms, the project injected large sums of money into the local economy, much of it in the form of salaries and other forms of compensation.

Both the consortium directly and its main contractors employed large numbers of mostly temporary and low-skilled workers during the pipeline construction period. Furthermore, residents whose farms or other property were affected by the construction received individual compensation (approximately 2,000 persons in Adamaoua and North Provinces). Beneficiaries used a significant portion of these payments to fund informal petty commercial enterprises— small village shops, itinerant market trade, and small restaurants—which catered to both local village populations and project workers. Of the regional compensation payments made by the project, a portion (144 million CFA francs in Adamaoua and North Provinces) was allocated for the construction of classrooms, dispensaries, and other facilities at village level, which in turn was subcontracted to Cameroonian firms.[5]

Beyond the economic activity stimulated by compensation payments and earnings from project salaries, local businesses also benefited from considerable project expenditure in the region. In compliance with the World Bank-inspired Environmental Management Plan (CCDP 1999), pipeline documentation abounds with references to the project's aim at "maximizing local business involvement" by "giving priority to host country subcontractors and suppliers who meet competitive standards of quality, cost, reliability, schedule and payment terms" (CCDP 2002: 81). As of mid-2007, the project had spent approximately US$1.5 billion in local goods and services, of which some US$600 million had been spent in Cameroon, although the level of expenditure sharply declined in early 2003 with the completion of major construction activities.

Bidding procedures and award of contracts

In December 2000, after the start of the pipeline construction phase proper, COTCO publicized a series of rules governing the contract bidding process. The first step was to establish a shortlist of Cameroonian companies that qualified legally and technically as potential project subcontractors. Once this was determined, both COTCO and its main contractors invited the shortlisted companies to bid for specific contracts.[6] The company that put forward the best bid was then awarded the contract. Shortlisting potential bidders ensured that no companies were unduly excluded and allowed the consortium and its partners to claim that all Cameroonian companies possessing the requisite capabilities had been identified and invited to bid according to their areas of specialization. These procedures aimed to guarantee the transparency and accountability of the consortium's decisions in the award of contracts. However, in practice, the procedures proved ill adapted and excluded many qualified operators.

The geographical location of the Adamaoua, East and North Provinces' business sector, for example, became a major handicap. Although COTCO's procedural norms could be accessed on the Internet, few people in these provinces appear to have been aware of them at the time. With no reliable flight connections, COTCO's headquarters in faraway Douala (575 km away from Bertoua, 906 km from Ngaoundere, and 1,173 km from Garoua, the main urban centers) offered limited access to information. At this stage, people interested in contacting the project found it a time-consuming, expensive and often futile enterprise. Lack of easy access to the consortium's decision-making centers was compounded by ExxonMobil's ignorance about the on-the-ground situation in these parts of the country. In such circumstances, businesses located in Douala had the best chance of obtaining contracts.

Nonetheless, the deficiencies in COTCO's communication approach and an inadequate flow of information to locations distant from its decision-making centers only partly explain the consortium's failure to find Cameroonian subcontractors from these areas in the early stages of construction. Even if they had been better informed about the bidding procedures, many potential subcontractors in these three provinces could not have qualified. Required documents included a location map of the business premises for tax purposes, personal and company tax certification, a business license, and a court certificate of registration in the national registry of companies.

Pipeline subcontractors also had to conform to Cameroon's labor legislation, in particular the registration of their employees with the National Social Insurance Fund (CNPS), and pay their contributions as employers to that fund.[7]

A second set of requirements related to the managerial and technical standards, which required subcontractors to show that they had adequate financial resources, equipment, personnel, and a satisfactory track record in their domain. Candidates were asked to submit a certificate of non-bankruptcy. Those who did not have a bank account had to open one. Financial endorsements and credit facilities, when needed, did not come through easily. The three provinces we studied are among those with the lowest density of bank branches in the country. Cameroonian banks are notorious for over-liquidity and their limited lending to small and medium-sized ventures (Monga 1997). Such financial services were only obtained at considerable cost—including at times payments on the side to the bank's local branch managers. Compliance with technical specifications could prove equally challenging.

Many subcontractors believed that the most onerous requirements were those concerning tax and social security obligations. To work with the pipeline, most aspiring contractors had to alter their relationship with fiscal enforcement agencies. In the new business environment, "regularization" became necessary, though it was by no means a straightforward move for the majority of contract bidders. Naturally, most subcontractors saw their tax and social security payments increase in degrees that corresponded with the growth of their annual turnover. In any case, the difficulties involved in complying with pipeline requirements were not insurmountable. Indeed, attracted by the new business opportunities, many went to great lengths to overcome such difficulties. Determined contractors had to plan in advance and move swiftly. They put to good use their previous experience working with parastatals and foreign companies, and relied on well-placed contacts for information and support.

Despite the "local business development" goals affirmed in the project's planning documents, it became apparent early on that they had failed to yield contracts for firms in the three provinces. To understand the failure to hire local companies it is important to recall the circumstances in which the consortium assumed its commitment to promote local business in the context of the World Bank's loan. The consortium had made its most significant choices of contractors before the rule of giving priority to in-country businesses became its official policy. Indeed, by the time the consortium subscribed to the principle of "locals first," foreign companies had already secured most major contracts, especially those related to pipeline construction, the transport of materials and equipment, the upgrading of the road system, and the building of most project facilities. Only retrospectively was this justified on the grounds that domestic companies could not compete in these sectors.

Even the majority of smaller contracts were awarded before any machinery aimed at prioritizing local firms took effect. The initial period of surveying the pipeline right of way in mid-2000, which involved housing and feeding substantial teams of workers in the field, provided evidence of the consortium's unsatisfactory arrangements. From COTCO's perspective, the chief concern was to move the work ahead in the most efficient and rapid manner. This led to contracting with a South African firm, SSI, to supply meals for the work teams. All the foodstuffs for these meals were shipped up from Cameroon's economic capital and main port Douala, with no expense spared. Ironically, the supplies of beef came from cattle raised in northern Cameroon that had been shipped as live animals to Douala where they were butchered and frozen and then returned to northern Cameroon for consumption by SSI. Moreover, SSI purchased its meat supplies in Douala from expatriate operators. Although COTCO, in response to protests from Adamaoua business circles, later found ways to involve local suppliers in such provisioning, this case shows how, in the early stages of the project, buying locally had not been a serious concern.

In its fourth quarterly report for 2000 (CCDP 2000: 26; our emphasis), the consortium itself acknowledged serious difficulties in meeting its engagements:

> It has been challenging for the Project to fulfil its commitment to buying locally as much as possible. Developing countries generally do not have economies that can support large companies with the resources to handle major construction jobs such as this one. One answer to this *dilemma* has been to require Project contractors to find *creative ways* to buy from local suppliers. In addition to local business development outreach, and building a computer database of potential suppliers, the Project has been identifying opportunities to build up local capabilities.

Among the measures mentioned in this passage that aimed to overcome the difficulties experienced in honoring the consortium's commitment to buy locally, one deserves special attention. That COTCO should require of the project contractors "to find creative ways to buy from local suppliers" reveals a tension that weighed heavily on the consortium's decisions as to how and when to work with Cameroonian firms. On the one hand, the consortium had to comply with World Bank-validated standards of environmental protection and working conditions for project employees. Moreover, COTCO was bound by its own rigorous procedural rules. On the other hand, the consortium had to satisfy its commitment to encourage local business development, which in places such as Adamaoua and East and North Provinces implied dealing with some economic informality. Sticking to the project rules while, at the same time, working extensively with Cameroonian firms involved an inbuilt tension: thus the "dilemma." The irony underlying the consortium's wording is that the project's foreign contractors, far from needing any encouragement, had already found "creative ways" of dealing with local suppliers. Indeed, many contractors' field managers tended to view project norms as a needless complication and as a reflection of Exxon-Mobil's scant African experience. Since many of the main contractors were French, this opposition was often phrased in terms of contrasting American versus French corporate cultures. Therefore, from the outset, foreign project contractors such as Doba Logistics had reached agreements with local firms. Such exercises of creativity often implied granting Cameroonian businesspersons favorable access to subcontracts in return for a portion of the profits.

Because of the project's strict norms, very few operators based in those three provinces made it to COTCO's shortlist. We even documented the case of an aspiring subcontractor who, after fulfilling the requirements for prequalification, passing the technical test, and being shortlisted, was subsequently never invited to bid. In contrast, the consortium's foreign contractors had succeeded where COTCO had failed. From the early stages of the construction phase, they dealt extensively with Cameroonian firms. This, however, was achieved while disregarding established procedures for contract bidding and allocation. In the face of this routine departure from project norms, such procedures lost credibility for everyone involved. Although appearances were kept by generating the appropriate paperwork, contacts with project contractors' personnel, mostly expatriates, located at key managing positions, became the determining factor in contract-awarding decisions.

With time, the consortium developed a series of principles to ensure that the nominal priority of locals translated into secured contracts for them. COTCO's liaison with the communities along the pipeline's right of way via the local community contact personnel (LCCs) played an important role in this process. The actions inspired in these principles included "conducting outreach" to recruit potential subcontractors, helping them achieve the required qualifications, and "breaking jobs into smaller increments when possible, so that domestic businesses have a better chance to bid competitively" (CCDP 2002: 81). A confirmation of how ineffectual formal procedural norms had proven thus far, this newfound flexibility increased the number of contracts for firms based in Adamaoua, and East and North Provinces. For instance, by late 2002, COTCO made sure that contracts relating to its community and regional compensation program showcased this revised approach. Indeed, in comparison with other pipeline activities, this program turned out to be a relatively transparent contract bidding process (although, the execution of the contracts themselves encountered numerous problems). But this constituted the exception rather than the norm.

In other spheres of activity, such as food supplies, personal relationships continued to play an important role and the levels of both expatriate and Cameroonian intermediation increased. Catering companies working for the main pipeline contractors facilitated this. Even with their most important suppliers they operated without written contracts. There were many routes to obtaining these small but repeated contracts, and a strategic position in the supply chain could even be traded. For example, a small supplier recounted how "with time I found a radically different occupation. So much so that well before the closing of the camp I had stopped doing the deliveries myself. Instead, I entrusted everything to an acquaintance. It was as if I had privatized the whole thing." At other times, intermediaries were eventually bypassed. Thus a farmer who owned one of the largest fruit and vegetable stores in the region and had initially sold produce to the pipeline companies through a local facilitator later set up an independent business supplying most of them.

The handful of operators from Adamaoua Province who came to control the majority of the pipeline food supplies up north, for example, belonged to a broad network of agents who could effectively and regularly provide produce. One of the main beef suppliers used a fellow cattle trader to provide the pipeline logistics contractor with eggs for months in one of their camps. An important food supplier helped a university student to resurrect his father's dormant "community initiative group" (GIC) and assisted him in supplying fruits and vegetables in a pipeline camp for more than a year.[8] This was, as he put it, "un travail de profanes (laymen's work)." It was also a line of business that he abandoned as soon as that camp was dismantled, in order to pursue a career in national NGO circles.

In the realm of transport, the pipeline logistics contractor used structures already in place to allocate contracts to numerous small trucking companies. Both the government freight bureau (BGFT) and the national union of transporters (SNTRC) had a role in ensuring the distribution of haulage work among transporters whose trucks met the project's specifications. Yet, because of power imbalances within the organization, the union privileged some members over others. Moreover, what were by local standards extremely important contracts simply bypassed these procedures. From the early stages in the construction phase, COTCO in a rather opaque manner singled out a series of well-connected transporters by signing special contracts. Some of these privileged subcontractors in turn informally outsourced part of their allocated freight to other transporters.

In short, most contracts secured by operators based in Adamaoua and East and North Provinces were obtained in ways that departed from project rules. This was the case for COTCO contracts as much as for those of its main contractors. Although COTCO never did away with procedural norms to the extent that its foreign partners did, as the construction phase progressed, it increasingly adopted a more pragmatic management style. After all, in a context of deficit of prior on-the-ground local experience, what seemed to matter most to the oil consortium's managers was to get good marks from the ECMG and the IAG, the two main bodies to whom international oversight of the project had been delegated. As long as they did so, they felt they had lived up to their part of the bargain on CSR. CSR as an operational notion hardly figured for those with longer experience in Cameroon, such as the French contractors. They resorted to familiar networking strategies to the benefit (as they saw it) of project efficiency and, at times, personal gains for members of the network.

Trajectories and profiles of Adamaoua's pipeline subcontractors

While pipeline subcontractors based in these three provinces present a varied range of backgrounds and professional itineraries, some dominant profiles emerge. They were overwhelmingly men. Despite the rhetorical importance that the project's documentation gives to the socioeconomic promotion of women, cases of female contractors in these three provinces were very few. To some extent, this reflects larger economic patterns of a region where, despite the enormous importance of their activities in economic terms, women remain poorly represented in business circles. The project did benefit women who owned (or subsequently opened) restaurants along the pipeline area and those who worked as petty traders in local markets. Indeed, one of these petty traders became one of the most successful food suppliers to COTCO and its contractors up north; however, her case is an isolated instance. In other areas where northern businesswomen have made modest inroads in recent years, such as NGOs or public works, neither the consortium nor its partners selected them as subcontractors. Religion is also a significant variable in explaining the differential involvement of men and women in pipeline contracts. There were no Muslims among the few female subcontractors who worked for the pipeline in Adamaoua Province, for example, despite the predominance of Muslims in the population.

In generational terms, most contractors in these provinces were in their mid- to late forties when the prospect of working for the pipeline arose. They were born around 1960, the year of Cameroon's independence, and began their professional lives in the late 1970s and early 1980s. However, they cannot be counted among the technocrats who became the iconic figures of their generation (Warnier 1994). Indeed, the careers of most northern Cameroonian technocrats have taken them to larger urban centers in the south or even abroad. Several pipeline contractors entertain client relationships with these *élites extérieures* (external elites),[9] and these ties were decisive for the award of some contracts. Nonetheless, high-profile elites remained remarkably uninvolved in the project. Unlike the technocrat members of their cohort, most pipeline subcontractors rarely had acquired higher education and lacked training in professional management practices. Neither were most of them what may be called *enfants de la crise* (children of the crisis). In fact, they came of age during the oil bonanza of the late 1970s and early 1980s, a time of economic optimism. Yet, from the mid-1980s onward, the economic crisis shattered many expectations and certainly marked the career trajectories of these future pipeline subcontractors. Like most Cameroonians, during the 1990s they had to weather the effects of a shrinking economy, the 1994 currency devaluation, widespread insolvency, and a turbulent business climate.

In these provinces' multiethnic society, the pipeline subcontractors' ethnic and religious identifications were far from irrelevant. Indeed, although such identifications are largely omitted in project documentation and reports, they played a key role in the COTCO's pragmatic determinations of who counted as local and who did not (Muñoz 2008). Ethnic and religious labelling affects everyday social interaction. COTCO and its main contractors mainly took on Muslim operators as subcontractors in northern Cameroon, reflecting the overrepresentation of Fulbe, Hausa, and other majority Muslim groups within the economy of Adamaoua and North Province. In the project's very modest attempts to promote local business, COTCO tended to accommodate the existing ethnic composition of the different business communities with which it interacted. Thus, in the Mbere District in south-eastern Adamaoua Province where the majority population is neither Fulbe nor Muslim, the consortium had a more ethnically diverse set of contractors. In East Province, the selected local partners in the regional compensation scheme were associated with Gbaya or other Christian groups who are most numerous in the province's population.

Some operators from distant West and North West Provinces, who are broadly identified as Bamileke, obtained contracts as transporters and food/drink suppliers, while others operated pump stations and ran restaurants along the pipeline. In the popular discourse about the allocation of pipeline contracts, this was interpreted as proof of the effectiveness of Bamileke networks of ethnic solidarity (Warnier 1993) and the marginalization of Adamaoua and East and North Provinces in Cameroon. Some Lebanese based in Adamaoua and East Province working in the auto parts trade, bakeries, logging and road transport (passengers and freight) benefited from pipeline contracts—and were included in the "local business development" section of the project's progress reports.

A sizeable number of Cameroonians with no prior exposure to the region also came to the north with pipeline contracts in mind. Aside from the realm of transport, their bids were for the most part not met with success. A building contractor based in Douala, for example, opened a temporary office in Ngaoundere in the hope of obtaining regional compensation program-related work. In order to put together a convincing file for COTCO, he paid the fee for a business license in Adamaoua, but in the end he failed to get any contracts.

The kinds of firm acting as pipeline subcontractors were not too different from the precarious business structures that generally make up those provinces' economic landscape. With only rare exceptions, these firms are relatively small ventures characterized by highly personalized management, very few permanent employees, low capital investment, and limited financial capabilities. Their business horizons have a marked short-term orientation. In some cases they were created ad hoc to bid for pipeline contracts. The pipeline dealt with Cameroonian counterparts who operated under different legal umbrellas. COTCO, for instance, chose several NGOs to carry out contracts related to its regional compensation scheme. Given their tax-exempt status, the NGO format is particularly attractive. However, until very recently, very few organizations based in these three provinces enjoyed official recognition as an NGO. As a result, most of them have an ambiguous legal status. Authorities treat them as simple associations and determine their obligations, including tax liabilities, on a highly variable case-by-case basis. Other counterparts in the regional compensation contracts were legally categorized as *enterprises individuelles* (individual enterprises) or *sociétés à responsabilité limité* (limited liability incorporated businesses). Some of them complained that the tax authorities discriminated against them vis-à-vis the NGOs that worked for the pipeline, even though the latter's activities did not differ that much from theirs. COTCO representatives themselves did not give much credit to the NGO label of some of its subcontractors, whom they referred to as "enterprises in NGO disguise."

Outside the regional compensation scheme, most subcontractors who worked with the consortium and its partners did so under established commercial formulas. As a matter of fact, some contractors were particularly exacting in this regard. For example, SOGEA-SATOM, the French contractor for road network upgrading, initially required that its subcontractors in charge of construction works or construction materials were corporate persons whose annual turnover placed them in the highest taxpaying category (above 100 million CFA francs). Contracts for food supplies were the exception to this general picture. Pipeline suppliers of vegetables, fish, meat, drinks, dairy and bakery products adopted, with varying degrees of opportunism, alternative forms such as cooperatives and the very-popular GICs, both of which benefit from favorable tax regimes and other legal incentives.

Contract performance and the afterlives of pipeline subcontractors

The award of an initial contract turned out to be a decisive threshold for Cameroonian operators interested in conducting business with the project. Once crossed, most subcontractors developed fluid working relationships with COTCO and its partners. This often led to further contracts and at times it also meant that the subcontractors expanded their services for the consortium into new areas. One of our informants exemplifies this dynamic. At different points and in different capacities, from local facilitator and food supplier to building contractor, he worked for five different companies linked to the consortium. "*J'ai piqué dans toutes les phases du pipe* (I've had a bite in all the stages of the project)," he proudly asserted. Similar cases include a supplier of construction materials for SOGEA-SATOM, the pipeline contractor in charge of road construction, who was later hired to construct several buildings for them; a transporter whose services for Doba Logistics were rewarded with a few additional construction contracts; and a food supplier whose connections enabled him to obtain COTCO support in bidding for the regional compensation contracts.

As a rule, not only the consortium and its potential subcontractors but also external monitoring groups, the media, and the general public paid considerable attention to the initial bidding process. However, the completion of those contracts and the award of successive ones to already tested subcontractors were not so closely scrutinized. Thus, the rigor that, at least nominally, had characterized the award of first contracts gave way to considerable room for maneuver in their completion, renewal, and the acquisition of new ones. In the phase of contract completion, the consortium's and its contractors' representatives continued to play the important gatekeeping and intermediary roles they had had during the initial phase of contract bidding, but with increased leverage. The widest departures from project guidelines on contract performance can be traced back to a few of these field managers, often expatriates, who enjoyed considerable autonomy—"*les fanfarons qui venaient nous casser les pieds* (the braggarts who came here to pester us)," as one of their disgruntled subordinates referred to them. Irregularities aside, contract terms varied considerably in practice depending on which of the consortium partners the subcontractors had to deal with, which locations they serviced, and which stage the project had reached.

One of risks faced by the consortium and its foreign contractors in their dealings with Cameroonian firms was overinvoicing. Practices aimed at inflating the cost of different budgetary items when doing business with both the Cameroonian state and certain parastatal companies are widespread. It is hardly surprising that the consortium tried to minimize such practices. The emphasis on competitiveness and transparency in the bidding process was to prevent, or at least reduce, overinvoicing. In addition, the consortium carried out consultations to establish the going rates for different services and commissioned a series of preliminary surveys to assess benchmark prices and price trends of different goods.

Given the widely documented difficulties of Cameroonian small and medium-sized enterprises in gaining access to credit, the consortium and its contractors tried in different ways to help its subcontractors finance their activities within the framework of the pipeline contracts. Another issue that arose throughout the project concerned payment methods and delays. Here again, despite the attempts of the consortium to follow uniform guidelines, experiences varied widely, depending on the partners involved and the different sectors of activity.

Depending on the extent of their previous business experience, the completion of contracts was more or less of a challenge for pipeline subcontractors. There was great diversity in their respective situations. Factors such as the financial challenge inherent in their participation in the project, or the incorporation of changes in management practices they had to introduce, meant that their experience working for the pipeline differed considerably. On the whole, the consortium seems to have found their overall performance satisfactory. During the construction phase, however, the benchmarks for subcontracting that the consortium had established were not systematically adhered to. Despite all the efforts of the consortium, overinvoicing was not always successfully avoided. Measures aimed at preventing overinvoicing, such as those of the regional compensation program, were sometimes counterproductive and often created additional problems. Subcontractors who received the consortium's financial support for the completion of their contracts generally welcomed its terms and thought it had made a difference. Yet, such financial support was not uniformly distributed. Some subcontractors were privileged over others for reasons that were not always entirely clear. Almost unanimously, subcontractors found the training received from the consortium and its partners extremely valuable in enabling them to comply with more demanding quality and safety standards. Tasks such as processing larger stocks and supervising more employees also contributed to the broadening of their management skills.

The pipeline project represented an unprecedented opportunity for most of the subcontractors. At the same time, they were painfully aware that once the construction phase came to an end, so would the possibilities for profit and expansion it had brought. A food supplier eloquently referred to this post-pipeline phase as the return to the "civilian economy" (CCDP 2002: 73). This return meant different things for different subcontractors.

Some, for example, who had created their enterprises with the exclusive object of capturing pipeline contracts, either let them become dormant or closed them down once the construction phase was over. An NGO whose pipeline contracts had attracted technical and financial partners saw these partners leave with their share once the project was over. The founder of another NGO, which had built schools and rural clinics for the consortium's regional compensation program and was pretty much a one man show, put his activities on hold and moved to a more strategically located town where he made a living as a retailer of imported computers. These are not rare occurrences in the regional context in recent decades. Years of economic crisis have habituated everyone to short-term business operations that translate into volatile structures and erratic trajectories.

Subcontractors who counted the work undertaken for the pipeline among their previous lines of activity showed more continuity. An obvious route was to find similar contracts with other important projects in the region, like the European Union-funded 390 km Ngaoundere-Moundou road between 2003 and 2007, or continued to work for pipeline contractors whose activities went beyond the construction phase, like the pipeline logistics firm Tchad Cameroun Logistics, a subsidiary of the French multinational Geodis. But this did little to cushion the sharp decline in turnover that the end of the pipeline construction represented. Similarly, NGOs based in these three provinces that had worked for the consortium tried to use their involvement in the pipeline to enhance their credentials with the promoters of several internationally funded development initiatives underway in the area.

There were several instances of less experienced subcontractors who, lacking clear alternatives, made risky or unwise investment decisions. Among those who abandoned their pipeline businesses, investments in vehicles, real estate, or cattle were the most common destinations for their savings. Nonetheless, a sizable group of operators expanded their business activities after the end of their contracts. The case of a cattle trader who had worked as one of the project's meat suppliers and put the refrigeration unit he had received from a pipeline contractor to good use was one of the most prominent successes. Aiming at the segment of the urban population with higher purchasing power, he opened one of the rare "modern" butcheries in the region.

Most trucking companies saw the purchase of more vehicles as the most straightforward avenue of business expansion. Others were more cautious and channeled part of their profits into trading or cattle ventures. This trend conforms to diversification strategies in the past during periods when transporters have needed to adapt to the sector's ups and downs—the early 1990s (the peak of the economic crisis) being the most recent period of massive disinvestments. The pipeline project had attracted other trucking companies from southern Cameroon to come north, and, in more recent years, the increased competition has translated into excess capacity and lower freight rates. More generally, the pipeline project has contributed to a renewal and improvement of the available trucking fleet in northern Cameroon, even though almost all vehicles purchased were secondhand.

Of all the subcontractors, suppliers of construction materials most clearly used their participation in the project as a platform to explore other markets. Some of them have opened stores elsewhere in the country. As far as the construction enterprises are concerned, those that benefited from the pipeline's contracts returned to business as usual after the end of the project. For a few of them, however, the balance of their work for the pipeline was more negative. Low budget estimations, unexpected tax audits, or both, led to a situation of de facto bankruptcy. In other instances, substandard works resulting from the consortium's budgetary constraints, or even uncompleted works, seriously undermined their reputation and led to protracted conflicts with COTCO, occasionally reaching the courts. For those in better standing with the consortium, the dismantling of some of the project's temporary facilities represented an opportunity to prolong their involvement. Most subcontractors went on to work for their more conventional clients, such as parastatal companies or the state itself. Almost without exception, they used the profits they made from the pipeline project to diversify the range of their economic activities rather than to expand their construction ventures.

NGO participation in the project, while generating considerable revenue for its promoters, did not produce far-reaching changes. Certainly, those with larger memberships saw their organizational capacities reinforced, and improved their reputation vis-à-vis future projects. But NGOs with a weaker presence on the ground reverted to the minimal structure they had before the pipeline. Above all, the project accentuated the increasing trend of NGOs taking on the role of public contractors.

In conclusion, the different courses of action pursued by pipeline subcontractors based in Adamaoua and North and East Provinces demonstrate that large portions of the profits they made did not feed a virtuous cycle of business expansion. Some used their income from the pipeline to buy imported consumer goods and to invest in real estate. The majority, however, adopted diversification strategies that are widespread in the regional economy. The rates of reinvestment in the same or similar lines of business were only modest.

Project rules, personal relationships, and business formalization

For many business people in these provinces, the cultivation of privileged relationships with field managers occupying key positions was an obvious way of capturing some of the many business opportunities that the pipeline offered. Whether these relationships had already reached a contractual form or not, some local operators went out of their way to accommodate project field managers' demands. Their transactions with the pipeline project took shape in the context of highly personalized relationships where loyalty and reciprocity, and not the respect of project norms, took priority. They tried to become useful in as many capacities as possible in the expectation that the services rendered would be well rewarded.

It is equally important to underscore that much of the courting of project field managers to create bonds transcending the purely commercial failed to bear the desired fruits. Sometimes these business operators made unrealistic assumptions concerning what the consortium or its employees were in a position to do for them. One of our interviewees offers an extreme illustration of this mismatch of expectations. He had had to work under a tight budget and a demanding timetable that involved construction work during the rainy season. He had also actively participated in a national television documentary in which he had praised the project's achievements. When COTCO disclosed the amounts of his contracts to the Tax Bureau he felt betrayed. He wondered how after all he had done for them they could sell him out to the tax authorities.

While patronage shaped the way many subcontractors understood their work for the pipeline, many others did not conceive their work primarily in such terms. In any case, everyone with a stake in the project, including the consortium, was well aware of the degree to which a large part of the pipeline business had been personalized. In the words of a disgruntled businessman from Adamaoua Province: "[The consortium] got into all the *magouilles* [wheeling and dealing] that Cameroonians hold dearly." Such views reproduced established narratives about the rootedness of corruption in Cameroon and the painstaking observance of regulations by ExxonMobil. And yet, COTCO and its major contractors left more room for irregular business practices than they would have cared to admit.

The subcontractors' involvement in the pipeline project had other consequences that are more tangentially related to the question of business consolidation and expansion. The depth of these transformations has depended on their respective points of departure, which differ considerably. For many subcontractors with more modest ventures, the project represented the first experience in bookkeeping, in documenting commercial transactions, and in conducting basic banking operations. Medium-sized enterprises, in turn, have moved to increased sophistication in their accountancy and financing. However, such steps can be undone with surprising speed. For example, the NGO that was awarded a large share of regional compensation contracts in the East Province, which at the time was seen as working with exemplary transparency, saw its activities suspended in 2009 as a result of falling out with its European sponsors over accounting irregularities.

The most substantial aspects of the process of formalization that accompanied subcontractor involvement in the pipeline project, nonetheless, impinged upon changes in their relationship with the state, and with tax authorities in particular. Contract bidders had to provide evidence of their compliance with regulations. Some of the largest subcontractors opted for new legal forms for their business ventures. We documented several interesting cases in which the performance of pipeline contracts was the occasion for a transition toward corporate status, with individual enterprises typically transforming themselves into limited liability companies.

As far as tax payments on the profits made from their pipeline contracts are concerned, subcontractors were subject to closer scrutiny than is the norm in the region. Not only had their successful bids for such a large project made their activities more conspicuous but also COTCO disclosed the amounts its subcontractors had received for their work to the tax authorities. It is certainly the case that, during the pipeline construction phase, there were loopholes in the contracting process that allowed some operators to diminish their tax liabilities and avoid other legal obligations. However, it did not take long before some subcontractors felt the effects of the authorities' closer scrutiny. The beneficiary of construction contracts quoted above who accused COTCO of having sold him out to the tax authorities, for example, was, in the course of a year, compelled to apply for a more expensive business license, fined for late payment of his company income tax, and forced to pay several million CFA francs in VAT arrears. Like him, many subcontractors saw the type of their business license change, which not only meant higher fees but more demanding accountancy standards and more frequent and detailed reporting.

Furthermore, the tax returns of some of the largest pipeline subcontractors were targeted for review and, more often than not, became the object of subsequent adjustment. The ensuing conflicts led to mutual tests of strength and some haggling. While some subcontractors settled for moderate additional tax payments—plus, possibly, payments under the table to officials—others took less conciliatory approaches and took their disagreements to the central tax authorities in Yaoundé, with varying fortune. Overall, pipeline subcontractors' relationships with the tax authorities have taken an adversarial turn. The exception to this pattern are subcontractors such as the NGOs, which on account of their nonprofits orientation, benefit from tax exemptions and have, for the most part, been spared this tighter tax surveillance.

The experience of many pipeline subcontractors demonstrates the open-ended nature of processes of formalization of economic activities. While the pipeline induced a move toward greater compliance with bureaucratic formalities and regulations, the outcome of this process varied widely. Formalization proved to be negotiable, often only partial, selective and, when needed, reversible.

Doing business with a corporate citizen

As Steve Coll (2012: 349) has written, for ExxonMobil's managers in the Chad-Cameroon project, applying the corporation's operations integrity management system involved "engineering Chad and its pathologies out of the equation to the greatest extent possible." In their view, the prime function of the corporation's standards was to enact the logic of modularity and the ethics of detachment that Hannah Appel and Jamie Cross respectively have discussed in other ethnographic contexts. The irony is that, as the opening quote from the Vice-President for Development in Africa underscores, in ExxonMobil's official discourse adhering to such standards and introducing other economic actors to them was singled out as an exercise in rather than an abdication of responsibility.

Cameroonian enterprises that adopted the consortium's standards in order to take advantage of the limited opportunities that the pipeline project made available had to introduce changes in their business practices and in their relationship with different state agencies. Indeed, many of COTCO's subcontractors were appreciative of project norms that departed from the terms (commercial and others) that they had experienced before. They often referred to aspects of project requirements that limited the potential for overinvoicing. A feature of COTCO's budgeting rules, for example, allowed NGOs in charge of construction within the framework of regional compensation to charge an institutional overhead on top of the costs of materials and labor. Similarly, contractors valued the ability to obtain payments without the need to pay "facilitating money" in return (unlike the common practice in public contracting). Yet, for all these favorable impressions, there is little evidence that the example of such new models has generated enduring changes. Despite the formal rules associated with the project, networks of contacts and influence, which included both Cameroonians and expatriates, continued to play an important part in the award and management of contracts. In this sense, to a significant degree, practices that circumvented project rules played a role in ensuring business as usual in Adamaoua and East and North Provinces.

This uneven exposure to project rules and standards, however, fell short of the inflated expectations around "local business development" that the World Bank and the oil consortium had fueled. On balance, in these three provinces, as far as capacity building, technology transfer and technical training went, the project had little to show for itself. In the domain of private sector promotion, what our informants called *les retombées du pipe* (the pipe's economic benefits) and the project literature referred to as "local spin-offs" were decidedly meagre. The project's role in introducing new standards and spreading bureaucratic formalities was in any case hardly surprising. In this same region, large corporations have historically had important structuring effects. During the French colonial period, for example, the Compagnie Pastorale played a decisive role in the formalization of the cattle sector in Adamaoua. Similarly, after independence, the cotton parastatal Sodecoton, the transport consortium Sogetrans, and the tobacco parastatal Société Camerounaise de Tabac mediated relationships between the state and small and medium-sized enterprises in the North Province, Adamaoua and East Province respectively. The same can be said about the impact of Camrail, the railway company, which undertakes substantial tax-collecting tasks on behalf of the authorities in Adamaoua and East Province. With this historical backdrop in mind, the Chad-Cameroon project appears somewhat less exceptional in this regard. What constitutes a novelty is that, through ExxonMobil's partnership with the World Bank, this exposure to laws and standards ended up being presented as a corporate gift to Chadian and Cameroonian businesses, workers and citizens.

ExxonMobil was only drawn to the moral fold of CSR as a relative latecomer. The project planning and pipeline construction took place in the days when the corporation was coming to terms with an incipient CSR agenda, which would find its tentative formulation in the first of successive annual reports on corporate citizenship (ExxonMobil 2002). In the case of the Chad-Cameroon project, this agenda was largely driven by contractual obligations acquired with the World Bank. By focusing on subcontracting as a dimension of CSR, we have called attention to the fact that sometimes CSR can be envisioned as giving less tangible things than school buildings or medical supplies. In the Chad-Cameroon project, ExxonMobil's initiatives toward "local business development" largely hinged on "demonstrating through their own example the benefits of corporate discipline and principled consistency" (Coll 2012: 164). The corporation saw the creation of a context in which adherence to rigorous rules and standards not only became possible but was even encouraged, as its trademark gift. The terms of the gift at issue here presupposed, on the one hand, American and European corporate persons who had mastered those tried-and-tested rules and standards and, on the other, Chadian and Cameroonian persons who needed to be educated in them. In Cameroon's Adamaoua and East and North Provinces, this was a gift that many businesses no matter how cognizant they were of its fragile, compromised and ephemeral nature, actually welcomed.

Notes

1. The OIMS was first formulated in 1992. In the words of a former executive quoted by Steve Coll (2001: 32), "so there could be no excuses," the system contained "every single goddamn aspect of how we operate." The OIMS is based on established principles of risk assessment and management and consists of eleven elements (ExxonMobil 2009). In 1998, Exxon ensured the OIMS complied with the International Organization for Standardization (ISO) 14001 guidelines. In 2002, in its first corporate citizenship report, ExxonMobil singled out the standards of business conduct enshrined in the OIMS as the "basis for corporate citizenship." Among other things, the report explained how the OIMS framework ensured that throughout the corporation's global operations "we focus on building local capabilities by endeavoring to use competitive local suppliers, hiring nationals to staff our operations and transferring technology and skills" (ExxonMobil 2002: 2–3).
2. The research on which this chapter is based was supported by an Economic and Social Research Council UK grant ("An ethnographic study of recent trends in business activity in Northern Cameroon," R000239960), in which we collaborated with Saïdou Abdoulaï Bobboy (Chamber of Commerce) and Martial Massike Loke (University of Ngaoundere), to whom we are deeply indebted. The main fieldwork period took place from June 2003 to November 2004. This was supplemented by shorter research trips between August and September 2005 and May and June 2011, which were funded

by Northwestern University's Program of African Studies and Emory University's Program in Development Studies respectively.

3. For a journalistic account of the World Bank's involvement in the project, see Mallaby 2004: Chap. 13. As Mallaby explains, at the time of the project, the Bank was at a crossroads, with its principal policy orientation veering away from support for large infrastructural projects and toward more social sector lending in reaction to pressures from environmentalist NGOs. This change in viewpoint was manifested within the Bank itself in the form of staff factionalism, with an evident resistance on the part of an internal environmentalist faction to any involvement by the Bank in the pipeline project.

4. In September 2000, the International Finance Corporation hired an Italian consultancy firm to act as ECMG and monitor compliance with the project's Environmental Management Plan, which contained the consortium's many environmental and socioeconomic commitments. To date, the ECMG has published 19 reports (http://www.ifc.org/wps/wcm/connect/region__ext_content/regions/sub-saharan+africa/investments/chadcameroon_ecmg). In February 2001, the World Bank's President appointed an IAG to advise him and the governments of Chad and Cameroon on the implementation of all projects related to the Chad-Cameroon pipeline. The IAG's mandate was "not primarily on monitoring compliance" but involved "identifying measures that can contribute to making this project a veritable instrument of development" (IAG 2001: 1). From 2001 to 2009, the IAG conducted fourteen statutory visits to Chad and fifteen to Cameroon (IAG 2009).

5. In June 2000, 1,000 CFA francs equaled 1.40 US dollars.

6. For the sake of readability, in what follows we refer to those foreign companies who secured major project contracts as "contractors" and we reserve the term "subcontractor" for Cameroonian firms, whether they were hired by COTCO directly or by one of its foreign partners.

7. It is worth noting that some of the project's foreign contractors themselves engaged in highly irregular labor practices—the case of the logistics contractor, Bollore's Doba Logistics, being the most notorious on the Cameroonian side of the project. On the problems faced by employees of contractors operating on the Chadian side, see Guyer (2011: 22).

8. In the context of political liberalization and economic crisis of the early 1990s, the "groupements d'initiative commune" represented the Cameroonian government's attempt to shape and promote associative arrangements in sectors of activity with very small units of production, such as agriculture, livestock, crafts, and petty trade. The GIC formula had proliferated considerably in Adamaoua and East and North Province by the time the pipeline project got underway. See Law n. 1992/006 of 14 August 1992, and the application decree n. 1992/455/PM of 23 November 1992.

9. "External elites" is the term used in Cameroon for the "sons and daughters" of a given area that have made successful careers either in business or in politics outside their hometowns. For an overview of the importance of the notion of "elites" in the imaginary of urban-rural connections in Cameroon and elsewhere in Africa, see Burnham (1996: 133–153) and Geschiere and Gugler (1998).

References

Appel, Hannah. 2012a. Walls and white elephants: Oil extraction, responsibility, and infrastructural violence in Equatorial Guinea. *Ethnography* 13(4): 439–465.
Appel, Hannah. 2012b. Offshore work: Oil, modularity, and the how of capitalism in Equatorial Guinea. *American Ethnologist* 39(4): 692–709.
Burnham, Philip. 1996. *The politics of cultural difference in northern Cameroon.* Edinburgh: Edinburgh University Press.
Chad-Cameroon Development Project (CCDP). 1997. *Chad export project (Cameroon portion) environmental assessment.*
Chad-Cameroon Development Project (CCDP). 1999. *Environmental management plan (Cameroon portion).*
Chad-Cameroon Development Project (CCDP). 2000. *Quarterly report no. 1. 4th quarter.*
Chad-Cameroon Development Project (CCDP). 2002. *Quarterly report no. 7. 2nd quarter.*
Coll, Steve. 2012. *Private empire: ExxonMobil and American power.* New York: Penguin.
ExxonMobil. 2002. *Corporate citizenship in a changing world.*
ExxonMobil. 2009. *Operations integrity management system framework.*
Frynas, George. 2009. *Beyond corporate social responsibility: Oil multinationals and social challenges.* Cambridge: Cambridge University Press.
Gardner, Katy. 2012. *Discordant development: Global capitalism and the struggle for connection in Bangladesh.* London: Pluto Press.
Gary, Ian, and Nikki Reisch. 2005. *Chad's oil: Miracle or mirage?* Baltimore: Catholic Relief Services.
Geschiere, Peter, and Josef Gugler. 1998. The urban-rural connection: Changing issues of belonging and identification. *Africa* 68(3): 309–319.
Gould, John, and Matthew Winters. 2007. An obsolescing bargain in Chad: Shifts in leverage between the government and the World Bank. *Business and Politics* 9(2): 1–34.
Grovogui, Siba, and Lori Leonard. 2007. Oiling tyranny? Neoliberalism and global governance in Chad. *Studies in Political Economy* 79: 35–59.
Guyer, Jane. 2002. The Chad-Cameroon petroleum and pipeline development project. *African Affairs* 101(402): 109–115.
Guyer, Jane. 2011. Blueprints, judgment, and perseverance in a corporate context. *Current Anthropology* 52(S3): 17–27.
Hernandez Uriz, Genoveva. 2002. The application of World Bank standards to the oil industry. *Brooklyn Journal of International Law* 28: 77–91.
Hoinathy, Remadji, and Andrea Behrends. 2014. Does rationality travel? Translations of a World Bank model for fair oil revenue distribution in Chad. In Andrea Behrends et al., eds., *Transfering models in African conflict management: Translating technologies of social ordering*, pp. 76–91. Leiden: Brill.
International Advisory Group (IAG). 2001. Report on first statutory mission to Cameroon and Chad, 19 July to 3 August, http://web.worldbank.org/archive/website01210/WEB/IMAGES/IAG_R-16.PDF
International Advisory Group (IAG). 2009. Final report, http://web.worldbank.org/archive/website01210/WEB/IMAGES/IAG_CHAD.PDF
Leibold, Annalisa. 2011. Aligning incentives for development: The World Bank and the Chad-Cameroon oil pipeline. *Yale Journal of International Law* 36: 167–205.
Mallaby, Sebastian. 2004. *The world's banker.* New Haven: Yale University Press.
Monga, Celestin. 1997. *L'argent des autres. Banques et petites entreprises en Afrique: Le cas du Cameroun.* Paris: Librairie Générale de Droit et de Jurisprudence.
Muñoz, José-María. 2008. Au nom du développement: Ethnicité, autochtonie, et promotion du secteur privé au Nord-Cameroun. *Politique Africaine* 112: 67–85.

US Congress. 2002. The Chad-Cameroon pipeline: A new model for natural resource development. Hearing before the Subcommittee on Africa of the Committee on International Relations, House of Representatives, 18 April, serial no. 107–175.

Warnier, Jean-Pierre. 1993. *L'esprit d'entreprise au Cameroun*. Paris: Karthala.

Warnier, Jean-Pierre. 1994. La bigarrure des patrons Camerounais. In Jean-François Bayart, ed., *La réinvention du capitalisme*, pp. 175–201. Paris: Karthala.

José-María Muñoz is a lawyer and an anthropologist who has conducted research in Cameroon since 2003. He is a lecturer of International Development at the University of Edinburgh's Centre of African Studies.

Philip Burnham is Emeritus Professor of Anthropology at University College London. He has been carrying out social and historical research in Cameroon since 1968. From 1998 to 2003, he undertook socioeconomic impact assessments of the Chad-Cameroon pipeline project as a consultant for ExxonMobil.

– Chapter 8 –

COLLECTIVE CONTRADICTIONS OF "CORPORATE" ENVIRONMENTAL CONSERVATION

Rebecca Hardin

In 2004, in Chile, Goldman Sachs announced the unprecedented gift of a sprawling wilderness to the New York–based Wildlife Conservation Society (WCS). The more than 680,000 acres (272,000 hectares) of land, about the size of the state of Rhode Island, but located on the island of Tierra del Fuego, are home to the world's southernmost stands of old-growth forests as well as unique grasslands, rivers, and wetlands containing extraordinary wildlife. Press accounts on the deal cited WCS Chief Executive Officer Steve Sanderson:

> Goldman Sachs, the Goldman Sachs Charitable Fund, WCS and the people of Chile will be pioneering a new kind of partnership for conservation of these precious wild lands, which reflect the importance of Chile for global conservation. Goldman Sachs has set a new standard for the private sector's commitment to the natural world, and deserves tremendous credit for their imagination and resolve that these lands and their wildlife should be protected now and forever.

How to make sense of such a new form of exchange, unfolding at such a vast territorial and temporal scale? Anthropologist Marcel Mauss powerfully stated that not only are there not, but "there should be no free gifts." His concept of *prestation*, a term evocative in French of both an intimate promise and a public exchange of money for particular services (in the form of dues, allowances, or loans), prompts me here to examine how anthropologists shape and analyze the ways that conservation and commercial organizations exchange money, knowledge, and gifts. For Mauss, gifts entail social reciprocity, and make actors responsible to one another in new ways. Seen thus, the mandate of an international conservation NGO such as WCS is redefined after receiving such a "gift."

This idea helps analyze an environmental conservation sector where mutual recognition among companies, countries, and a few particularly powerful NGOs has implications for new forms of governance at community levels. Lemos and Agrawal (2006) have used the term "hybrid governance" to describe systems where communities, state agencies, corporations, and nongovernmental organizations forge new partnerships and norms for the use and protection of natural resources. This opens up environmental governance relations that were once dominated by either state institutions or corporations interacting directly with rural populations. Ethnographic description of such arrangements, and theoretical and conceptual insights about how they emerge and change is still needed, however.

In Africa, state-NGO or community-NGO dyads have been richly documented by a generation of development anthropology monographs (see, e.g., Dupré 1982, Ferguson 1999). Recent anthropological monographs take field conservation projects and protected areas as units of analysis (Walley 2004; Lowe 2004; West 2005). As noted recently in the pages of this journal (Cepek 2010) there is increasing attention to the ways that organizational imperatives in either development or conservation belie actual implementation and outcomes (Ferguson 1990; Carrier and West 2009). Less work has been done to document the transformations within corporate and nongovernmental organizations that emerge from new objectives and mechanisms for environmental governance.

When, for instance, did environmental organizations begin to have chief executive officers, rather than directors, or chairs? Such shifts in the institutional cultures of NGOs toward more corporate norms and terms both reflect and shape changes in their actions and their partners in field sites. Let us again take an example from WCS. In 1991, they undertook collaboration with an organization representing some of the Guaraní people, the Capitanía de Alto y Bajo Izozog (CABI), to protect the Bolivian part of the Chaco. This is one of the most unspoiled portions of an ecoregion that stretches across Argentina, Paraguay, and Brazil. Its health was threatened by hunting, trade in wildlife products, farming and ranching, road and infrastructure development, and energy exploration. The WCS-CABI collaboration led to the creation of the Kaa-Iya del Gran Chaco National Park and Integrated Management Area in 1995, which designates 3.4 million hectares as a protected national park and 1.9 million adjoining hectares as indigenous territory. The Guaraní are responsible for managing these two areas, a level of ownership no other South American indigenous organization has achieved.

After the park was created, the Bolivian government awarded to Gaz Transboliviano (GTB) the concession to build the Bolivia-Brazil gas pipeline, slated to go through both the national park and the indigenous territory. Initially uninterested in addressing the long-term objectives of the indigenous people, eventually the company gave 1.5 million dollars to a financial mechanism that would sustain their development by securing the titles over their land, a further $1.5 million to support their resource-management activities, and also a trust fund of one million dollars to secure the management of the national park. Avecita Chicchón is an example of those on the front lines of forging and following up on such partnerships. An anthropologist working with WCS on a variety of fronts in Latin America, she commented on such efforts at a recent Woodrow Wilson Center workshop on "Innovative Partnerships for Peace: The Role of Extractive Industry." Describing the Bolivian case, she asserted that "the alliance between an indigenous people and a conservation organization was the key" to avoiding conflict between GTB and the Guaraní. She noted that "ultimately, the corporation also became an ally for conservation and a promoter of indigenous development, but the road to ... that outcome was not an easy one."[1]

These negotiations taught WCS that extractive industry companies have long planning horizons—frequently forty or fifty years. Chicchón argues that that is a time frame environmental groups should emulate. NGOs are in fact revising the timelines and performance parameters of projects in light of expectations from within their donor base of young, results-oriented retirees from early careers in industries such as the dot.com and financial sectors. Such individuals are managing philanthropic portfolios with focused attention to outcomes and often rapid results need to be demonstrated from any "gift." This can be incompatible with adaptive management approaches in which monitoring of complex ecological and social systems over time is intended to redefine policy directions, in cycles of adjustment and assessment. However, organizational theory has its own versions of adaptive management and long-range planning (Haeckel 1999); businesses are also constrained by weather, economic cycles, market volatility, and other factors to measure their performance over time. Mauss himself asserts a wide range of time frames over which mutual indebtedness can play out.

The exchanges between WCS and Goldman Sachs, or between WCS and some Guaraní actors, make powerfully illustrative jumping-off points for this essay on the contradictions implicit in changing relationships within and between the conservation and business sectors. In the article I will not consider the Latin American case in more detail, but will instead describe emerging field strategies for forest conservation in African regions where my own ethnographic work has been carried out, and where many of these issues are most starkly linked to a set of related challenges in health and conflict prevention.[2] I seek to illustrate how and why ethnographers should attend to the ways that both NGO and corporate actors are participating in social forms such as trusts, certification schemes, and task forces to forge new modes of environmental governance. Doing so offers useful conceptual advances regarding reciprocally transformative gifts in an era of emergent hybrid environmental governance marked on the one hand by spectacular gestures, and on the other hand by the less visible creep of corporate institutional cultures into sectors such as rural development and resource management.

Anthropology and conservation accountability

As noted above, the scholarly literature describing and critically engaging "big international nongovernmental organizations" (or BINGOs) has matured. Only in the last decade or so has the scale of the conservation BINGOs (whether at the levels of budgets, staffs, infrastructures, or wider professional networks) corresponded to a major force in environmentalist careers, driving enrollments and placement strategies in professional schools of environmental management. This professionalization is in part due to the expansion of conservation funding beyond "the individuals and family foundations that seeded the movement to include very large foundations like Ford, MacArthur, and Gordon and Betty Moore, as well as the World Bank, its Global Environment Facility, foreign governments, USAID, a host of bilateral and multilateral banks, and transnational corporations" (Dowie 2005; see also Rubino 2000). The Wildlife Conservation Society, for example, has nearly doubled its operating budget in the last ten years, from 30 million to 70 million dollars annually. This expansion of conservation NGO budgets, personnel, and purview is not unique to WCS, but includes Conservation International (an early recipient of significant funds from Gordon Moore's Intel empire), as well as The Nature Conservancy and the World Wildlife Fund (both of whom are actively courting corporate partners). It has occurred in the wake of several key debates about conservation approaches over the course of the 1990s.

One is about the relationship between conservation organizations and the resource bases they protect; the other is about their relationship to corporations versus rural populations. A flashpoint publication for the first came in 2000, when anthropologist and primatologist John Oates published his book *Myth and reality in the rainforest: The failure of conservation in West Africa* (Oates 2000). It was part memoir, part monograph, and part militant argument against the kind of "integrated conservation and development project" (or ICDP) that WWF was spearheading in the Dzanga Sangha Dense Forest Reserve, or RDS, in the Central African Republic (CAR). ICDPs had emerged as an alternative to the coercive colonial conservation efforts that had created a first generation of parks, and caused social frictions in many parts of the world during postcolonial eras (Brandon, Redford, and Sanderson1998; Wilshusen et al. 2002). Oates argued that the approach led to increased infrastructural, demographic, and economic pressures on resources under strain, without accomplishing more sustainable livelihoods for inhabitants of species-rich regions. Responses to his argument included assertions that the conservation bottom line should include not only the integrity of isolated resource bases, but also contributions to the capacity for improved environmental governance at regional, national, and international scales in developing countries. Advocates of ICDP approaches noted that they were ambitious in scope, and needed time to play out. Most acknowledged, however, that better monitoring of key resources should be more common practice.

A second flashpoint publication referred to the integrity not of ecological systems, but of social contracts between rural residents and conservationists. In 2004, Mac Chapin's piece in *World Watch* entitled "A challenge to conservationists" expressed outrage and accused BINGOs in the conservation sector of having "sold out" to corporate interests, forsaking their previous partners in environmentalist work, the indigenous peoples. He wrote in a scathing tone of upscale conferences, hushed boardrooms, and donor-driven dynamics' having replaced field-based, ecologically and culturally driven advocacy work to save biodiverse environments and those humans who have inhabited them over history. For Chapin's critique to make sense, much about the imperial history of environmentalism and environmental actors must be ignored. It has been amply documented that many of the guiding principles and institutional cultures of conservation emerged from structures of imperial and colonial control over natural resources and landscapes. Further, many of the actors involved in establishing international environmental organizations such as the International Union for the Conservation of Nature (IUCN) had direct links to colonial commercial, scientific, and administrative networks (Cock and Fig 2002; Neumann 2002).

From smug (even triumphant) accounts of "innovative corporate partnerships" by conservation professionals to scathing (even moralistic) criticism by advocacy professionals functioning in their own competitive economies, the tone of debates is prone to extremes. Where are the more nuanced analyses of the conservation sector as, itself, a kind of industry? NGOs are not all alike as neocolonial instruments that commoditize wild lands. They differ in terms of their specific histories, strategies, and support bases. For example, there are tensions between an advocacy-based NGO such as the International Federation for Animal Welfare (IFAW) and a more scientifically oriented *in situ* conservation organization such as WCS. One effect of the full-tilt normative debate about whether corporate conservation entails the betrayal of indigenous peoples, grassroots environmentalism, and particular ways of valuing nature outside of markets has been to obscure finegrained comparison of the range of approaches emerging and their transformative roles within institutions or individual lives.

Critics of the growing influence of BINGOs as they manage proliferating protected areas worldwide have been most specifically and prolifically focused on the displacement of people in the interest of environmental protection; that literature is beyond the scope of this article, but introduces welcome specificity in ethical and empirical terms of debate. More broadly, arguments are emerging about the relationship of conservation to food security. Some argue that the influence of BINGOs has grown alongside biotechnology and the vertical integration of food and medicine production such that farmers are linked to chemical and pharmaceutical industries in new ways, in an era of biocapital that will be far more exclusionary and rapacious than industrial and imperial expansion was (see Moran, King, and Carlson 2001; Nattrass and Altomare 1999; Werhane 1985).

Others counter these cautionary arguments, and fear throwing conservation babies out with bathwater. Some advocate partnerships between corporate sectors and BINGOs for the protection of natural resources and wildlife, given the frustrating pace of public response to current trends in forest conversion and mass extinction. Effective action on timelines and geographical scales that matter, they argue, must sidestep unwieldy political and policy processes, or at least complement them with other approaches that remain accountable to norms of civil society and global good governance (Sanderson and Bird 1998). They further note the effectiveness of protected areas or private conservation set-asides, despite their exclusionary history. Such arguments highlight the importance of multiple political and institutional approaches to conservation in order for it to have any hope of success (Brandon, Redford, and Sanderson 1998; Naughton Treves, Holland, and Brandon 2005).

Few analysts have looked carefully, however, at global flows of funding into the preservation of biodiversity. One preliminary result, summarized in a post by Ananyo Battacharya to the blog for the journal *Nature*, comes from a presentation by Daniel Miller at recent Conservation Biology meetings in Canada. Miller's argument attracted attention for his statement that "starting from an average of $200 million per year, biodiversity aid rose dramatically after the creation of the Global Environment Facility in 1991 and the Earth Summit in Rio de Janeiro in 1992, which set international aid targets at $1.75 billion per year. Although the international community has never met that target in 1992 dollars, it has since hovered at about $1.25 billion per year." This contradicts OECD figures on conservation funding that were used by an international team to obtain an estimate of $3.13 billion spent on conservation aid in 2007 (Butchart et al., *Global biodiversity: Indicators of recent declines*, cited in Aldhous 2010). On one hand, these figures clarify the need for more funding to preserve biodiversity in many sites worldwide. They also highlight the need for better information about the types, targets, and transformations of such funding flows.[3] Such backdrops also relate to specific strategies emerging on the ground for hybrid governance, their effectiveness for conservation, and their other social consequences.

Pioneering partnerships

Recent years have seen an increase in the number of protected areas in the western Congo Basin. This has entailed a flurry of wildlife censuses, proposing of limits, classifying and managing territory, and forging international agreements. These intertwined efforts reached their peak in the Yaoundé Summit of 1999, which crystallized national and regional support levels for conservation. The Project for the Management of Ecosystems Adjacent to the Nouabalé-Ndoki National Park (PROGEPP) laid out WCS's efforts to work with and improve the ecological impacts of logging in the concession of the company Congolaise Industriel des Bois (CIB) in the northern Congo Basin, along the border with the RDS area in the CAR.

The PROGEPP experiment was an unprecedented effort at integrating conservation and logging activities. It originated in the early 1990s from the wary mutual respect built between WCS field biologist J. M. Fay and logging company manager M. Mevellec, both of whom were based along the Sangha River and had mandates to monitor and manage one of the largest concessionary forested expanses in Africa. If the cornerstone of the partnership was the mutual regard of these two men in their concessionary rivalry, the mortar and the motivation came from a wider context in the 1990s. The logging sector in those regions was intensifying at the same time the ascendance of animal-rights movements both challenged and bolstered the growth of international conservation NGOs, This contributed to a popular drive among consumers and green political movements in Western Europe and the US to protect animals and their habitat from the violence of commercial hunting that characterizes extractive industry in these tropical areas. Such concerns prompted demonstrations outside CIB headquarters in Germany, and enabled the emergence of the bushmeat issue as a "crisis" back in Washington, giving rise to a "Bushmeat Crisis Task Force" (or BCTF) that linked wildlife conservation agencies, zoos, animal welfare organizations, and policy communities. In the field, these highly mediatized issues fostered more formal WCS partnership with Congolese timber interests, specifically for stricter monitoring and enforcement of antidefaunation policies at the concession level.

In April 2000, WWF convened an expert workshop in Libreville, during which biologically important areas were identified, covering 54 percent of the basin. This led to the delineation of eleven "priority landscapes" for conservation intervention (more than 700,000 square kilometers).[2] Local administrations in some cases imposed conditions of service and infrastructural provision by the NGOs and private companies (such as tourism or hunting operators). These latter thus become, in effect, "concessionaires," either in partnership with or in competition with one another. As one key advisor to BCTF, Elizabeth Bennett (2001) has noted, "Logging companies are often the only significant institutional presence in large swathes of tropical forests ... [and] they are often the only institutions in a realistic position to solve [the problem of wildlife trade]." Components of such projects include preventing outside hunters and wildlife traders from using roads, restricting logging staff hunting practices, establishing "protected zones" within concessions, and hiring and training "ecoguards" to enforce regulations through concessions.

The project in northern Congo Brazzaville played out, however, on a field shaped by the Congo Basin Forest Partnership (CBFP), launched in 2002 as a USAID-sponsored, broad-based effort improve forest management in equatorial Africa. CBFP was a key part of nearly 200 million dollars in aid to the forest sector in the countries of Cameroon, Congo, the CAR, Gabon, the DRC, and Gabon. It fostered new dialogue between NGO, private-sector, and state actors. Building on the data and training of initiatives like the late 1990s "Global Forest Watch" under the auspices of the Washington-based World Resources Institute, as well as significant European campaigns to suppress and control illegal logging, the CBFP sought to concretize the use of good conservation science to inform policy, build institutions, and foster community-level monitoring of logging and hunting practices.

Yet the status of the guards in CIB's concessions, as employees of both the conservation project and the timber company, and further as sworn state officials with the power to make arrests, was unprecedented in conservation. They embodied new managerial alliances in the direction of monitoring and surveillance. Perhaps this also made them easy targets for those who were building movements in support of the rights of indigenous peoples in these forests, where such movements lag far behind those in other tropical forest regions worldwide. In PROGEPP territory in 2006, the process of Forest Stewardship Council (FSC) certification of the timber interests in that regionevaluated both ecological and social sustainability. It thus entailed inspection of conservation projects and company partnerships in its relationships to logging labor and other residents of the region. As a senior staff member of WCS in New York put it in recent meetings with the University of Michigan research team on these issues: "It is like you could see the human rights framework moving in to displace the animal rights framework that got us into the PROGEPP partnership in the first place."

The lead anthropologist involved in the team of researchers reporting on those relationships was University College London cultural anthropologist Jerome Lewis. The team's report opened serious dialogue with the company about allegations of abuse against forest foragers and other hunting groups within its concession area, involving the activities of conservation guards. The struggles to monitor and improve concession-level management of overhunting and to minimize its negative human-rights impacts on forest dwellers who rely on hunting and gathering fed into a broader project for

Lewis. He began to combine participatory methods for mapping forest use and conveying those data to timber industry planners and managers, with new efforts to train logging professionals in criteria of "social excellence."

That project, funded by the Tropical Forest Trust (TFT)[4] and the Fondation Chirac,[5] employed not only Lewis but also Congolese anthropologist Norbert Gami, who traveled between Congo Brazzaville and Cameroon to found and staff "Centers of Excellence." Prompted by the fact that effective controls on wildlife hunting and trade can all too often conflict with the enforcement of what have recently become more formal international frameworks such as the U.N. statement on indigenous rights of 2007, the work of the TFT and Chirac Foundation project came ultimately to rest more centrally on meeting goals of certification compliance in the Congo basin timber industry. These centers were intended to train young forestry professionals and potential state officials in environmental sectors from several states in the equatorial Africa region in the criteria and practices compatible with FSC certification of harvested timber.[6]

In a historical moment when NGOs are themselves proliferating, and those with more advocacy-based agendas are also eager for corporate partnerships, competition can be stiff for the purveyors of "best practices." In this case, critiques of conservation practice fed into and laid the groundwork for transformations in the timber sector, as its most prominent actors come to resemble NGOs in some of their concerns and mandates to manage concessions more sustainably.

As with NGOs, however, not all timber companies are alike. Younger or smaller-scale operators face larger challenges in meeting the criteria of FSC certification than does a transnational operation of such vast scale as CIB.[7] In discussions with timber professionals and their technical associations,[8] the ascendance of FSC certification over other possible certification options was not always a given. In meetings and discussions, suggestions arose that to embrace FSC criteria would mean the consolidation of power among large, mostly European-owned logging companies. Many of these were waiting in line to attain FSC certification status, managing their own staff and resources for both ecological and social monitoring of production systems for sustainability, and thus projecting a "greener" image (see Figure 8.1).

My visits to various professional timber companies and associations in Paris revealed the ways that environmental and health concerns had become central to the commercial success and social image of timber operations. The offices were far from opulent, and their shelves were filled with newsletters and manuals featuring photos of

Figure 8.1. Image on homepage of French Forest Products Group, Rougier, with slogan "Manage the forest, give life to the wood".

cuddly wildlife and smiling indigenous peoples. Younger staff members included a woman with a background in sociology, who had worked for several years to improve HIV testing, information, and medical service among the logging companies of Cameroon. Her mandate was not limited to health issues, however. It extended to possibilities that logging companies could participate in clean development mechanisms through renovation and restructuring of their own energy use and deforestation-related activities. For companies struggling to stay afloat in the wake of the recent financial crisis, during which worldwide demand for tropical hardwoods plummeted, such new directions and possibilities are not merely gestural; they are crucial to their survival.

Initiatives to improve ecological and social impacts in source sites for tropical timber fit like jigsaw puzzle pieces with the aforementioned activities of affiliated anthropologists in training personnel and fostering dialogue with local populations. They also engendered interventions in consumer countries, such as the training and education of young architects within France in the sourcing and use of certified timber from African forests. And yet, there were those in the logging sector's most affluent inner circles who dragged their heels about embracing NGO partnerships and certification criteria. At one joint meeting of ATBIT and IFIA (see footnote 8) I witnessed a heated discussion that would not have surprised Marcel Mauss, about the extent to which such partnerships and exchanges would transform or betray the core mission of timber companies, and their investors.

The Congo basin is a surprising crucible for an emerging international class of "green" scholars and professionals, working at the intersections of corporations, academic institutions, state and intergovernmental initiatives, and conservation NGOs. The leader of IFIA had come from a previous career in the petrochemical industry, but had a Ph.D. in philosophy. The President of ATBIT had come from an early career in fieldwork on wildlife conservation, and later research and teaching on community-based forest management; his Ph.D. was in tropical veterinary medicine, and his former students staffed and wrote reports for institutions such as the World Bank, Chatham House, and universities and E.U. offices in Belgium. Back at the University of Michigan, as Daniel Miller completed his PhD thesis, moving first into a professional post at the World Bank's Forest Program, and then into a faculty position at University of Illinois (Champagne Urbana), other students on whose committees I sit are studying monitoring mechanisms for the reduction of illegal logging, perfecting tools such as agent-based modeling and remote-sensing analysis of how forest cover responds to initiatives such as conservation aid and certification schemes.

Such evolving economies of green expertise pose their own challenges to questions of corporate social responsibility, for they create dense networks of actors who share intricately in the elaboration and confirmation of what constitutes "sustainability" from both ecological and social perspectives (Reed 2002). We thus see the emergence of several key strategic axes along which state, corporate, scientific, and community actors together—but not necessarily in commensurate power relations—elaborate a complex of new professional skills for "sustainable" forest management (see Kamdem Toham et al. 2003; Karsenty et al. 2008). Consequences include: harmonizing fiscal and forest exploitation regimes; elaboration and implementation of international conventions and agreements; formulation and reform of forest policies; production, circulation and analysis of datasets regarding forest resources (through inventories, regional observations, and remote sensing technologies); pioneering of management strategies on the ground; conservation planning (especially focused on transborder conservation areas); certification; and dialogue about supply chain transparency, traceability, and accountability.

Specific adjustments concern the approval of free prior informed-consent mechanisms; the preparation, review, and implementation of management plans; the timing and validity of monitoring efforts and sanctions; and the challenges of building effective social platforms that can transcend colonial and postcolonial legacies of patronage for dialogue with populations. Such systems elaborate upon and sometimes either elide or extend the limits of formal corporate responsibility. The image of forest industries as key authors of sustainable outcomes is especially easily produced given a dearth of ethnographic attention to their activities, relative to abundant studies that consider the various kinds of violence done in the name of conservation policies and practitioners.

None of this has happened overnight. In recent decades, as logging companies became more and more concerned with sustainable development and forest management, large conservation NGOs were internalizing corporate norms, metrics, and micropractices. These same NGOs were being taken as topics of study and professional apprenticeship by business schools, professional environment schools, and other organizations related to international management (Casadesus-Masanell and Mitchell 2007). Such developments seemed initially to favor both large-scale NGOs and large companies, and even to produce partnerships among them for certification and experiments with integrated management, while smaller-scale NGOs played watchdog roles. Meanwhile African nationals emerged from universities and international projects to form new networks of expertise in ecological and economic arenas, working on contract to conduct monitoring and management activities in ways perhaps best captured by the phrase "subcontracted sustainability." All these hybrid governance practices emerged from waves of decentralized natural resource management policies and neoliberal reforms, which drive the professionalization of regional- and local-level resource use planning and monitoring. However, they have proven contingent on fluctuating timber markets, and changing geopolitics of forest trade.

Conclusion:
relational norms and reciprocal transformation

The problems of scale and social density in corporate environmental and social accountability have been taken up in earnest in the literature on international law and business, particularly with respect to industries such as mining and oil and concepts such as climate justice (Osofsky 2007; Reibstein 2007). This article raises an even more nebulous set of arrangements among improbable but privileged partners, across code-law and common-law systems. The arrangements such as certification efforts, retraining of staff, and membership in trusts or task forces all hinge on largely voluntary practices, elaborated with respect to market mechanisms in volatile economies. Actors are grappling with scientific imprecision about ecological thresholds, and with competing definitions about human development standards. Their actions unfold within extremely impoverished settings that contain some of the most significant biodiversity on the planet. In this sense, my description of African forest sectors is not comparable to the Goldman Sachs Gift. Rather, these examples from the Congo Basin offer a set of norms and practices for corporate accountability that are relational, not always effective, but most often reciprocally transformative in the practice of commerce and conservation.

The past decade's sweeping critiques of BINGOs, or conservation approaches, has done little to explore variations in this sector, and ask where it can be effectively differentiated from related ones, such as monitoring, or advocacy, or even commerce. Few conclusions have been drawn about structural challenges that many of these organizations are themselves trying to solve—sometimes together, but often in competition with one another. For all their differences, environmental conservation organizations are constantly comparing themselves to one another, and competing with one another— territorially, financially, scientifically, and symbolically. They have historically looked to one another for models and lessons far more than to private sector actors. They thus present a fascinating case of corporate creep within their internal institutional cultures, which nonetheless remain distinct from many corporate strategies and features. One senior conservation scientist and administrator recently told me that he has learned two things in the course of his work within a BINGO: to be patient (results take time), and to allow others credit for their ideas (even, often, for his). The first bit of wisdom contradicts much about what private donors desire and require; the second contradicts basic (if informal) rules about work in competitive scientific sectors. These are lived contradictions, working themselves out over the course of careers that span enormous social change, such as the birth and maturation of NGOs.

Some conservation NGOs boast modern histories of alignment with environmental and social justice causes such as the opposition to large dams, nuclear power, and oil development. This makes trends toward increased reliance on partnerships with and financial patronage from private industry all the more difficult for professional conservationists to justify, even as such trends are difficult to avoid (Büscher and Whande 2007). Hoffman (2000, Hoffman and Bertels 2010) notes that only Greenpeace, among nearly one hundred US-based environmental organizations, effectively maintains a policy of no corporate ties at this point. Despite the cheery news in NGOs' annual reports, such trends are not all about clear forward movement toward new strategies. Conservation professionals at various levels are still engaged in multiple, competing endeavors each day, as the parameters of "sustainable" practice shift in many sectors concomitantly (Bartley 2003). Conservation organizations are faced with steep learning curves about corporate structure and function, including key arenas that are transforming conservation practice, such as marketing and advertising, time frames for strategic planning, and information and management systems for personnel within NGOs.

This article does not report on the results of institutional ethnography within conservation organizations, so much as it offers ideas in a call for more such work. The contradictions of contemporary conservation merit ethnographic attention not only for their consequences in developing regions and among marginalized populations, about which an increasingly robust literature spearheaded by anthropologists has emerged (West and Brockington 2006). They also create political conflict and social change within the boardrooms and conference corridors of NGOs, about which ethnographers have been more silent (though Brosius is working with teams of students to study such issues; see his reflections on these issues in Brosius 1999).

As ethnographers experiment with new modes of research on these issues, WCS is by no means alone in experimenting with the new conservation forms chronicled here, and they have many avid potential business partners (Groves, Klein, and Braden 1995; Kate and Laird 2000; Reichert, Webb, and Thomas 2000). Whether they are capable of pushing for positive environmental change in the public and other sectors through such partnerships remains to be seen; the current trend toward timber certification in Congo's logging operations could be seen as an example in the affirmative. However, it required politically engaged anthropologists and NGOs with specific advocacy mandates to catalyze and direct such trends. Rather than WCS "pushing," one might argue that they are caught up, along with companies and states, in a "push me-pull you" situation from which emerge new standards and practices, many of which are still only scattered or ephemeral in their purview.

To further explore these differences would entail developing an analytical approach that distinguishes between the generation of profit and these NGOs' increasingly competitive and market-savvy searches for public, philanthropic, and member-based support. It might also require attention, across sites and along new commercial circuits, as well as more deeply within organizations, to the contradictions between upper-level leadership practices and discourses and the work of field personnel. The changing strategies described here raise questions I have addressed elsewhere (Hardin 2011) about how conservation NGOs are historically entangled with corporate actors.

All of us who are involved in education, research, and policy on these issues are perforce enmeshed in entire sectors that are being transformed. This article has shied away from discussing the extent to which the very gifts that enable my academic unit to improve its infrastructure and function competitively in a rapidly changing world come from companies doing damage to communities and ecosystems across the world (but see Kirsch 2010). Crowding around this article are also other urgent unanswered questions about future trends (for instance the growth in rates of global land transfers, or the massive transition in capital investment in Africa away from European and toward Asian economies). Overnight, during my revisions to this essay, the news broke of stolen credits in Europe's landmark scheme for trade by industries seeking to mitigate their high carbon emissions. Considering the newest instruments available for protecting standing forests and limiting the ravaging effects of climate change was already an urgent imperative; it is now on even shakier ground. Such developments call for an even more expansive application of core anthropological methods and concepts than those I sketch here for the conservation sector. What might Marcel Mauss have made of the notions of mitigation currently being adopted, tested, and contested through such policy options as cap-and-trade? These, more than timber certification or biodiversity conservation, appear as new frontiers of exchange that will shape forest life.

Taking Mauss's notion of the gift seriously compels us to study gestures or events in their social context for how they illuminate the complicated relationships among ostensibly distinct or even opposed communities of actors. Here, that means questioning CSR as a dominant idea for finding solutions to contemporary asymmetries in wealth production and distribution and environmental health, or even for describing the way that various organizations are facing such challenges. State power persists amidst new mandates for corporations and NGOs. Thus power relations that are not at all new are nested within and reinforced by emerging matrices of professional expertise, self-regulation, and intervention by nongovernmental organizations in local and transnational institutions. Ethnography is key to understanding how organizations are undergoing internal transformations, elaborating relational norms in their interactions with one another, and accepting that certain tensions will persist, unresolved.

Ideas of corporate accountability are confronted daily by a growing and increasingly diverse community of conservation professionals. They also confront contradictory ideas of themselves as local experts, scientists, managers, and moral crusaders for the protection of remaining wilderness against human encroachment. Their days are spent at the crossroads of rapid, results-oriented private-sector practices, long-range financial and scientific planning for risk management, incremental interdisciplinary analysis of ecological and social complexity, and incessant political and institutional challenges that characterize the messy business of conservation implementation. They labor under the weight of what Mauss and Durkheim would call "collective representations" about what is worth saving, and why. They share some of that labor with private sector professionals who engage with conservation goals. All of them work, alongside growing numbers of anthropologists, under the constraints and possibilities of what we might call "collective contradictions" such as those I have sketched here: wilderness transactions, developed protected areas, the regulated primitive, and the executive environmentalist.

Notes

1. I draw from her talk in January of 2008, posted to a website compiled by Rachel Weisshaar (edited by Meaghan Parker), last accessed on January 10, 2011: http://www.wilsoncenter.org/index.cfm?topic_id=1413&categoryid=A82CCAEE-65BF-E7DC-46B3B37D0A3A575F&fuseaction=topics.events_item_topics&event_id=345945.
2. The Wilson Center event at which Chicchón spoke launched a series "New Horizons at the Nexus of Conflict, Natural Resources, and Health," funded jointly by USAID's Office of Natural Resources Management, its Office of Population and Reproductive Health, and its Office of Conflict Management and Mitigation. The series serves as a useful archive of applied perspectives on the links between business, politics, and human security issues worldwide.

3. Working for the Macarthur Foundation before his doctoral study, Miller found it difficult to obtain accurate information about quantities and flows of money from private donors or governments. Using the independent international development aid database AidData.org offered an opportunity to investigate and revise recent figures.
4. TFT is an organization with "supply chain expertise" that works to ensure "responsibility" in products from tropical forests' being delivered to worldwide markets. For more information see http://www.otabenga.org/node/140 (last accessed January 19, 2011)
5. The Fondation Chirac, created in 2007, works to combat deforestation; see http://www.fondationchirac.eu/programmes/lutte-contre-deforestation-et-desertification/ (last accessed January 19, 2011); for Chirac's address to European architecture students on using certified wood, see http://vimeo.com/18527283 (last accessed January 19, 2011).
6. For information about how Lewis and Gami designed radio- and Palm Pilot–based communication and mapping strategies for conveying forest dwellers' preferences, see http://www.otabenga.org/node/140 (last accessed January 19, 2011).
7. Created in 1996, the Interafrican Forestry Industries Association (IFIA) represents the interests of the private-sector forest industries in the Congo Basin and West Africa. It is based in Paris, out of shared offices with the Association International des Bois Inter-Tropicale (ATBIT).
8. A recent survey of logging in Central Africa suggested two distinct periods: a phase (1950 to 1970) dominated by large, foreign concessions; and the last 15 years, with more national concessions, more varied in size, ownership, and markets (Ruiz Pérez et al. 2005: 225, 234).

References

Lemos, Maria Carmen, and Arun Agrawal. 2006. Environmental governance. *Annual Review of Environment and Resources* 31: 297–325.
Aldhous, Peter. 2010. Rio hopes of conservation cash were never met. *The New Scientist.* http://www.newscientist.com/article/dn19128-rio-hopes-of-conservation-cash-w (last accessed 1 September 2010).
Bartley, Tim. 2003. Certifying forests and factories: States, social movements, and the rise of private regulation in the apparel and forest products fields. *Politics and Society* 31 (3): 433–64.
Bhattacharya, Ananyo. 2010. Biodiversity aid lags in corrupt countries. http://blogs.nature.com/news/thegreatbeyond/2010/07/biodiversity_aid_lags_in_corru.html.
Brandon, K., K. H. Redford, and S. E. Sanderson. 1998. *Parks in peril: People, politics, and protected areas.* Washington: Island Press.
Brosius, J. Peter. 1999. Analyses and interventions: Anthropological engagements with environmentalism. *Current Anthropology* 40: 277–309.
Büscher, Bram, and W. Whande. 2007. Whims of the winds of time? Emerging trends in biodiversity conservation and protected area management. *Conservation and Society* 5(1): 22–43.
Carrier, James G. and Paige West, Eds. 2009. Virtualism, governance and practice: Vision and execution in environmental conservation. Oxford: Berghahn Books.

Casadesus-Masanell, Ramon, and Jordan Mitchell. 2007. *World Wildlife Fund for Nature.* Cambridge, Mass.: Harvard Business School Publishing.

Chapin, Mac. 2004. A challenge to conservationists. *World Watch Magazine* 17 (6): 17–31.

Cock, Jacklyn, and David Fig. 2002 From colonial to community based conservation: Environmental justice and transformation of national parks in South Africa (1994–1998). In *Environmental justice in South Africa,* by D. A. McDonald. Cape Town: University of Cape Town Press.

Cepek, Michael L. 2010. Can nature be governed? Design, practice and power in environmental conservation. *Focaal—European Journal of Global and Historical Anthropology* 58: 131–34.

Dowie, Mark. 2005. Conservation refugees: When protecting nature means kicking people out. *Orion Magazine,* November 2005 (http://www.orionmagazine.org/index.php/articles/article/161/; accessed April 20, 2010).

Dupré, Georges. 1982. *Un rdre et sa destruction.* Paris: Editions de l'Office de la Recherche Scientifique et Technique Outre-Mer (Collection Mémoires no. 93).

Ferguson, Jim. 1990. *The anti-politics machine: "Development," depoliticization, and bureaucratic power in Lesotho.* Cambridge: Cambridge University Press.

Ferguson, Jim. 1999. *Expectations of modernity: Myths and meanings of urban life on the Zambian copperbelt.* Berkeley and Los Angeles: University of California Press.

Groves, Craig R., Mary L. Klein, and Thomas F. Breden. 1995. Natural heritage programs: Public-private partnerships for biodiversity conservation. *Wildlife Society Bulletin* 23 (4): 784–90.

Haeckel, Stephan. 1999. About the future and nature of interactive marketing. *Journal of Interactive Marketing* 12 (1): 63–71.

Hardin, Rebecca. 2011. Concessionary politics. *Current Anthropology* 52 (4): S113–S125.

Hoffman, Andrew. 2000. Integrating environmental and social issues into corporate practice. *Environment* 42: 22.

Hoffman, Andrew, and Stephanie Bertels. 2010. Who is part of the environmental movement? Assessing network linkages between NGOs and corporations. In *Good cop bad cop: Environmental NGOs and their strategies toward business* 48–69. Washington: Resources for the Future Press.

Kamdem-Toham, A., A. W. Adeleke, N. D. Burgess, R. Carroll, J. D'amico, E. Dinerstein, D. M. Olson, and L. Some. (2003) Forest conservation in the Congo Basin, *Science* 299 (5605): 346.

Kate, Kerry T., and Sarah A. Laird. 2000. Biodiversity and business: Coming to terms with the "grand bargain." *International Affairs* 76: 241–64.

Karsenty, A., I. Garcia Drigo, M. G. Piketty, and B. Singer. 2008. "Regulating industrial forest concessions in Central Africa and South America. *Forest Ecology and Management* 256: 1498–1508.

Kirsch, Stuart. 2010. Sustainability and the BP oil spill. *Dialectical Anthropology* 34: 295–300.

Lowe, Celia. 2004. *Wild profusion: Biodiversity conservation in an Indonesian archipelago.* Princeton: Princeton University Press.

Elisabeth L. Bennett, 2001. The joint effort of timber certification. *Conservation Biology* 15(2): 318–319.

Moran, Katy, Steven R. King, and Thomas J. Carlson. 2001. Biodiversity prospecting: Lessons and prospects. *Annual Review of Anthropology* 30: 505–526.

Naughton Treves, Lisa, M. Buck Holland, and K. Brandon. 2005. The role of protected areas in conserving biodiversity and sustaining local livelihoods. *Annual Review of Environmental Resources* 30: 219–52.

Nattrass, Brian F., and Mary Altomare. 1999. *The natural step for business: Wealth, ecology, and the evolutionary corporation.* Gabriola Island, B.C.: New Society Publishers.

Neumann, Roderick. 2002. *Imposing wilderness: Struggles over livelihood and nature preservation in Africa*. Berkeley and Los Angeles: University of California Press.

Oates, John F. 1999. *Myth and reality in the rain forest: How conservation strategies are failing in West Africa*. Berkeley and Los Angeles: University of California Press.

Osofsky, Hari. 2007. Local approaches to transnational corporate responsibility: Mapping the role of subnational climate change litigation. *Pacific McGeorge Global Business & Development Law Journal* 20: 143–50.

Reed, Darryl. 2002. Resource extraction industries in developing countries. *Journal of Business Ethics* 39: 199.

Reibstein, Richard. 2007. Time to get real: The necessity of legal accountability for responsible transnational commerce. *Environmental Law Reporter* 37: 10414–32.

Reichert, Alan K., Marion S. Webb, and Edward G. Thomas. 2000. Corporate support of ethical and environmental policies: A financial management perspective. *Journal of Business Ethics* 25: 53.

Rubino, Michael C. 2000. *Biodiversity Finance*. International Affairs. 76 (2): 223–240.

Ruiz Pérez, M., D. Ezzine de Blas, R. Nasi, J. A. Sayer, M. Sassen, C. Angoué, N. Gami, O. Ndoye, G. Ngono, J.-C. Nguinguiri, D. Nzala, B. Toirambe, and Y. Yalibanda. 2005. Logging in the Congo Basin: A multi-country characterization of timber companies. *Forest Ecology and Management* 214: 221–36.

Sanderson, Steven E., and Shawn Bird. 1998. The new politics of protected areas. In *Parks in peril*, eds. K. Brandon, K. H. Redford, and S. E. Sanderson, 441–54. Washington: Island Press.

Walley, Christine. 2004. *Rough waters: Nature and development in an African marine park*. Princeton: Princeton University Press.

West, Paige. 2005. *Conservation is our government now: The politics of ecology in Papua New Guinea*. Durham: Duke University Press.

West, Paige, and D. Brockington. 2006. An anthropological perspective on some unexpected consequences of protected areas. *Conservation Biology* 20 (3): 609–16.

Werhane, Patricia. 1985. "Introduction." In *Profit and responsibility*, eds. P. Werhane and K. D'Andrade, 1–13. Lewiston, N.Y.: Edwin Mellen Press.

Wilshusen, Peter R., Steve R. Brechin, Crystal L. Fortwangler, and Paige C. West. 2002. Reinventing a square wheel: Critique of a resurgent "Protection Paradigm" in international biodiversity conservation. *Society and Natural Resources* 15: 17–40.

Rebecca Hardin holds her degree in anthropology from Yale University. She has taught at Yale, Paris I (Sorbonne), the National Museum of Natural History in Paris, McGill University, and the University of Michigan. She has held research fellowships in the US at Yale's Center for International and Area Studies, the Harvard Academy of International and Area Studies, and in France at the Institut de la Recherche pour le Développement and the University of Orleans. She is grateful for support for this article from her collaborative work with UM colleagues on an NSF-coupled human and natural systems grant, number 0709545.

– Chapter 9 –

ENGINEERING RESPONSIBILITY
Environmental Mitigation and the Limits of Commensuration in a Chilean Mining Project
Fabiana Li

"Responsible mining" has become a ubiquitous term in the mining industry, and is meant to convey a company's commitment to the environment and the people living in the vicinity of its operations. Mining corporations usually showcase "responsible mining" initiatives by establishing environmental monitoring programs, adopting industry codes of conduct, and implementing community development programs. These examples of Corporate Social Responsibility (CSR) could be seen as efforts to incorporate ethical considerations and moral values into a "good neighbor policy," or they could be dismissed as marketing strategies aimed at obtaining community consent and increasing profit (see Raman 2010). While scholars have called attention to the inherent contradictions of "sustainable mining" and the rhetoric of corporate accountability (see Benson and Kirsch 2010), CSR is presented by the mining industry as an effort to balance "the diverse needs of communities and the imperative to protect the environment with the ever present need to make a profit" (Jenkens 2004:24).

My aim in this chapter is to elucidate how various actors enable or challenge efforts to balance community demands with corporate interests. I examine how CSR takes shape at a time when *environmental* concerns have become the focus of corporate efforts to demonstrate a commitment to ethical practices. While a growing literature on CSR has analyzed the social dimensions of corporate practices (e.g. Frynas 2005; Sharp 2006; Watts 2005; Welker 2009), less attention has been paid to the work of engineers, scientists, and other mining professionals whose work informs CSR initiatives. As transnational mining illustrates, CSR does not relate only to a company's investment in communities and good relations with local institutions. Corporations must also convince the public that mining will not generate pollution or reduce the availability of water resources. Increasingly, CSR depends on the production and dissemination of scientific data and technical information about a company's environmental management plans.

In Chile, increased attention to environmental management in CSR has gone hand in hand with a move toward privatization in the mining industry and an increase in foreign investment. Like many other developing countries, Chile experienced a "mining boom" following the adoption of economic liberalization policies during the 1980s and 1990s.[1] Some of these policies were implemented during the military dictatorship of Augusto Pinochet, but were maintained after Chile's return to democracy in 1990. In a context of democracy and political stability, the government's acceptance of this neoliberal model already in place helped usher in a series of "mega-projects" in the mining sector (Danús 2007: 171). One of the most controversial of these new projects was Pascua-Lama, a gold mine owned by the Canadian Barrick Gold Corporation, which entered the construction phase in November 2009 with the aim of producing its first bar of gold by 2013. The mine, which straddles the border with Argentina, is at the source of a watershed that sustains agricultural production in the Huasco Valley, home to small-scale agriculturalists and producers of grapes for the national and international markets. As environmentalist campaigns against the project gained international notoriety, Barrick sought to create an image of "environmental responsibility" to counter accusations of depleting water resources, destroying glaciers, and putting the valley's agricultural production at risk.

This chapter focuses on Pascua-Lama to examine the cultural dynamics that shape what companies broadly conceive as "environmental mitigation." My analysis is based on two months of research between November 2009 and January 2010, conducted in the capital city of Santiago and in communities in the Huasco Valley. In addition to talking to agriculturalists, NGO representatives, and activists, I interviewed 20 engineers, geologists, anthropologists, and other professionals either directly or indirectly involved with the mining industry. Some of them were employed by mining companies, while others worked for consulting firms, research institutes, and universities.

Compensation agreements, environmental management, and other CSR initiatives rest on what I call a *logic of equivalence* that makes the possible consequences of a mining project commensurate with the mining companies' mitigation plans.[2] Espeland (1998) defines *commensuration* as the comparison of different entities according to a common metric; two values or goods can be said to be commensurable if they can be measured in the same units, such as money. In the context of mining, commensuration makes it possible to compare (and ultimately reconcile) different forms of value, such that, for example, water pollution can be offset with monetary compensation, or a company's water usage can be measured against the needs of agriculturalists downstream from the mine. According to Espeland, price, cost-benefit ratios, and other forms of quantification and standardization make different entities comparable. My concern with *equivalence* draws on but seeks to broaden this conception of commensuration by examining other ways in which disparate entities are brought into relation.

Although people do not always use the concept explicitly, a concern with equivalence is central to many aspects of mining controversy, including disagreements about water availability, adequate compensation, and the value of resources. To shed light on these controversies, I explore attempts to make various entities measurable and comparable, or conversely, to challenge the mechanisms that allow for such comparisons. Specifically, I show how the law serves as a common standard that facilitates commensuration in the context of mining, but also leaves room for contestation. In the first part of this chapter, I describe how legal mechanisms allow engineers to make mining impacts commensurable, and to design environmental mitigation plans in compliance with environmental regulations. Commensuration enables companies to balance their economic interests with their ethical responsibilities, and to restrict their social and environmental commitments to the mandates of the law while emphasizing their adherence to CSR principles.

In the second part of the chapter, I focus on the Pascua-Lama mine to show how a logic of equivalence influenced ways of evaluating the project's effects on water resources and the negotiations between the company and local agriculturalists. I examine the processes of inclusion and exclusion involved in these processes of commensuration. While legal codes make commensuration possible and enable engineers to measure, compare, and reconcile the costs and benefits of a project, the law is neither fixed nor uncontestable. Faced with mounting public pressure, companies must negotiate the ambiguous boundaries of the law as they respond to the growing demands of communities, governments, and international actors. In the final part of the chapter, I describe how local and international campaigns against the mine challenged the company's claims of environmental responsibility by focusing on the presence of glaciers in the mine's area of operations. Glaciers came to represent an incommensurable value, something that could not be negotiated and thus made the project inherently unviable.[3] By changing the scale of the problem (making a local problem into one of planetary dimensions), glaciers brought into view elements that disrupted the logic of equivalence, as well as new forms of ethical reasoning that extend beyond the usual concerns of CSR.

Engineering solutions through commensuration

Chile's characterization as a "mining country" (a phrase commonly used in the mining industry and in popular discourse) is usually justified by its ranking as the world's leading producer and exporter of copper. Chile's copper mines account for more than 35 percent of total world copper production, and more than 50 percent of the country's exports (Ruiz-Dana 2007). Pascua-Lama might have gone largely unnoticed in a country of intensive mining activity, but the project had some distinguishing characteristics that are significant for understanding the challenges and notoriety that it brought with it. First, Pascua-Lama is touted by the industry as the world's largest remaining gold deposit, and the first binational mining project. The mine is considered a model for a number of mines to be developed along the Andes mountain range that marks the border between Chile and Argentina. The Mining Integration Treaty ratified by the two countries in 1997 aimed to open up this area to mining activity by creating what some critics have called a "virtual territory," administered according to the interests of transnational companies (Luna, Padilla, and Alcayaga 2004). Like other attempts to create cross-border regions to facilitate the flow of money, technology, and goods,[4] the Treaty could be seen as a form of reterritorialization that gives the illusion of a borderless world, yet is driven by and serves to advance strategic neoliberal interests (cf. Sparke 2005).

Another important characteristic of the Pascua Lama project was the geography of the mine site. The key controversy that emerged from Barrick's public presentation of its Environmental Impact Assessment (EIA)[5] related to the mine's location at the top of the watershed. Opponents of the project argued that glaciers at the mine site served as water reservoirs that were critical in regulating the water cycle in this arid region. It was this argument, more than any other, which captured the imagination of environmental activists nationally and internationally. The notoriety of Pascua-Lama was unprecedented—no other mining project had sparked such strong opposition in a country where many people equate mineral extraction with the nation's progress and development.

The controversies surrounding Pascua-Lama provided a rich site to explore processes of commensuration in the early stages of a mine's development. To do this, I focused my attention on engineers and their ways of transforming a project's "impacts" into measurable, quantifiable data. The engineers I interviewed were not a homogeneous group, nor did they have the same level of involvement with the Pascua-Lama project. As in other industries operating within a globalized economy, mining companies typically delegate different parts of a project to specialists in multiple locations: the company's headquarters, local offices, or transnational consulting firms. The organization of labor within the mining industry makes commensuration necessary, since information must be aggregated (or discarded) as it passes through the company's various divisions and levels of management.

For some of the engineers that I talked to, the specific nature of their tasks—and their sense of disconnect from the larger project—framed out complex ethical considerations from their technical work. Few people see the "complete picture," one engineer told me, recalling that he had been hired as a consultant at an early stage of the Pascua-Lama project many years earlier to help the company determine how much water was available for the mine's operations. "As consultants, we limit ourselves to the question that is put to us," he said. In this case, the question was "How much water is there (in the watershed)?" His role was not to make a judgment on whether that amount was sufficient for the mine's processes, or to determine the mine's possible effects on water quantity for agricultural uses. For people in the Huasco Valley, "How much water is there?" is a question of vital importance and a source of constant preoccupation, since they associate water scarcity with profound consequences for their agricultural livelihoods and ways of life. For the mining company, however, water scarcity is not in itself an impediment to mining. Alternatives can always be found, even if it means transporting and desalinating sea water (a costly but increasingly common practice in newer projects). The determinant factor is whether the value of the minerals to be mined justifies additional expenditures.

This way of framing a problem facilitates commensuration, allowing project managers to make cost-benefit calculations using the quantitative data produced by their consultants. Implicit in this approach is an attempt to separate the "technical" work of engineers from "social" and "ecological" considerations. Sandra, who worked for an engineering firm in Santiago, explained how she saw this separation with relation to her work:

> We are engineers, and we are an engineering firm. Our commitment is to the client, and we have to help clients carry out their project. We [cannot] get fundamentalist with environmental themes. We help clients so that they can abide by the legal norms, and we try to also inculcate 'good practices.'… But in the end it's their decision.… In general, clients have sustainable development policies, and in their mission statements there is a commitment to the environment, but at the moment of deciding whether to accept a project investment or not, they limit themselves to what the law mandates.

Sandra made it clear that generally, companies do not go beyond the legal requirements when implementing a mitigation plan, and while she can make recommendations based on "good practice" guidelines, companies will not adopt them unless it is considered cost-efficient. The law served as the basis for making equivalences, enabling her to design technologies that met the legal permissible limits for particulate emissions or water quality standards, and allowing the client to evaluate her recommendations based on its legal obligations and economic objectives. Unlike conventional systems of metrics that facilitate commensuration, however, the law is not a fixed, unambiguous, or uncontested standard. Companies today face increasing pressure to adopt international standards (e.g. international certification schemes or protocols on indigenous rights), and their codes of conduct are scrutinized by a more vigilant public (see Bendell 2004).

Sandra was cognizant of the law's gaps and ambiguities, which were particularly problematic when it came to community relations. Although she emphasized the purely technical nature of their job, which did not involve dealing with communities, there were ways in which the "social" increasingly encroached upon their work. She and her colleagues had to figure out how to mine around cemeteries to avoid community conflicts, or how to obtain water for the mine's operations without inciting local opposition. In the last decade, she had seen that communities had begun to demand more from corporations. For Sandra, the difficulty of dealing with communities was precisely the fact that there were no legal norms to follow, and companies' attempts to quell conflicts by offering compensation were creating a new set of problems:

> What is happening right now is something very peculiar.... [M]ining companies are kind of regretting, or backing out of, these compensation programs because they're finding that communities never stop asking for things. One of the complexities that I see is that none of this is legislated. Because if you have a standard for air quality, or for particulate matter emissions, you know exactly how much you can emit, at what moment you have to take precautionary measures and when you don't need to. But with the community there are no such laws that tell you what you should do to maintain control of the community.

Other engineers and community relations people that I spoke to also mentioned the absence of legal guidelines for handling social concerns. Something as incommensurable as alterations to the aesthetic quality of the scenery (which companies had begun to include in their EIAs), or relocation plans, could not be easily quantified and were not legislated. In these cases, compensation allowed communities to form direct relationships with the mining companies and negotiate on their own behalf, bypassing third parties such as governments and NGOs (Kirsch 2006: 127). Monetary compensation thus became another way of making equivalences, but this was problematic precisely because it blurred the boundaries of the law.

Some mining critics consider monetary compensation a way of co-opting local actors, and indeed, the way compensation agreements are negotiated is often legally questionable (the case of the canal users' association, discussed below, is a case in point). For the engineers, however, the possibility of compensation meant that the potentially negative consequences of a project could always be mitigated—if not with a technical solution, with a monetary one (the latter being sometimes more economical). In their feasibility studies, a logic of equivalence served to characterize mining projects as technically viable, legally sound, and economically justified. Indeed, the engineers I talked to considered that every mining project they had ever worked on was technically feasible and executable—even one as controversial as Pascua-Lama. This was because from their point of view, most technical issues in mining had already been resolved; the technologies used were familiar and standardized, and all risks could be controlled. In the next section, I explore how this logic of equivalence became fundamental to Barrick's claim of "environmental responsibility."

Water equivalence:
Measurement, compensation, and the law

As in other conflicts over mining (see Bebbington and Williams 2008), water became a central point of contention in debates about Pascua-Lama. What is significant about Pascua-Lama, however, is that it involved a particular kind of water: bodies of ice situated around the ore deposit to be mined. When the company presented its Environmental Impact Assessment (EIA) for approval in 2000, it contained a plan to "relocate" three glaciers at the mine site. According to a report submitted to the regional environmental authorities, the company would use a hydraulic digger to remove almost 20 hectares of ice sitting on top of the mineral deposit. Trucks would transport blocks of ice to another glacier of similar geological and geomorphological characteristics (Barrick 2000), where they would fuse together over time. Barrick's EIA was approved by Chilean authorities in 2001, but the project was put on hold because of the low price of metals. Over the next few years, the company identified additional gold reserves, bringing up estimated reserves from 2.3 million to 17.8 million ounces of gold. In 2005, Barrick presented a modified EIA to account for this and other changes in the project. As part of a 15-month consultation process, Barrick organized door-to-door information campaigns and public hearings to present its EIA to the public. It was during this time that opposition to the project intensified and gained international notoriety.[6]

Over the project's long trajectory, the glaciers became a prominent symbol in international environmentalist campaigns, and the focus of debate whenever Pascua-Lama was discussed. Scientific studies commissioned by the company and government institutions called into question whether these bodies of ice were "true" glaciers. Responding to comments made on its EIA, the company argued that the bodies of ice at Pascua-Lama did not share many characteristics with "traditional" glaciers, such as movement and basal sliding (Barrick 2005). In newsletters and public presentations, the company downplayed their significance by calling them "ice reservoirs" or "glacierettes" that were insignificant in terms of their contribution to the hydrological balance of the watershed.

Amidst disagreement about the nature of the glaciers, water availability emerged as a key issue in arguments presented by the company as well as by its critics. In spite of the common focus on water, however, each party involved had a different understanding of how water availability should be measured, managed, and safeguarded. According to the company, the water to be drawn from freshwater sources on the Chilean side was a small amount: a total flow of 43 l/s (liters per second). For local people, however, even this small an amount was significant, given the low levels of precipitation in the area and the periodic droughts characteristic of the valley.

Antonio, a Barrick engineer I interviewed, dismissed the importance of the glaciers by focusing on the use of water by the mine compared to the total amount of water in the watershed:

> According to the EIA, the water that will be used for the project is not even one percent of the river flow…. Let's imagine that all this [he motioned to the office where we were sitting] is the Huasco River watershed. This is the glacier [holding up his keychain]. Do you think the glacier is going to contribute water to the river? No. It's the snowfall, which is part of the normal water cycle. If there is no snow, there is no water…. If you see photos you will realize that [the glaciers] are very small, they are irrelevant….

Glaciologists calculate the amount of water that a glacier holds based on its size and density, which gives the glacier's "water equivalent" (Azócar and Brenning 2008). Compared to other glaciers, the water equivalent of the Pascua-Lama glaciers is small. Yet when I mentioned this to local agriculturalists, they insisted that while the amount of water used for the project might be small, it was significant when seen *proportionally* to the very small amount of water that they have available. Over the years, the valley has experienced periods of drought and floods, a cyclical pattern that agriculturalists are attuned to. When I visited the valley in early 2010, it was during a period of drought and people said it had been more than ten years since the last heavy rains, the kind of rain that makes the nearby desert bloom. The "blooming desert" (*desierto florido*) is a phenomenon usually seen every ten years or so, but the last one had happened in 1997.

Even more worrisome for people was the fact that a section of the river had dried up, something they had never experienced in their lifetimes. Some people attributed this change to the mine's operations, including prospecting, road building, and other construction activities they believed were already depleting the glaciers and disrupting surface and subterranean water flows. Yet the idea that mining activity could affect water levels was simply "mythological," according to Antonio, and was only used by people opposed to the mine because it "sells." He was convinced that water availability was simply not a problem—there was enough water, it was just a matter of using it responsibly. And agriculturalists, rather than mining companies, were the ones that needed to learn to use it more efficiently:

The issue is not water. The issue is: How do I manage the water, how do I use it efficiently? Here people are super irresponsible with water use. In this watershed, because of its climatic characteristics, the losses just from channeling the water are about 40%. So it's a simple calculation. If in this valley there are 11,800 water shares, and if 40% is lost by channeling, you lose 4000 water shares just by channeling the water. And out of these 4000 shares, we are going to use 0.01% (43 liters per second). Today the issue in the valley is not the resource, but how I *use* it, how I *manage* it....

These calculations did little to assuage the fears of those who see their most valuable resource threatened by mining activity. For some local farmers, what was at stake was not simply the amount of water to be used for the project, but that building a mine at the top of the watershed might further reduce water levels in a valley where water scarcity had been a constant challenge.

The company's calculations may have failed to convince some agriculturalists, but they supported the company's claim that it was safeguarding the valley's water resources and abiding by Chilean law. Indeed, the company had legally acquired the rights to the water it needed. According to the Chilean Water Code, water rights are separate from land rights, meaning that ownership of a piece of property does not automatically give the owner rights over the water that flows through it (Bauer 1998). Water rights (in the form of shares) can be bought, traded, and sold in the market. The company was following the laws, but as the Water Code illustrates, Chilean laws—widely lauded by free-market proponents as a model for neoliberal restructuring that other countries should emulate—facilitate the operations of mining companies.

Critics of the Pascua-Lama project argued that the approval of Barrick's EIA demonstrated the collusion between private and state interests, and even outright corruption. Those who defended the project, however, pointed to the fact that Pascua-Lama was subject to one of the most thorough and exhaustive reviews in the country's history. After the EIA was submitted for evaluation, environmental authorities presented the company with a series of questions and observations, which included those submitted by the public. In response, the company produced a 529-page addendum responding to each of these observations and proposing improvements and modifications to the project.

While the company followed and even went beyond the legal requirements for public consultation in the EIA process, this was not enough to gain the approval of local communities. Most crucially, Barrick needed the support of the Junta de Vigilancia del Rio del

Huasco, the administrative entity that represents canal users and manages water use in the valley. The Junta was initially opposed to the project, but during the EIA consultation process, Barrick entered into an agreement with its board of directors, effectively turning the Junta into an ally of the company. As part of this agreement, Barrick offered the Junta USD 60 million in compensation for "direct or indirect potential damages to the canal users" (Jarur and Maldonado 2005). The money would be payable in yearly USD 3 million installments over the mine's 20 year lifespan, and was to be invested in the maintenance, construction, and improvement of irrigation infrastructure.

Putting a price on potential damages to canal users was one way of making equivalences, but the participatory process of evaluating the EIA could also be seen as a form of commensuration. As Espeland (1998) shows, public participation is sometimes seen as the commensuration of values, an attempt to turn all actors into equal players in the decision-making process. From this perspective, commensuration is a way to make the environmental evaluation process more rational and democratic. This form of commensuration has become central to Corporate Social Responsibility, which aims to align the different interests of "stakeholders" as equivalent in relation to a common goal (cf. Blaser 2009); in this case, that common goal was the management of water resources. CSR thus incorporates communities, governments, NGOs, and other actors into the participatory process, creating relations of collaboration that give an illusion of consensus (see Li 2009). In the Pascua-Lama case, Barrick's strategy was to enroll the Junta in the elaboration of the EIA. As part of the agreement, the company transferred funds so that the Junta could hire an environmental consulting company to conduct an "independent" environmental study, and asked the board of directors to collaborate with the company to improve its environmental mitigation plans. The aim was to incorporate the Junta's proposals and recommendations in order to "jointly" bring the project to fruition (Jarur and Maldonado 2005).

It could be argued that the agreement was simply a way to "buy" compliance, with little regard as to whether it would actually compensate for the mine's potential damages. Indeed, the agreement was negotiated without the full participation of water users, and before the project's EIA had been approved by the government. Adding to the controversy surrounding the agreement was that fact that, as a water rights holder, Barrick was also a member of the Junta. In spite of these irregularities, Barrick made its agreement with the Junta public and presented it as a successful CSR initiative, which implied that the mine's negative effects were commensurate with the economic compensation offered. The agreement was also intended to show that the commensuration of values and interests of the different constituencies represented a more democratic approach rooted in collaboration and public participation.

What this ignored, however, was that for small farmers living in the upper part of the watershed, the agreement was simply a reflection of a historical power imbalance within the Junta. The Junta represented more than two thousand water users, who were divided into four sections of the watershed, stretching from the mountains to the coast. The eight directors on the Junta's board were elected by the canal users, and the number of directors for each section was proportional to the number of water shares in that section. What this meant in practice was that some sections were more powerful than others, and some shareholders had so many shares they essentially had the power to elect themselves as directors. Meanwhile, farmers with a single share or a fraction of a share felt they had no voice in the decisions taken by the Junta.

Only the board of directors of the Junta voted in the negotiations with Barrick, while the rest of the water users were informed of the decision after the agreement had been signed. The agreement was ratified through a system that reflected a recent concentration of land and water rights in the hands of a few landowners, especially with the introduction of vineyards for export production over the past two decades. Meanwhile the majority of people living closest to the mine site saw themselves increasingly marginalized, and mining represented an additional threat to their water resources and their way of life.

As I have sought to show, technical arguments, calculations about water flows, legal standards, and compensation agreements were necessary for establishing equivalences in the Pascua-Lama case. As the case of the Junta illustrates, compensation agreements can sidestep legal frameworks and exploit existing power asymmetries. However, companies face increasing public scrutiny, and must present their actions as legitimate and in line with their commitments to CSR. A logic of equivalence can help create an image of environmental responsibility and accountability to the public, but it can also bring about unexpected consequences.

Glaciers and the limits of commensuration

When Barrick acquired the concession for Pascua-Lama, the mine site's specific geography inspired anti-mining campaigns that put the future of the project in doubt. For the territory to be mined was not simply *land* that the company could buy or acquire rights to, nor was it *water* in the form of a lake or lagoon, which are sometimes engulfed by open-pit mines. That the mineral deposits lay beneath *glaciers*—a particularly symbolic form of water and earth—put Pascua-Lama in the international spotlight and at the center of debates around climate change, water scarcity, indigenous rights, and the politics of gold.

In company statements and personal conversations, those who defended the Pascua-Lama project tended to present the glaciers as a symbol that had been introduced by outside actors (activists and NGOs from Santiago, North America, and Europe) and used strategically in anti-mining propaganda. Yet the effectiveness of the image of the glaciers in galvanizing local, national, and international opposition suggests that there was something more at work. The glaciers were not simply a "prop" introduced by radical environmentalists, since in order to draw people into the movement against the mine, it had to resonate with people's own understandings of what was at stake in the conflict. For the valley's local residents, "glacier" was not a term they had used before the arrival of the company. Although they are not visible from any of the communities in the valley, animal herders were familiar with the area, and most people talked in more general terms about the snow and ice on the Cordillera. Some people said their parents and grandparents had talked about the "eternal ice" (*hielos eternos*), and these ideas became incorporated into campaigns against the mine as they converged with scientific and environmentalist discourses about glaciers.

The glaciers touched upon the environmentalist sensibility of some activists who took an interest in the case. A university student whom I interviewed acknowledged that the glaciers had initially drawn her to the cause. As she began to learn about mining, however, the Pascua-Lama case came to represent much more than the protection of glaciers. She learned that it was a *socio*-environmental problem that brought together a range of issues: government corruption, neoliberalism, foreign investment, and social injustice. The glaciers bridged the diverse and sometimes contradictory interests of the many actors that took an interest in Pascua-Lama: university students, grape-growers and small farmers, Catholic priests and their congregations, artists, and the Diaguitas, a group of indigenous peoples that gained official recognition from the Chilean government in 2006. This diversity was sometimes a source of tension, as some people favored nationalizing the nation's resources, others demanded better environmental safeguards, and some opposed mining altogether.

Scholars have used the concept of "boundary object" (Star and Griesemer 1989) to explore how various entities inhabit intersecting social worlds, flexibly acquiring new meanings and forms but maintaining their identity. It could be said that boundary objects have the ability to commensurate various forms of life along a common standard of measurement. It may be useful, therefore, to think of glaciers as boundary objects that made different entities commensurate across local, regional, national, and global scales. Glaciers have themselves become (controversial) standards of measurement, useful to scientists as markers of climate change. Their value has come to be understood not simply in terms of their economic importance (e.g., for tourism and recreation), but also in terms of their aesthetic qualities and ability to elicit an affective response (Orlove, Wiegant, and Luckman 2009). In the case of Pascua-Lama, glaciers allowed the convergence of multiple interests, including those of scientists, environmentalists, agriculturalists, and corporations. Glaciers bridge social and natural worlds (Cruikshank 2005), and made it possible to bridge the interests of canal users concerned with water scarcity and those of environmentalists wanting to protect fragile ecosystems.

It could also be argued that for activists opposed to the project, glaciers were an *incommensurable* value, and that this ultimately proved to be a challenge for the company. Defining something as incommensurable can serve as a political strategy, as when land is described by indigenous groups as something that is not simply a resource, but that is constitutive of their identity (Espeland 1998). In the mining case, the glaciers defied a logic of equivalence, not only from the perspective of local residents and environmentalists, but also of some scientists and engineers who saw that the glaciers signified new risks. For Sandra and her colleague Roberto, for example, the glaciers seemed to disrupt their certainties about environmental management:

> *Sandra:* When I heard about the plan to relocate the glaciers, as an individual, it really worried me. For me it's inconceivable to relocate glaciers and have them remain the same in another place.

> *Roberto:* We don't have the experience [with relocation]. Tailings management, waste rock deposits—these are proven technologies; the projects exist, and I can show that they work…. But glaciers? Also, moving glaciers is not good, moving them from one place to another … there are changes in temperature, the wind, the sun's rays. Tailing dams, waste rock piles—that we know … they have existed for a very long time. The problem with glaciers is something new.

While commensuration is central to engineering practices, the commensuration implicit in Pascua-Lama's glacier relocation plan was unacceptable to these engineers.

The difficulty that the glaciers posed, however, went beyond technical questions regarding their relocation. Pascua-Lama shows how glaciers brought an *affective* dimension to the controversy, and this was something that corporations could not control. This affective quality of the glaciers—their ability to evoke sentiments that coincided with but also exceeded preoccupations about water scarcity—placed it outside the realm of calculations and beyond a legal and scientific rationale. This way of looking at the role of glaciers has implications that extend beyond the Pascua-Lama mine. What it shows is the way new concerns are enabling different forms of political action and, at the same time, changing the way mining companies conceive of social and environmental responsibility.

Conclusion

This chapter has explored how processes of commensuration inspire conflicts that are often cast as ethical (Espeland and Stevens 1998), posing new challenges for corporations. On the one hand, an inherent logic of equivalence in environmental mitigation plans and compensation schemes makes it possible for companies to claim that they are acting responsibly. On the other hand, new concerns that have emerged in controversies over mining—from glacier retreat to water scarcity and climate change—are forcing companies to rethink their approach to ethics and corporate accountability. These issues—and the unusual entities, like glaciers, that they introduced into debates— connect different actors across local, regional, and international scales, producing new ways of thinking about equivalence. In some cases, they can also produce *incommensurable* values, which challenge the legal and scientific rationality that informs the work of engineers and other professionals responsible for environmental mitigation.

In the case of Pascua-Lama, glaciers became a powerful symbol that revealed the inadequacies of science and the law, and in so doing challenged the company's claims to environmental responsibility. The glaciers drew a wider public into the discussion, and new witnesses to events unfolding in another part of the country or the world. In this way, they introduced a new moral dimension to debates around mining, bringing to the table issues such as biodiversity and climate change. Significantly, glaciers also redefined the concept of responsibility, which was no longer limited to local communities but extended to future generations and the planet as a whole. As mining activity expands into new territories, corporations will continue to confront issues that challenge established strategies of commensuration and existing ethical guideposts.

Acknowledgments

I am grateful to the many people who facilitated my fieldwork in Chile and to the engineers who agreed to be interviewed for this study. Research and writing was conducted while a postdoctoral fellow at the University of Manchester, and was made possible by the Royal Society's Newton International Fellowship Scheme. I owe special thanks to Penelope Harvey for inspiring conversations and invaluable feedback. I would also like to thank Dinah Rajak and Catherine Dolan for putting together this collection of essays.

Notes

1. Between 1990 and 2001, Chile was the largest target of global mining investment out of more than 90 countries, receiving 18% of the total investment during this period (Bridge 2004).
2. Anthropologists have long been interested in the ways things are made comparable and exchangeable. For example, anthropological theories of value and exchange have been foundational and remain influential in the discipline (see, e.g., Graeber 2001, Guyer 2004, Humphrey and Hugh-Jones 1992). My own interests have been shaped by scholarly work that has moved discussions about equivalence and commensurability in new directions. These concepts have been used in explorations of number as a site of anthropological enquiry (see Guyer et al. 2010, Verran 2001), the anthropology of money (Maurer 2006) and medical anthropology (e.g. Lakoff 2005; Hayden 2006). Studies of commensurability have queried how people interpret and negotiate radically incompatible knowledge practices and forms of ethical reasoning (Povinelli 2001), a question that is especially relevant for examining environmental politics.
3. In 2013, Barrick Gold announced a temporary suspension of the Pascua Lama project, a decision made due to ongoing opposition from local groups, problems related to environmental permitting, and accusations of failing to build an adequate water treatment system and not meeting its commitments to protect the glaciers. A sharp drop in bullion price and cost overruns also contributed to the company's economic problems. The estimated cost of the Pascua Lama project (set at $1.5 billion in 2004) went up to $8.5 billion in 2012.
4. The proposed creation of Cascadia, a crossborder region encompassing the Canadian province of British Columbia and the states of Washington and Oregon, provides an interesting point of comparison (see Sparke 2005). While the ideal of borderless economic development results from the conjunction of capitalist interests, these are nevertheless challenged by environmentalist groups that espouse competing ecoregional visions and form crossborder activist alliances which also represent a challenge to national sovereignty.

5. Pascua-Lama was the first project subject to Chile's System of Environmental Impact Assessment laws, introduced in 2000, including requirements for community participation. Barrick's EIA received unprecedented public scrutiny, and put social and environmental responsibility at the forefront of discussions. The company submitted two separate EIAs, following the different legal requirements in Chile and Argentina.
6. Pascua-Lama was made known internationally through a widely disseminated email petition, numerous documentaries, and articles published in mainstream and alternative media.

References

Barrick. 2000. *EIA proyecto Pascua-Lama* (EIA Pascua-Lama project). Santiago, Chile: Barrick Gold.

Barrick. 2005. *EIA modificaciones proyecto Pascua-Lama.* Adenda n° 2. (EIA Pascua-Lama project modifications: Addenda 2). Santiago, Chile: Barrick Gold.

Bauer, Carl. 1998. *Against the current? Privatization, water markets and the state in Chile.* Boston: Kluwer.

Bebbington, Anthony, and Mark Williams 2008. Water and mining conflicts in Peru. *Mountain Research and Development* 28: 190–95.

Bendell, Jeremy. 2004. Barricades and boardrooms: A contemporary history of the corporate accountability movement. *Technology, Business and Society Programme Paper* No. 13. Geneva: UNRISD.

Benson, Peter and Stuart Kirsch. 2010. Corporate Oxymorons. *Dialectical Anthropology* 34: 45–48.

Blaser, Mario. 2009. The threat of the Yrmo: The political ontology of a sustainable hunting program. *American Anthropologist* 111 (1): 10–20.

Bridge, Gavin. 2004. Mapping the bonanza: Geographies of mining investment in an era of neoliberal reform. *The Professional Geographer* 56 (3): 406–421.

Azócar, Guillermo, and Alexander Brenning. 2008. *Interventions in rock glaciers in the Los Pelambres mine, Coquimbo Region, Chile — technical report.* Department of Geography and Environmental Management. Waterloo: University of Waterloo.

Cruikshank, Julie. 2005. *Do glaciers listen? Local knowledge, colonial encounters, and social imagination.* Vancouver: University of British Columbia Press.

Danús, Hernán. 2007. *Crónicas mineras: 1950–2000* (Mining journal: 1950–2000). Santiago, Chile: IRL.

Espeland, Wendy Nelson. 1998. *The struggle for water: Politics, rationality and identity in the American Southwest.* Chicago: University of Chicago Press.

Espeland, Wendy Nelson, and Mitchell Stevens. 1998. Commensuration as a social process. *Annual Review of Sociology* 24: 313–43.

Frynas, Jedrzej George. 2005. The false developmental promise of corporate social responsibility: Evidence from multinational oil companies. *International Affairs* 81 (3): 581–98.

Graeber, David. 2001. *Toward an anthropological theory of value: The false coin of our own dreams.* New York: Palgrave.

Guyer, J. 2004. *Marginal gains: Monetary transactions in Atlantic Africa.* Chicago: University of Chicago Press.

Guyer, Jane, Naveeda Khan, Juan Obarrio, Caroline Bledsoe, Julie Chu Souleymane Bachir Diagne, Keith Hart, Paul Kockelman, Jean Lave, Caroline McLoughlin, Bill

Maurer, Federico Neiburg, Diane Nelson, Charles Stafford, and Helen Verran. 2010. Introduction: Number as inventive frontier. *Anthropological Theory* 10: 36–61.

Hayden, Cori. 2006. Generic medicines and the question of the similar. *Cinvestav* 50–60. Mexico City: Cinvestav.

Humphrey, Caroline, and Stephen Hugh-Jones, eds. 1992. *Barter, exchange and value: An anthropological approach.* Cambridge: Cambridge University Press.

Jarur, Paola, and Germán Maldonado. "Pascua Lama anuncia: Estamos dispuestos a modificar el proyecto" ("Pascua Lama announces: We are willing to modify the project"). *El Mercurio*, 6 July 2005.

Jenkens, Heledd. 2004. Corporate social responsibility and the mining industry: conflicts and constructs. *Corporate Social Responsibility and Environmental Management* 11 (1): 23–34.

Kirsch, Stuart. 2006. *Reverse anthropology: Indigenous analysis of social and environmental relations in New Guinea.* Palo Alto: Stanford University Press.

Lakoff, Andrew. 2005. *Knowledge and value in global psychiatry.* Cambridge: Cambridge University Press.

Li, Fabiana. 2009. Documenting accountability: Environmental impact assessment in a Peruvian mining project. *Political and Legal Anthropology Review* 32 (2): 218–36.

Luna, Diego, César Padilla, and Julián Alcayaga. 2004. *El exilio del cóndor: Hegemonía transnational en la frontera* ("Exile of the condor: Transnational hegemony at the border"). Santiago, Chile: Observatorio Latinoamericano de Conflictos Ambientales.

Maurer, Bill. 2006. The anthropology of money. *Annual Review of Anthropology* 35: 15–36.

Orlove, Ben, Ellen Wiegant, and Brian H. Luckman, eds. 2008. *Darkening peaks: Glacial retreat in scientific and social context.* Berkeley and Los Angeles: University of California Press.

Povinelli, Elizabeth. 2001. Radical worlds: The anthropology of incommensurability and inconceivability. *Annual Review of Anthropology* 30: 319–334.

Raman, Ravi, ed. 2010. *Corporate social responsibility: Comparative critiques.* Basingstoke: Palgrave Macmillan.

Ruiz-Dana, Alejandra. 2007. Commodity Revenue Management: The case of Chile's copper boom. Winnipeg, Canada: International Institute for Sustainable Development (IISD).

Sharp, John. 2006. Corporate social responsibility and development: An anthropological perspective. *Development Southern Africa*, 23 (2): 213–22

Sparke, Matthew. 2005. *In the space of theory: Postfoundational geographies of the nationstate.* Minneapolis: University of Minnesota Press.

Star, S. L., and J. R. Griesemer. 1989. Institutional ecology, "translations," and boundary objects: Amateurs and professionals in Berkeley's Museum of Vertebrate Zoology, 1907–1939. *Social Studies of Science* 19: 387–420.

Verran, Helen. 2001. *Science and an African logic.* Chicago: University of Chicago Press.

Watts, Michael. 2005. Righteous oil? Human rights, the oil complex, and corporate social responsibility. *Annual Revew of Environment and Resources* 30: 373–407.

Welker, Marina. 2009. "Corporate security begins in the community": Mining, the corporate responsibility industry and environmental advocacy in Indonesia. *Cultural Anthropology* 24 (1): 142–79.

Fabiana Li is Associate Professor of Anthropology at the University of Manitoba, Canada. Her research interests include the anthropology of water, social movements, resource extraction, and environmental politics in Latin America. She is the author of *Unearthing Conflict: Corporate Mining, Activism, and Expertise in Peru* (Duke University Press, 2015).

– Chapter 10 –

GLOBAL CONCEPTS IN LOCAL CONTEXTS
CSR as "Anti-Politics Machine" in the Extractive Sector in Ghana and Peru
Johanna Sydow

When I arrived in New Abirem, Eastern region, Ghana in August 2009, the multinational mining company Newmont had not yet started its operations. Negotiations for compensation for potential impacts were ongoing between community and company representatives. While Newmont was waiting for its Environmental Impact Assessment (EIA) to be approved by the Ghanaian government, it was establishing alternative livelihood programs, community-administered develop- ment funds and training for affected communities. It was in this context that local traditional authorities told me about the jobs and development that Newmont would bring to the region and expressed their anger toward certain NGOs that hinder Newmont's work. Newmont was, it seemed, welcomed by the community and considered more responsible than other mining companies operating in Ghana. Newmont's corporate social responsibility (CSR) programs and environmental protection facilities, administered through a newly established NGO, were praised by different local institutions as being unique and extensive. Meanwhile, at the global level, the US-based mining company, one of the world's leading gold producers, is a signatory of both the UN Global Compact and the Voluntary Principles on Security and Human Rights, which set benchmarks for best practice for participating multinationals.

In Peru, where Newmont has been extracting gold since 1993, a very different picture of corporate-community dynamics emerged. Rather than the apparent optimism and sense of expectation I encountered in New Abirem, Ghana, community relations with Newmont in Peru were marked by deep mistrust and open contestation. Here also, as in Ghana, Newmont had established an NGO to manage its CSR issues and community relations when it began operations in the early 1990s. Yet, as we will see, the NGO was regarded in a rather different light—more as an instrument of corporate interests than a vehicle of community upliftment—to that newly set up in New Abirem.

CSR, which this chapter examines more closely in the context of Newmont's operations in Ghana and Peru, has become common practice within the extractive sector over the past two decades, and has become the subject of increasing interest from governments, international NGOs and multilateral agencies such as the UN, as well as the focus of an increasing body of academic research in business and management studies, development studies, and anthropology. Scholarly perspectives on CSR often attribute to it impacts that are diametrically opposed. While some see CSR optimistically as a way of humanizing business (Matten and Crane 2003), many doubt that CSR prevents the negative social and environmental impact of multinational enterprise (Gilberthorpe and Banks 2012). Going a step further, some argue that CSR grants the company more control and power over the government and local community (Rajak 2011). This chapter will investigate this argument further, elaborating on the capacity of CSR as a standardized strategy and set of corresponding technologies to exercise corporate power and discipline in very different local contexts.

This chapter explores how Newmont approaches local communities on different continents in a standardized way following its one global model developed in abstraction from the particular contexts of operations. By applying standardized methods it aims for standardized, manageable outcomes. James Scott (1998) has shown how a state gains power over its citizens, to a large extent, by making society administrable through the simplification of qualitative matters into measurable units. From this perspective people are uniform, measurable units without any specific skills or experience (Scott 1998: 346). In the same way, CSR models produce a standardizing view on communities, which can facilitate greater control for a company.

According to Ferguson (1994) the application of a standardized development program is possible when the problem that is meant to be addressed is decontextualized and discursively transformed into a technical problem. Through this decontextualization, power structures are made invisible, so depoliticizing both the causes of poverty and the development measures deployed to address them.

Consequently, Ferguson argues that development programs act as "anti-politics machines," enabling highly political agendas to be implemented without seeming to be political. Yet, as he points out, these standardized solutions in development often fail to achieve the targeted development result, yet still have an (unintended) side effect. It is an influential "instrumental effect" that enables the exercise of power over the target population (ibid.: 256). This power is a "bureaucratic power" exercised through the administration of development projects, over the surrounding population (ibid.: 274). CSR in the extractive sector is promoted as a similar kind of standardized solution (Rajak 2011: 18). In this sense, CSR can provide mining companies with just such a depoliticizing mechanism, to veil or contain the underlying and emerging issues of inequality and marginalization; for example, in the case of displacement and resettlement of local populations. Instead of working with the state, CSR works in the "spaces where the state fails to deliver," which "creates opportunities for new unintended consequences to flow from CSR interventions" (Sharp 2006: 220).

However, the ethnographic evidence presented in this chapter from Newmont's operations in Ghana and Peru show that standardized methods do not necessarily produce standardized effects of control. Newmont had been present in Peru for much longer than in Ghana and should therefore have been able to adjust its standardized concepts to the local context and make use of instrumental effects. But its grand plan for CSR could not prevent huge protests against its new mining project "Conga." Violent clashes with the police led to a temporary suspension of the venture (Osterman and Wilson 2012), and Newmont investors even considered a possible transfer of assets from Peru to Ghana, because they considered the latter to offer a more secure investment climate (Els 2012).

While Scott (1998) and Ferguson (1994: 2005) give great insight into the workings of power, which will be particularly useful in the discussion of Newmont's techniques, they neglect the relevance of counter-conduct and fundamentally, as I will show, underestimate the agency of local actors. Here, I set out to examine both the power and *limitations* of corporate techniques, alongside the perspectives and agency of local actors, in response to those technologies of CSR. I do this through a comparison between local responses to standardized corporate techniques, based on ethnographic fieldwork at Newmont operations in Ghana and Peru from 2009–2010. The comparative angle of one company operating in two different places across two continents serves as a unique basis to better comprehend the dynamics of standardized tools in different contexts by highlighting the specificities and the similarities of the two cases. Moreover, the different stages of the two operations—one being an expansion of a long-standing project, the other being a prospective operation far away from other operations of the same company—reveal how a temporal dimension (the stage of operation) influences corporate strategies as well as local responses. The geographical and temporal dimension of this comparative approach thus provides a lens through which to examine the scope and limits of global standardized techniques in local contexts. This comparative framework brings into view the crucial contextual specificities—not only differing legal frameworks but a different history and memory of mining, divergent discourses on the promise and risks associated with mining, and, crucially, different networks and mobilization around mining. This serves to highlight how standardized techniques cannot always adequately deal with complexities at the local level nor fully absorb counter-conduct and the agency of local actors. Ultimately, I challenge the conception that standardized techniques of governance yield standardized effect of domination and argue conversely that local agency in fact shapes the effects of corporate techniques.

The power and function of CSR: The academic debate

Much academic work has been published on the social and environmental issues of mining across different disciplines. Studies reach back to colonial times when mining was an integral part of colonization (Lentz 2008). Today mining is still promoted as a key driving force for development (Akabzaa 2000). It forms the basis of many economies, in Africa, Asia and Latin America, even though the risks of resource extraction are well known. The so-called resource curse—that is, the link between resource abundance and high levels of violence, civil war and poverty has been the focus of an extensive body of literature (see for example Luong and Weinthal 2006; Sachs and Warner 1997). Many scholars see this issue as a matter of resource and revenue management, implying that when mining is done well it leads to development. But more critical voices have emerged that question resource-based economies and resource extraction in general, especially in Latin America (Gudynas 2012).

In response to this general critique, CSR programs have emerged in the extractive sector (Gilberthorpe and Banks 2012: 185). And CSR itself has become the focus of an increasingly polarized literature. On the one hand, we find authors who welcome the emergence of CSR and endorse initiatives like the Global Compact as the foundation for voluntary engagement in environmental issues and human rights (Cetindamar and Husoy 2007). Others go so far as to argue that companies should step into the empty space where governments fail to provide and correct this failure (Hopkins 2012). Gifford and Kestler's study (2008) on Newmont in Peru can be located in this school of literature viewing CSR as a vehicle to earn the "social license" to mine. On the other hand, many see this development more critically, arguing that CSR is a facade that helps companies to formally satisfy different expectations, while maintaining practices that are strongly decoupled from the rhetoric of compliance (Hiß 2006). In this sense, CSR merely distracts the observer from the real impact of mining and from the demands for stronger regulations (Cetindamar and Husoy 2007). Other authors go further, arguing that CSR is more than a "smokescreen" but a tool that shapes "social relations and projects according to a particular set of corporate interests and values" (Rajak 2011: 12). Rajak points to a discursive power of CSR that is often overlooked, and which provides companies with a "moral mechanism through which their authority is extended over the social order" (ibid.: 13). By creating cohesion and local bonds with actors of the community, companies can gain strength. Thus CSR, rather than being a philanthropic and altruistic act, offers mining companies a way to increase their agency and control. This insight is the starting point of my analysis.

Among the studies that examine CSR as a corporate tool to manage company-community relations, a few key studies highlight the way in which companies use social programs to achieve control at the local level. In South Africa, Paul Kapelus identifies various corporate strategies to stay in "good stead with potential financiers and local elites" (2002: 291). He shows how a subsidiary of the company Rio Tinto gains control by limiting participation to a kind of symbolic participation, which is similarly observed by Sawyer (2004) as corporate strategy used by oil companies in Ecuador. A further strategy to prevent destructive conflicts against the company that Sawyer identified is the creation of allies and inequality through the strategic implementation of social programs. In this way the conflict is transferred to the local inhabitants themselves, as allies defend the mine against opponents. This "divide and rule" strategy has been observed in various places (Gilberthorpe and Banks 2012). Thus scholars have described the destabilizing and conflict-generating character of CSR resulting from the distinction between stakeholders and non-stakeholders in various settings (see for example Sharp 2006: 217–220). These studies give detailed insight into the power of CSR to channel local actors' behavior, while also revealing the common corporate logic and techniques in diverse contexts. Nevertheless, as Arellano-Yanguas (2011: 634) argues, companies are not always successful at eliminating conflicts over their operations through their CSR programs, and other factors also play an important role. Indeed, as this chapter shows, CSR does not always achieve its intended ends and yield the expected benefits to companies.

Global yet local

In 2006 Sharp argued that CSR programs applied in host communities are still too new "for a cadre of experts to have emerged and be able to circulate among business corporations" (2006: 218). He argued that these techniques are not yet a standardized set of tools applied in different contexts. CSR has been further established since this statement, and Rajak (2011: 218) argues that "the power of CSR lies, to a great extent, in its capacity to claim global applicability (underwritten by supposedly universal market values)." Thus CSR is promoted as a universally applicable and locally adjustable tool that is implemented by globally active companies like Newmont in different local contexts. Various institutions and standards, such as the international protocol of Voluntary Principles on Security and Human Rights provide a scheme into which local CSR programs are meant to fit (Gilberthorpe and Banks 2012). Thus global norms shape the content and processes of CSR, not least by ensuring a respectable global image, which is important for multinational companies when mobilizing future investments. Hence CSR seems to fit the credo "think global, act local" (Rajak 2011: 18). This construction of CSR implies that global schemes can be designed in abstraction of local specificities but capture, adjust to and deal with local structures in a more or less predictable way. It implies that standardized CSR can shape, control and keep its "community" content by abstracting from cultural, historical etc., differences.

There are several studies that analyze the impact of CSR and other corporate techniques at *one* site of extraction (Bury 2004; Gifford and Kestler 2008; Welker 2009; Li 2009; Rajak 2011; Gardner 2012). But there is little academic literature that systematically analyzes and compares the reaction of communities to similar techniques by the same company in different national contexts in order to interrogate the claims of its global applicability. Consequently, we know much less not only about the reach of these so-called global tools, but about their limits; and more specifically, the extent to which contextual factors, as opposed to corporate techniques, influence local inhabitants' agency and reaction toward mining operations.

Through a comparison of Newmont's community-company relations at different places of operation I will provide further insight into the impact of standardized corporate techniques in different local contexts on different continents. For, when set alongside Li's (2009) study of a Newmont mine in Peru, and Welker's ethnography of the company's operations in Indonesia (2009), my study of Newmont's community engagement in Ghana and Peru reveals that, despite the great geographical, social, environmental and political-economic differences, the company deploys the same toolkit and technologies in its attempt to manage the community. At the same time, the ethnographic evidence presented in this chapter reveals how Newmont's claims to universal applicability are highly problematic and how contextual factors, in particular the agency of local actors, have a huge impact on its effects. Ultimately, I argue, standardized technologies of governance do not lead to standardized effects of domination.

Community relations management: "Global thinking" in Denver

Today, our vision is to become the most valued and respected mining company through industry leading performance. Our staff of around 40,000 employees and contractors works in eight countries on five continents — North America, South America, Asia, Australia and Africa. (Homepage Newmont)

In this section I sketch out Newmont's standardized management of corporate responsibility from its headquarters in Denver and outline the official global standards the company aims to implement across its operations. Newmont's management is highly centralized. In the context of CSR this means that the "ultimate oversight responsibility for the management of community relationships at Newmont lies with the Board of Directors, and, specifically, the ESR [Environmental and Social Responsibility] Committee in Denver" (Smith and Feldman 2009: 17). It has to develop the company's standards according to both management goals and global standards like the Global Compact, the Extractive Industry Transparency Initiative (EITI), or ISA 14001 (ibid.: 17). The company's standards are then rolled out to the regional Environmental and Social Responsibility offices to be implemented.

This task is based on what is often referred to as "global thinking" and demands a reduction of complexity by abstraction. This is seen clearly in Newmont's Community Relations Review, which was demanded by a shareholder's meeting in 2007 in response to protests at operational sites in Ghana, Indonesia and Peru that started to hamper Newmont's operations (Smith and Feldman 2009: 1). The review was conceptualized by the Environmental and Social Responsibility team and conducted by an external team. Certain mining sites were selected as representative, to be analyzed in regard to the impact of Newmont's Community Policies. All were ongoing operations, as opposed to prospective mines. This shows how experiences from different places are gathered, generalized and then transformed into strategies with intended universal applicability. The review provided a tool for "global learning," offering general "lessons learned" that since 2010 have become the criteria according to which the different mining sites are evaluated in an annual letter to the company's shareholders. In other words, they have become a standardized scheme corresponding to global initiatives and norms.

One such "lesson learnt" is dealing with the implementation of a better monitoring system for community relations at the regional level. It results from the identification of a gap between implemented programs and Newmont's global standards on paper. The external reviewers relate this gap to the weakness of its reporting scheme for social relations. It is argued that metrics drive performance and that if community relations cannot be measured the Environmental and Social Responsibility team cannot successfully "establish effective systems of accountability" (Smith and Feldman 2009: 133). In order to do so, the review instructs, "Newmont will need to develop key performance indicators and metrics for community relations performance. Newmont must have objective mechanisms for evaluating the performance of its employees in achieving the company relations goals" (ibid.). This follows the logic mentioned by one executive, "[w]hat gets measured, gets managed" (ibid.: 85). Inevitably, the processes of measurement and evaluation themselves have a significant impact on the object of evaluation (Scott 1998: 348) as community relations are transformed into numbers in order to produce the necessary standardization and therefore better "manage performance."

An essential element in this strategy is the establishment of local Consultative Committees and Social Responsibility Forums, prescribed by head office to all its operations in order to manage diverse and potentially unpredictable situations. In Ghana, this committee is used to channel "community concerns and frustration" and "the potential for community frustration to find expression in unproductive ways" (Smith and Feldman 2009: 99). The Social Responsibility Forum is celebrated as a best practice mechanism for participatory community investment and concern management to be implemented in other places. The success of the Social Responsibility Forum and the Community Consultative Committee is, the company claims, due to its transparency, inclusiveness, independence, and strong community mandate. As general advice, the Community Relations Review argues that this kind of advisory panel must include locally elected community members and be "organized or supported by third parties to establish the perception of independence and credibility" (ibid.: 53). Thus the company seeks to enable a degree of local agency but within a controlled realm. At the same time, the company gains insight into the perspectives of local actors and a strong community mandate lends legitimacy to the measures implemented. By bureaucratizing and institutionalizing the interface between community and company, new structures are implemented to exercise power. Moreover, the engagement with governments at all levels is seen as a vital company standard. Each site is supposed to have a list of key governmental contacts. Yet there is no further guideline to give each site the flexibility to engage the list according to their needs (ibid.: 53).

Beyond giving an insight into Newmont's global standardizing approach, the Community Relations Review itself can be seen as an instrument to depoliticize the operations. Merely focusing on procedural strategies and standardized measurements to better meet the population's expectations conceals the fact that CSR can serve to influence certain processes in a less transparent way. This hides how CSR is used to "transform social relations and projects according to a particular set of corporate ideas and interests" (Rajak 2011: 12). From the global standards generated in Denver, I now move on to explore their implementation at the company's local operational sites in Ghana and Peru. In doing so, I show that, while Newmont approaches its community relations in a standardized way, the very same CSR tools and standardized strategies do not lead to standardized outcomes.

Ghana—the application of a
global concept in a local context

The Chief of Abirem in the Eastern Region, Nana Amo Kyeretwie ... has admonished the NGOs to allow the company to engage in fruitful negotiations with the communities in the Newmont Akyem Project area for mining to commence for the benefit of the people and the country as a whole. ("Chiefs worried about propaganda against Newmont project" 2009)

In the context of Structural Adjustment Programs, Ghana was forced to open up its markets in 1983. A mining law with extremely low environmental and social standards, and favorable foreign direct investment (FDI) conditions were implemented. The ensuing mining boom led to immense and violent resettlements. Moreover water pollution and conflicts between large- and small-scale mines led to dissatisfaction and to violent clashes between local communities and both private and public security forces (Akabzaa 2000). In this context the NGO Wassa Association of Communities Affected by Mining (WACAM) was founded, supporting local communities in disputes with mining companies. In 2009 in New Abirem (Eastern region) at approximately 120 km from the place of these incidents, the mining company Newmont was preparing its second project in Ghana, 200km from their first project in the Brong Ahafo region.

When I conducted my research, the mining company was waiting for the approval of its Environmental Impact Assessment (EIA). In the meantime, the company's local CSR personnel devoted their attention to building up key strategic relations with specific community actors. Due to upcoming resettlement and compensation issues, the management of community relations is paramount for the company in the early stages of an operation. In this context Newmont established two institutions following the principle of an advisory board with elected representatives to enable broad community support. One of them is a Social Responsibility Forum following the best practice example of the Ahafo region and the strategy of participatory community investment. Elected community representatives, the chief, members of the district assembly and Newmont representatives came together to discuss ways to improve the communities, focusing primarily on infrastructural investment and development such as the renovation or construction of schools.

The task of a Compensation Negotiation Committee, the second institution following the same principles of election, was to negotiate the amount Newmont would pay in compensation for crop, land use, and property loss. According to the standards, representatives from all affected communities were elected into the committees. Together with Newmont's representatives and the community chiefs, procedural rules for the negotiation were established. Although the Ghanaian government prescribes negotiation of compensation payments by law (Republic of Ghana 2006: Art. 73 (1), 74 (2)), the company praised itself as especially participatory and transparent in this process. It invited representatives from the district assembly and other district institutions to observe the process, but at the same time the objectives of the Compensation Negotiation Committee forbid the reporting of decisions as well as recording or note-taking without permission. Through the implementation of the Compensation Negotiation Committee, following globally applied principles of representative democracy, Newmont avoided multiple individual negotiations, instead aiming for a collective solution, namely a standardized price for everybody's land, crops, and property. By electing a representative, the company enlisted local inhabitants to formally legitimize the procedure (Luhmann 2008), thereby inducing them to accept the outcome. Legally, Newmont has the right to use these collective solutions for compensation payment (Republic of Ghana 2006: Art. 74 (3)). Yet the standardized treatment of people, land and property is perceived negatively by some of the farmers, who want to negotiate the price themselves and see the standardized method as failing to account for the complexity of local structures and value.

Instead of representing the concerns of their community in the Compensation Negotiation Committee, local farmers argue that the position of the chiefs is strengthened in the committee. Moreover some indigenous farmers do not want to be represented by settler farmers, as they see settler farmers as having alternative opportunities and less attachment to the land. This blanket treatment is also critiqued with regard to the payment system introduced by Newmont, which is based on a standard price per acre. It assumes a monoculture and does not take into account the variety of plants in the fields, or the remaining lifetime of the trees. Farmers see this system as being ill-suited to an agrarian economy. However, despite these conflicts of interests, by implementing the Compensation Negotiation Committee, Newmont effectively forestalled many individual conflicts and deferred the responsibility of the price to the representatives. This sharing of the responsibility is also described by Li (2009) in the context of the EIA in Peru. It suggests that local communities are participating in shaping the future. It is a side effect that empowers Newmont to achieve formal legitimacy for an established price and compensation practice. At the same time, the individual agency of farmers to negotiate what they see to be a fair deal is decreased.

Newmont stated at the time that it did not know where people would be resettled. Thus the representatives did not know the extent to which they would actually be affected while negotiating in the committee. Here we can see that the emphasis is on monetary compensation, which, in comparison to what people normally earned, seemed substantial. Thereby attention was drawn to what farmers would get, and away from what they would lose. This attempt to obscure the actual future impact for every individual effectively depoliticizes the highly contentious processes of compensation and resettlement. This can be interpreted as a strategic form of information politics, also mentioned in the Community Relations Review, which points out that it can be advantageous not to fully provide information about impacts of prospective operations (Smith and Feldman 2009: 85).

Local employment and business opportunities

A key element of Newmont's CSR strategy, generated at its Denver HQ and exported to its various mine sites, is a set of measures designed to create local employment and business opportunities (Smith and Feldman 2009: 97). By establishing an NGO called Olives, which provided alternative livelihood programs, the company showcased one of its core values: sustainability. At that early prospective stage not many jobs were available; nevertheless people expected a job in the near future. Those who worked with the mine were seen to earn a comparatively high salary. Many hoped that at least one family member would become a mineworker. Others were hoping that a big influx of migrants to the mine would create new business opportunities. For many, the loss of farmland seemed to be redeemed by these tantalizing prospects. As Sharp puts it, the "odds of this happening are probably, in the cold light of business reality, rather slim, but the beauty of the convoluted CSR apparatus is that it continually holds out the possibility that the poor may—one day—get lucky" (Sharp 2006: 221). Some people, such as the chiefs, had already been promised work by the company and in response Newmont received their support.

By constantly referring to its commitments to sustainability and participatory approaches, Newmont aimed to establish an image distinct from other mining companies. The company organized trips for community leaders to its other operation site, showing them its water management, and organized talks at the site to demonstrate its sustainability. Films shown in Community Information Centers supported the statements and enhanced the good message, further endorsed by its Social Responsibility Forum. This information campaign successfully eclipsed rumors of negative environmental and social impacts that people had heard from other places like Obuasi and Prestea.

The politics of depoliticization

Newmont's special involvement of members from the district assembly and chiefs in the Compensation Negotiation Committee and the Social Responsibility Forum corresponds to the standard of engagement with the government at all levels. As the chiefdom in Ghana is a traditional parallel structure to the governmental system, Newmont had simultaneously to engage with them when adjusting its standards to the local context. Traditional chiefdom was strongly enhanced during colonial times, as it served the British in the execution of indirect rule (Lentz 2008). Newmont builds on this structure or even enhances it. A calculated effect of this is that chiefs react with reciprocity toward the company and try to keep resistance down. As Welker puts it, in Indonesia "Newmont managers ... nourished local patron-client relations by relying on elites to keep the peace, hiring them and their sons as Community Development and Community Relation offices, and rewarding them with contracts" (Welker 2009: 144). Just as in Indonesia, similar practices employed by Newmont in Ghana successfully enlisted the alliance of chiefs, who openly stated that they did not want NGOs like WACAM to come to the Akyem area. As I was told by a researcher and an employee of FIAN (Food-First Information and Action Network), representatives of the NGO FIAN were even detained by chiefs when coming to the communities without permission. The custom of only entering a foreign community with the permission of the chief is strong. People did not want to talk to me before I had received the approval of the chief. Here we see Newmont managing and preventing local opposition by mobilizing the local authority of the chiefdom recast in the global discourse of participatory stakeholder engagement.

At the same time, Newmont used these relationships to project discourses of accountability and transparency back onto critical NGOs. In doing so, Newmont attempted to disqualify accusations against the company in order to hide the political dimension of its own operations. Welker observed similar practices of divide and rule at work at a Newmont operation in Indonesia (Welker 2009). By comparing politics at different mining places, these unofficial global strategies become visible. In 2009 Newmont (Ghana) was accused of environmentally and socially damaging behavior toward local farmers by the NGO FIAN (working together with WACAM). This complaint was channeled through the Office of the United Nations High Commissioner for Human Rights. In response, the Public Relations Officer of Newmont accused WACAM of lying about its operation and of being unwilling to cooperate. At the same time, in the newspapers one could read quotes from a chief stating Newmont was very welcome and doing great work; that WACAM was lying and they did not want anymore interference from this organization ("Chiefs worried about propaganda against Newmont project" 2009; Kofoya-Tetteh 2009).

Of course, the control executed through chiefs is not total. According to WACAM, a chief openly admitted in an interview with a journalist that Newmont paid them money for doing this media campaign. In response Newmont published a report on its website stating that they promised chiefs an allowance of $8,000 for all extra work upcoming in the context of the mine (Newmont 2009). With this it aimed to meet the accusation of bribery with transparency, showing the chief's huge financial gain. Meanwhile doubts emerged in regard to Newmont's claims of sustainability, yet these were few and far between. The brother of a sub-chief, for example, commented that the trip to the other mining site did not convince him of their promises of sustainable development. Nevertheless, at the project site, nobody talked openly about the disagreement with the company. It was only in Accra that I became aware of a protest letter that was written by the son of a community chief, signed by 270 inhabitants, arguing against the Compensation Negotiation Committee; whereas at the mine site, a virtual consensus had emerged amongst informants, all hoping that the company would start operations quickly, so contributing to a general feeling that the majority supported the mine. More critical or dissenting actors were geographically distant from the mine site and dispersed, so that most often they did not even know of each other, precluding the possibility of any organized dissent and solidarity.

Mobilizing both CSR strategy and unofficial means of securing local alliances, Newmont managed to create a widely recognized image of being different from other companies, generating widespread popular support for their mining operations. In this context the traditional structure of chiefdom was instrumentalized by the company in order to help keep resistance low. The prospect of work, compensation payments and local improvements stemming from the Social Responsibility Forum were, for many, powerful inducements, despite potential losses to land, livelihoods, and likely environmental damage.

Peru: The limits of standards

In 2012 hundreds of people marched through the streets of Lima protesting against Yanacocha's new venture "Conga" (mainly Newmont-owned) in the highlands of Peru, close to its other operations. Some weeks later, local protests led to a violent clash with the police, resulting in several deaths, the temporary suspension of the project, and a state of emergency (Osterman and Wilson 2012). A key question running through this chapter is, then, how did the very same techniques of CSR that proved so powerful in enlisting local consent in Ghana fail to do the same and even contribute to dissent and resistance in Peru. As the next section reveals, standardized tools have their limits in forming company-community relations according to corporate interests.

Figure 10.1. Sign within the Newmont concession: "Yanacocha cares for the environment" (author's photograph and translation).

Present in Cajamarca since 1992, Yanacocha is one of the most influential mining companies in Peru (Bury 2004: 80). Much like Ghana, Peru has a history of mining dating back to colonial times and possesses legal and favorable conditions for FDI and low environmental legislation (Arellano-Yanguas 2008: 18–19). Thorp argues that the extraction processes "influenced the early shaping of institutions" (2012: 113). Institutions now are seen to be weak at all levels of government. Internationally, Peru ranks very low in terms of security, political stability, and socioeconomic agreements, and ranks high on conflicts over land on indigenous issues (Arellano-Yanguas 2008: 1). "Conflicts harm the profits of operation and put the viability of large planned investments at risk. In response to this situation, mining companies, in collaboration with the national government and international institutions, are trying to apply international prescriptions to the Peruvian context" (ibid.: 23).

CSR in the local context—an attempt at depoliticization

Much like the NGO Olives in Ghana, the mine established an NGO named Association Los Andes Cajamarca (ALAC). It was founded as an independent organization in 2004. By establishing this NGO, Newmont attempted to position itself within civil society in order to state its closeness to the people on the ground and its benign character. At the same time, ALAC emphasized its uniqueness in being the only NGO that funded the programs of other NGOs. This can be seen as a kind of participatory investment, as money is distributed to various local organizations. This NGO has a far more extensive reach than the one in Ghana and greater financial standing. However, several actors I interviewed described Newmont's financing as a dangerous way to secure reciprocity and to defend the corporate idea. ALAC is accused of influencing election results by financing special activities for favored candidates, or by giving certain benefits to a community to create social pressure. For example, a police car can be a gift to a mayor, which in turn helps him gain legitimacy in the community, as observed by a community member of Celendín. But, at the same time, this police car, like the construction of a police station by the company in both Indonesia (as observed by Welker) and Ghana, will always represent a certain dependency on Newmont (Welker 2009: 146).

Influence on an election can be crucial for the mining company, as the mayor plays a decisive role in the process of land-use management. This regional zoning process, invoked by the regional government in response to the conflicts, makes it possible to declare certain zones within the concession as conservation areas and represents an attempt by the regional government to (re)gain control over the territory. This unintended side effect of Yanacocha's operations, shaped by local actors' agency and the regional government, challenges the position of the company. A conservation plan is needed in order to identify the varied potentials of a territory and to divide it into different productive zones (Daffós 2003: 35). In this way, a more finely woven grid perspective is established (Scott 1998; Bebbington et al. 2013: 323). These plans can only be carried out by experts. Several actors have accused ALAC of hiring these experts and then asking for reciprocity in the outcome of the study, pointing to the mining company's attempt to control bureaucratic processes through the brokerage of the independent NGO it established.

According to the standards, ALAC also focuses on local employment and business opportunities in the form of local entrepreneurial capacity and income generation. It supports agricultural and agro-industrial production and introduces microcredit systems. A key element of this is *desarollo empresarial soledario* (creation of entrepreneurial solidarity), "which uses a method to create incentives to save money despite rural poverty" (Employee of ALAC, translated by the author). Here ALAC intends to teach people to value money and savings. Teaching the value of money is a powerful tool that is also fostered by Newmont's discourse on the importance of economic development (Bebbington et al. 2013: 329–330). Compensation mechanisms will only work if money is valued and only then will people willingly hand over certain rights to the company in exchange for cash. Several interviewees stated that Newmont's job policy has led to significant inequalities. Others accused Newmont of using job promises as a tool to silence participants in land-use management workshops.

Another of ALAC's enterprises is institutional capacity-building, fitted to the global standard of government engagement. Officially this involves the implementation of planning and budgeting for results, replacing an old and less structured system. This budgeting is intended to be participatory and is implemented in various municipal governments, including the regional government of Cajamarca. Here ALAC also worked to establish the concept of a development plan, according to an employee of ALAC. Through this intervention, Newmont was able to forge relations with government officials and gain insight into local planning processes. However, this close relationship is viewed negatively by many actors, who point to the impartiality of the government. The government's failure to provide services to the community of Alto Peru, which was opposed to mining, was interpreted by an activist as a way to force the community to accept mining.

If compliant, they would receive the company's support in the form of CSR and revenues from the operation (in Peru called "canon minero"). Moreover, activists involved in an organized resistance against the mine stated that both the mine and the "local" government approached them to offer money when attempting to quell the resistance. Newmont's involvement in planning processes can lead local governments to plan huge investments, locking them into their support for the mine in order for them to "repay" the debt. Nevertheless, it is precisely this kind of collusion that, in the end, has heightened the opposition to the mine in this context and ultimately led to the failure of Newmont's CSR strategies to prevent the powerful counter-effects — in particular a strong opposition from the regional government itself, with the regional candidate elected by Cajamarca's population on the basis of his critical stance on the mine and his support for the resistance against Newmont's prospective project, Conga (Archivan caso contra Gregorio Santos por el delito de apología a la rebelión 2013).

Corresponding to its standards for community concern management, and far more extensively than in Ghana, Newmont has implemented various modes of public participation and community consultations in the context of its planned expansion, the Conga project, since 2007. As in Ghana, these include a bulletin and a community information center (Newmont 2012). However, as Li similarly highlights in the context of Yanacocha's EIA, these participatory methods are only perceived as symbolic participation and do not provide the grounds for any real agency:

> The introduction of mechanisms of accountability such as the EIA, including recent modifications to incorporate public participation and community consultation, have not eliminated the tensions generated by the continual expansion of extractive activity. In communities affected by mining, some people argue that the EIA only provides them with an opportunity to ask questions and make comments, which may lead to some modifications in the company's environmental mitigation plans, but cannot stop a proposed project from being approved. (2009: 232)

Yanacocha sees itself as representative of modern mining in Peru and with its CSR programs it portrays itself as efficient and socially and environmentally responsible (Arellano-Yanguas 2008: 23). As in Ghana, it points to its utilization of modern techniques in the context of water management as demonstrative of this. Moreover, in comparison to subsistence farming it tries to position itself as the more environmentally friendly development option (Budds and Hinojosa 2012: 130). This moral depreciation of subsistence activities is a discursive strategy not unique to Peru but also utilized by Newmont in Ghana and in Indonesia (Welker 2009: 152–153). As natural springs are going to be destroyed by the new mining venture, Yanacocha is building water reservoirs. By arguing that this will provide more water than before, Yanacocha tries to transform the accusation of being water-greedy to being the very provider of water itself (Bebbington et al. 2013: 329–330).

Despite all these efforts to command local consent and support, several key events have derailed attempts to negotiate a working relationship between the company and the community. In 2000 a truck providing the company with mercury spilled several tons outside the village of Choropampa (Smith and Feldman 2009: 51). According to local inhabitants, the company did not warn the nearby community and people took mercury to their homes in the belief that it was a precious metal. Newmont is accused by local inhabitants of having manipulated the results of medical testing in order to avoid the health compensation costs. The impact of the incident on the health of those in the area is still present and the topic is brought up repeatedly in the local elections, as observed by an employee of ALAC. Company documents confirm that their credibility and support has suffered significantly as a consequence. Mistrust runs high and the mine is accused of repeatedly making bilateral promises that go unfulfilled (ibid.: 51). When Yanacocha wanted to expand its operations to the mountain named Cerro Quillish, which provides the whole city with water, even people employed by the company Newmont protested, according to a local actor. This led to the suspension of this expansion. Yanacocha's new mining venture, Conga, which is much bigger than all its previous projects, would similarly affect the many lakes that provide the surrounding communities with water.

Mining is seen by many to lead to a change in lifestyle and a move away from a healthy environment toward a greater dependency on money. Local actors in Peru have observed these changes in many affected communities (Bebbington et al. 2013: 324). The presence of the mine has led to reduced access to natural and social resources for some actors, while increasing availability of capital and human resources for other actors has led to immense social inequality. Many families are left without capital after low compensation payment (Bury 2004).

There is the consensus in the population that this mining brings a lot of environmental and social problems to the area … It pollutes the water, the air, the plants, the animals and the people. It does not take care as it should … therefore we make huge protests against the mine Yanacocha. (Activists of the community of Alto Peru, translated by the author)

The widespread mistrust has led to intensified scrutiny of corporate discourse and techniques, as well as more organized forms of activism, which defy the kind of "divide and rule" effects of CSR that worked so well in Ghana. Local activists inform potentially affected communities with detailed presentations about the scope and impact of the planned operations, challenging the company's control of information. The company's promise to construct water reservoirs did not convince all local actors (Bebbington et al. 2013: 339). Since an independent expert stated that the reservoirs technically do not work without being refilled, locals are fearful that they will be left without water when the mining company leaves.

As the trust in governmental institutions is also low, people do not expect any support from the government after the mine's closure (Muradian et al. 2003: 787). The fear of loss of water access is so high that people are willing to risk their lives in protest (Bebbington et al. 2013: 326). With the gradual changes in protest law in recent years, the criminalization of protest has facilitated and legalized the use of force by police (Chérrez et al. 2011: 133). This has made it more likely for protests to escalate to violent clashes.

The rejection of the mining project could only be achieved if the territory was declared a conservation area or agricultural area in the process of zoning (Li 2009). While the potential identification of a zone is seen as a technical task, the pressure to pursue this route almost always comes from protest and is seen as the chief way in which the affected population can express their desire for a non-mining alternative. This so-called technical option is at the same time political. Twice protests have led to the suspension of a mining project by declaring the site an area of conservation. This in turn motivates other protests. Thus the technical legislative framework is what provides the space or opportunity for political protest. For it is the very possibility of establishing no-go zones in the first place that does not exist in Ghana, much to the lament of the NGO WACAM, as it much reduces their grounds for formally fighting the development of new mining ventures in greenfield territories.

Moreover, as one of the activists of Celendín pointed out, old structures like the *rondas campesinas* (peasant rounds) are used to mobilize the affected communities. These structures, which emerged as communal self-defense against cattle theft in the 1970s (Gitlitz 1998: 24–26), are powerful and their participants are involved in multiple modes of resistance beyond street protests (Cajamarca: Ronderos retiran primera tranquera en el proyecto Conga 2013). In July 2013, *ronderos* decided to punish everybody who sold their land to the company (Cajamarca: Rondas prohibirán vender tierras a empresas mineras 2013). Many people reported the company's strategy to threaten active opponents with legal measures. At the same time, support letters between activists created greater strength and solidarity in the face of the company's attempt to criminalize them. With possible support from rondas campesinas, actors around the mines in Cajamarca have more independence from their elected leaders and a notably less hierarchical structure in relation to those leaders than their Ghanaian counterparts have toward the chiefs.

Many of my interviewees commented that inequality has risen dramatically. This inequality is at least partly an instrumental effect of CSR (Bebbington et al. 2013: 333). While inequality was just as much an outcome of Newmont's community investment program in Ghana, it proved much more difficult to manage and control in Peru. Bebbington et al. (2013: 336–340) argue that inequality can be seen as one reason for conflicts. Instead of inducing conflicts within and between the communities (Sawyer 2004), in Cajamarca it provided a rallying point for protest directed toward the company. Through this process, new solidarities across social and ethnic boundaries were created (Cajamarca: Paro indefinido contra la expansión minera 2013), which in turn reinvigorated the protest movement *internally* (Kirsch 2013: 362). Meanwhile, environmental and regional discourses of post-extractivism promoted by national and international NGOs provided legitimacy and moral support to the protest *externally* (Gudynas 2012; Cajamarca: Paro indefinido contra la expansión minera 2013).

Despite its extensive CSR apparatus, the company is not able to depoliticize its already politicized operations. While in Ghana Newmont argued that it is more responsible than other mining companies, in Peru people had shared a long experience with the company, which made such claims impossible. The company's discourse that it wants to improve has lost much credibility. Mistrust once created is difficult to reverse. Although Newmont implements the same strategies in Peru as in Ghana, it cannot make use of bureaucratic power and the depoliticizing effects in the same way as in Ghana. Ultimately, the standardized techniques do not lead to favorable instrumental effects for the mining company. Meanwhile, the persistent mistrust leads to scrutiny of Newmont's behavior and a resistance against the ways in which the company's development discourse and intervention devalues current modes of living.

Conclusion

"What gets measured gets managed" argued one of Newmont's CEOs in the context of its community relations management. This statement reveals the mining company's objective to control its community relations worldwide through the implementation of standardized, global CSR concepts, the success of which can be measured through quantifiable metrics. Global norms like the UN Global Compact and the Voluntary Principles on Security and Human Rights signed by Newmont, frame, endorse and validate their engagement in these standardized techniques of CSR.

This chapter examined the implementation and impact of these standardized CSR concepts in different local contexts within the extractive sector. In contrast to much research conducted in this area, the chapter explored the limits of these corporate techniques to influence company-community relations. The comparative approach based on ethnographic data involved both a temporal and geographical dimension, challenging the conventional wisdom of globalized corporate practice and revealing the specificities of local responses to standardized techniques. Ultimately, I argue that standardized technologies of governance do not yield standardized effects of domination.

While Newmont's expansion plans were widely accepted or even welcomed in Ghana, they resulted in violent conflicts and the mine's suspension in Peru, despite the company applying the same strategy. At both sites, Newmont engaged with community concern management, involved itself in participatory investment, established NGOs on the same model, and engaged with the government at different levels. They also installed programs for the creation of local business opportunities and job creation, as prescribed by its Environmental and Social Responsibility Unit in Denver. In both places Newmont tried to create a discourse of sustainable and responsible mining. Apart from these official strategies, some unofficial global strategies could also be identified. Newmont could not present these controversial strategies as CSR policies but used them to complement the official CSR. Correspondingly, the official strategies were used strategically to shape social relations in a way that benefited corporate interests. Corporate-government alliance at all levels was used to influence political processes and to take advantage of bureaucratic power. Job policies were used at both places to create reciprocal relationships. But in contrast to Newmont's official standards, nowhere were they deployed transparently. Participatory investment was much less effective at depoliticizing Newmont's operations in Peru than in Ghana, even though it was used to a greater extent. Community concern engagement resulted in criticism of its standardizing outcomes but still secured a broad acceptance in Ghana, whereas it was perceived as a corporate maneuver in Peru.

As this chapter has shown, the power of global concepts to depoliticize mining operations and control social relations in the interest of corporations has limits. In practice, they are not universally applicable tools for corporate control, as they cannot be adapted to local complexities throughout the world. Across these diverse geographies there are variances in social structure, political processes and historical context that these standards cannot fully account for. While global standards are mostly disconnected from local history, people's reactions are not. In Peru, the project was in the vicinity of Newmont's already ongoing operations, where Newmont itself admits many mistakes created huge mistrust amongst community members. Local actors consequently examined corporate techniques very closely, which, to a certain extent, prevented some of their instrumental effects. Here, CSR failed to redeem mistrust or expunge the memory created by the corporation's earlier misdemeanors. In response, rather than being divisive, these corporate techniques of alliance-building provided a focal point for resistance, and shared experience of the adverse impacts of mining became a foundation for solidarity and the biggest weapon against the company.

References

Akabzaa, Thomas. M. 2000. *Boom and dislocation: The environmental and social impacts of mining in the Wassa West District of Ghana.* Accra: Third World Network-Africa.
"Archivan caso contra Gregorio Santos por el delito de apología a la rebelión." 2013. *La Republica*, http://www.larepublica.pe/16-08-2013/archivan-caso-contra-gregorio-santos-por-el-delito-de-apologia-a-la-rebelion (accessed 14 September 2013).
Arellano-Yanguas, Javier. 2008. A thoroughly modern resource curse? The new natural resource policy agenda and the mining revival in Peru, http://www.ids.ac.uk/idspublication/a-thoroughly-modern-resource-curse-the-new-natural-resource-policy-agenda-and-the-mining-revival-in-peru (accessed 17 December 2012).

Arellano-Yanguas, Javier. 2011. Aggravating the resource curse: Decentralisation, mining and conflict in Peru. *Journal of Development Studies* 47(4): 617–638.

Bebbington, Anthony, Leonith Hinojosa, Denis Humphreys Bebbington, Maria-Luisa Burneo, and Ximena Warnaars. 2008. Contention and ambiguity: Mining and the possibilities of development. *Development and Change* 39(6): 887–914

Bebbington, A., Denis Humphreys Bebbington, Leonith Hinojosa, Maria-Luisa Burneo, Ximena Warnaars, and Jeffery Bury. 2013. Anatomia des conflicto: La negociación de las geograficas de la industria extractiva en Los Paises Andinas. In Antony Bebbington, ed., *Industrias extractivas: Conflicto sociales y dinámicas institucionales en al Región Andina*, pp. 321–347. Lima: IEP, CEPES, Grupo Propuesta Ciudana.

Budds, Jeffery, and Leonith Hinojosa. 2012. The co-production of waterscapes in Peru. *Water Alternatives* 5(1): 119–137.

Bury, Jeffery. 2004. Livelihoods in transition: Transnational gold mining operations and local change in Cajamarca, Peru. *The Geographical Journal* 170(1): 78–91.

"Cajamarca: Paro indefinido contra la expansión minera". 2013. *Mi mina corrupta*, http://minacorrupta.wordpress.com/tag/rondas-campesinas/ (accessed 15 September 2013).

"Cajamarca: Rondas prohibirán vender tierras a empresas mineras." 2013. *La Rebublica*, 30 July, http://www.larepublica.pe/30-07-2013/cajamarca-rondas-prohibiran-vender-tierras-a-empresas-mineras (accessed 30 September 2013).

"Cajamarca: Ronderos retiran primera tranquera en el proyecto Conga." 2013. *RPP NOTICIAS*, 20 August 2013, http://www.rpp.com.pe/2013-08-20-cajamarca-ronderos-retiran-primera-tranquera-en-el-proyecto-conga-noticia_623785.html (accessed 15 September 2013).

Cetindamar, Dilek, and Kristoffer Husoy. 2007. Corporate social responsibility and environmentally responsible behavior: The case of the United Nations Global Compact. *Journal of Business Ethics* 76: 163–176.

Chérrez, Cecilia, César Padilla, Sander Otten, and Maria Rose Yumbla. 2011. Cuando tiemblan los derechos: Extractivismo y criminalizacion en America Latina, http://www.biodiversidadla.org/Objetos_Relacionados/Extractivismo_y_criminalizacion_en_America_Latina

"Chiefs worried about propaganda against Newmont project." 2009. *Daily Graphic*, 15 September.

Daffós, Juan Aste. 2003. Perú: La expansión minera y la necesidad de una zonificación ecológica-económica para el desarrollo sostenible, *Aportes al Debate* (8), http://library.fes.de/pdf-files/bueros/peru/02154.pdf (accessed 12 October 2013).

Els, Frik. 2012. Newmont could redirect Conga billions to Ghana if delays continue, http://www.mining.com/2012/02/08/newmont-could-redirect-conga-billions-to-ghana-if-delays-continue/ (accessed 6 July 2012).

Ferguson, James. 1994. *The anti-politics machine: Development, depoliticization, and bureaucratic power in Lesotho*. Minneapolis: University of Minnesota Press.

Ferguson, James. 2005. Seeing like an oil company: Space, security, and global capital in neoliberal Africa. *American Anthropologies* 107(3): 377–382.

Gardner, Katy. 2012. *Discordant development: Global capitalism and the struggle for connection in Bangladesh*. London, New York, NY: Pluto Press; Palgrave Macmillan.

Gifford, Blair, and Andrew Kestler. 2008. Toward a theory of local legitimacy by MNEs in developing nations: Newmont mining and health sustainable development in Peru. *Journal of International Management* (14): 340–352.

Gilberthorpe, Emma, and Glenn Banks. 2012. Development on whose terms? CSR discourse and social realities in Papua New Guinea's extractive industries sector. *Resources Policy* 37(2):185–193.

Gitlitz, John. 1998. Decadencia y superviviencia de las rondas campesinas del Norde del Perú, http://www.cepes.org.pe/debate/debate28/02_Articulo.pdf

Gudynas, Eduardo. 2012. Der neue progessive Extraktivismus in Südamerika. In T. Lambert, ed., *Der neue extraktivismus: Eine Debatte über die Grenzen des Rohstoffmodells in Lateinamerika,* pp. 46–62. Berlin: FDCL-Verlag.

Hiß, Stefanie. 2006. *Warum übernehmen Unternehmen gesellschaftliche Verantwortung? Ein soziologischer Erklärungsversuch.* Frankfurt/Main: Campus Verlag.

Hopkins, Michael. 2012. Corporate social responsibility and international development: Is business the solution? Oxford: Taylor and Francis.

Kapelus, Paul. 2002. Mining, corporate social responsibility and the community: The case of Rio Tinto, Richard Bay Minerals and Mbonambi. *Journal of Business Ethics* 39(3): 275–296.

Kirsch, Stuart. 2013. Los conflictos sobre las industrias extracitvas: Una visión comparativa desde afuera. In A. Bebbington, ed., *Industrias extractivas: Conflicto sociales y dinámicas institucionales en al Región Andina,* pp. 349–369. Lima: IEP, CEPES, Grupo Propuesta Ciudana.

Kofoya-Tetteh, Kwae. 2009. Akyem Kotoku chiefs, communities support Newmont, *Daily Graphic,* 26 August.

Lentz, Carola. 2008. *Ethnicity and the making of history in northern Ghana.* Edinburgh University Press for International African Institute.

Li, Fabiana. 2009. Documenting accountability: Environmental impact assessment in a Peruvian mining project. *Political and Legal Anthropology Review* 32(2): 218–236.

Luhmann, Niklas. 2008. *Legitimation durch verfahren,* first edition. Frankfurt am Main: Suhrkamp.

Luong, Pauline Jones, and Erika Weinthal. 2006. Rethink the resource curse: Ownership structure, institutional capacity, and domestic constraints. *Annual Review of Political Science* 9(1): 241–263.

Matten, Dirk, and Andrew Crane. 2003. Corporate citizenship: Towards an extended theoretical conceptualization. *ICCSR Research Paper Series* (4): 1–21.

Muradian, Roldan, Juan Martinez-Alier, and Humberto Correa. 2003. International capital versus local population: The environmental conflict of the Tambogrande mining project, Peru. *Society & Natural Resources* 16(9): 775–792.

Newmont. 2009. Letter from Newmont to Nana Kwandwo Amo II.

Newmont. 2012. Citizen participation fact sheet l, http://www.newmont.com/files/doc_downloads/fact_sheets/south_america/Citizen-Participation-Fact-Sheet-04-15-12-Final.pdf (accessed 11 October 2015).

Osterman, Cynthia, and Christopher Wilson. 2012. Peru protest against Newmont leaves one dead, leader detained, *Reuters,* 4 July, http://www.reuters.com/article/2012/07/05/us-peru-newmont-idUSBRE86402820120705 (accessed 24 October 2012).

Rajak, Dinah. 2011. *In good company: An anatomy of corporate social responsibility.* California: Stanford University Press.

Republic of Ghana. 2006. *Mineral and Mining Act: Act 703.*

Sachs, Jeffery, and Andrew Warner. 1997. *Natural Resource Abundance and Economic Growth.* Cambridge: NBER Working Paper Series. http://www.nber.org/papers/w5398.pdf?new_window=1 (accessed 24 October 2012).

Sawyer, Suzana. 2004. *Crude chronicles: Indigenous politics, multinational oil, and neoliberalism in Ecuador.* Durham, NC: Duke University Press.

Scott, James. C. 1998. *Seeing like a state: How certain schemes to improve the human condition have failed.* New Haven: Yale University Press.

Sharp, John. 2006. Corporate social responsibility and development: An anthropological perspective. *Development Southern Africa* 23(2): 213–223.

Smith, Gare A., and Daniel Feldman. 2009. Community relationships review: Global summary report, http://www.newmont.com/files/doc_downloads/crr/CRR-Global-Summary-Report-and-Appendices-English.pdf (accessed 11 October2015)

Thorp, Rosemary. 2012. The challenges of mining-based development in Peru. In Rosemary Thorp, Stefanie Battistelli, Jose Carlos Orihuela and Maritza Paredes,, eds., *The developmental challenges of mining and oil,* pp. 110–130. Basingstoke: Palgrave Macmillan.
Welker, Marina. 2009. Corporate security begins in the community: Mining, the corporate social responsibility industry, and environmental advocacy in Indonesia. *Cultural Anthropology* 24(1): 142–179.

Johanna Sydow conducted field research in Ghana, Peru and Ecuador on the social impact of large- and small-scale mining, especially on the implications of CSR and the role of local contexts and the criminalization of protest 2009, 2010, and 2013. She holds an MA in Environment, Development and Policy from the University of Sussex, UK, and a BA in Sociology and Social Sciences from the University of Bielefeld, Germany. She currently works as Policy Advisor for the NGO Germanwatch, Berlin, and is Visiting Research Fellow at the University of Sussex working together with the University Andina Simón Bolivar, Ecuador.

— *Afterword* —

BIG MEN AND BUSINESS
Morality, Debt, and the Corporation: A Perspective
Robert J. Foster

⁂

Corporate executives today routinely admit that companies owe a debt to society over and above operating within the law. Companies, we are told, need to do more — to give back — even if the necessity is sometimes justified as smart business practice.

In what does corporate social responsibility (CSR) consist? Any answer of course presupposes a perspective on the corporation. In the legal scholarship of the past century, two competing perspectives emerged, prompting divergent responses to the question of who owes what to whom. Anthropological analysis, however, would regard these perspectives as mutually entailing. From such a vantage point on the corporation, CSR appears elusive. Indeed, the corporation — or, more precisely, the corporate form that separates ownership from management — appears as an instrument for severely limiting if not completely disabling the recognition of debt relations.

* * *

The issue of CSR was debated vigorously in the pages of the *Harvard Law Review* during the Great Depression. Professor E. Merrick Dodd, Jr. argued that the corporation has a social service function as well as a profit-making function; a business enterprise should not be treated solely as the private property of stockholders. Dodd appealed to emerging ethical standards for support, but he also invoked the idea that the corporation was a sui generis entity distinct from its constituent stockholders and their agents (managers and directors): "If we think of it [a business association] as an institution which differs in the nature of things from the individuals who compose it, we may then readily conceive of it as a person, which, like other persons engaged in business, is affected not only by the laws which regulate business but by the attitude of public and business opinion as to the social obligations of business" (1932: 1161). Therefore, Dodd concluded, corporate agents should be regarded as trustees of the institution obliged to consider the interests of the employees and consumers, for instance, with whom the institution deals.

Dodd was responding to the argument of Professor A. A. Berle, Jr., who reiterated his position in a sharp rejoinder to Dodd (Berle 1931, 1932; see also Dodd 1935). For Berle, there was no question that corporate managers and directors are trustees for the stockholders in whose interest the powers of any group within a corporation ought to be exercised; without such a fiduciary obligation, corporate agents are free and likely to enforce their own claims on the wealth assembled under the corporate form. Besides, he asserted, there is no current legal framework for recognizing any other obligation: "Now I submit that you can not abandon emphasis on 'the view that business corporations exist for the sole purpose of making profits for their stockholders' until such time as you are prepared to offer a clear and reasonably enforceable scheme of responsibilities to someone else" (1932: 1367). The alternative would be, according to Berle, a situation in which the various groups that have a claim on the revenue stream of the corporation—investors, workers, customers, and the public at large—would be left to take, perhaps violently, what each could get.

The Dodd-Berle debate hinged not only on different assessments of the ethical standards of corporate managers and directors, but also on how to imagine the personhood of the corporation. For Berle, the corporation was ultimately identified with its shareholders, not with its non-shareholder participants. Although Berle never addressed the issue of personhood directly, he implicitly appealed to what can be called the aggregate theory of corporate personality. In this view, the corporation, while legally distinct, *is* the association of owners; it is a collective "organism" (a metaphor that Berle favored). This view of the corporation as a not fully separate personality was common in the early nineteenth century, before the rise of liquid share markets and large-scale enterprises (see Ireland 1996). It is a view that foregrounds property relations, especially the relations between owners (shareholders in Berle's day) and their agents (managers and directors).

Berle worried that shareholders, as dispersed and "passive" property owners, had little control over how their investments were used by corporate managers. His emphasis on the fiduciary obligations of managers was meant to highlight the property rights of the increasingly large number of people in 1931 with direct or indirect investments in securities. Henceforth, Berle's name became coupled with the phrase "shareholder primacy." That position often misleadingly represents shareholders as owners of the corporation (as opposed to owners of shares), an assertion made baldly by Milton Friedman in his celebrated 1970 *New York Times* manifesto, "The social responsibility of business is to increase its profits." In Friedman's extreme version of shareholder primacy, the corporation owes no debt to society besides operating within the law. CSR is thus in effect theft by corporate managers and directors of other people's property.

Dodd, by contrast, explicitly invoked the entity theory of corporate personality. In this view, the corporation is a distinct person (whether natural or artificial is irrelevant)—a reification, independent of the individuals who compose it. This view foregrounds the external relations between the corporation and the various groups with which it interacts. It underwrites a position of "director primacy," in which directors hold the power to allocate profits to non-shareholder participants in the corporation, such as workers. It is a view that makes ample room for the practice of what is now spoken about as CSR.

* * *

The debate between Dodd and Berle continues unresolved. We can get critical purchase on it by way of a rather different provocation about personhood. I refer to Marilyn Strathern's discussion of the Big Man, that famous Melanesian manager of debts in pigs and pearl shells. For Strathern (1991), the Big Man personifies "unitary identity," one of two complementary modes of sociality along with "particularized difference" that alternate with each other, taking the respective forms of same-sex and cross-sex relations. In Highlands New Guinea, the Big Man in action thus presents a singular form, isomorphic with a male collectivity ("one clan") capable of acting purposively in external relations of ceremonial exchange with other such collectivities. The particular kinship (male-female) relations— multitudinous and diverse—that compose the clan in effect disappear; the clan's female components (sisters and wives) are externalized, mobilized in marriage relations that grow the clan.

The Big Man contrasts with the Great Man, a powerful leader who establishes authority by means of a distinctive competence, such as military prowess or ritual expertise, rather than through competitive giving designed to overwhelm the recipient with disproportionate generosity (Godelier 1986 [1982]). Embodying one of many capacities, the Great Man does not stand as one man; there can be no single Great Man. Nor is he isomorphic with a male collectivity. On the contrary, "the great man differentiates between categories of men in order to substitute for an external relationship with females or enemies an internal male heterogeneity" (Strathern 1991: 213). What is taken for granted here is the homogeneous capacity of men in their collective state—precisely what must be achieved in the case of the Big Man. Great Men in action create the internal divisions—between male and female, ally and enemy—necessary to grow the collective body of men by turning sons into fathers.

For Strathern, one mode of sociality emerges from and turns on the other; social life takes shape as the alternation and enactment of same-sex and cross-sex relations. The difference between Big Men and Great Men, then, is ultimately one of perspective. Each figure provides a different focal point from which "people can both look out from and look in on themselves" (Strathern 1991: 209). Perhaps the same can be said of the difference between Dodd and Berle's understandings of both the corporation and its debt relations.

* * *

From Dodd's point of view, the corporation is a person, a discrete entity seen as if from the outside looking in. This person owns assets; it (most likely, he) is the active subject of a property relation. The corporation is oriented to its external relationships. Furthermore, its debts are construed as same-sex relations between autonomous and equal collective individuals (two patriclans)—that is, as debts that can and should be canceled. No debt is a possibility. Hence the conceit of CSR: corporations, although chartered by the state, act as if they preexist and are equal to society, capable of paying off all debts incurred through their operations.

From Berle's point of view, the corporation is a thing; it is an owned asset, itself property. The corporation is thus seen as if from the inside looking out, a field of contractual relations and implicit obligations among diverse particular persons (principals and agents) whose interests potentially conflict with each other. As a result, its debts are construed as cross-sex relations of mutual but asymmetric dependency between principals and agents (husbands and wives). Like capital and wage-labor, each calls the other into existence; each defines the identity of the other.

These two perspectives, the public and private dimensions of corporate law, have alternated with each other over the last 150 years or so in both jurisprudence and civic discourse. Friedman's manifesto signaled the return of both "shareholder primacy" and the view of the corporation as an aggregate of property owners and their agents after a period beginning in the 1940s in which corporate statesmen—Dodd's enlightened directors of national enterprises run as autonomous social institutions—held sway. Since the protests in Seattle in 1999, and after the financial crisis of 2008, the view of the corporation as a distinct person (entity) has re-emerged incongruously as an object of critique on the left, as settled law for the US Supreme Court majority in *Citizens United*, and as a device for authoring declarations of CSR.

*   *   *

What propels or motivates the alternation of perspectives? There appears to be an irreducible tension in the corporate form itself, but one that looks different from each point of view. From the inside— the dominant perspective of corporate law—the tension stems from the agency problem that Berle identified. This perspective comes to the fore historically when shareholders seek to assert their interests over those of their agents or, indeed, anyone else. For example, it accompanied the insistent claim during the 1990s that "shareholder value" should supersede all other concerns.

From the outside, however, the root of the tension appears to lie elsewhere, namely, as Berle sensed, in the peculiar nature of the alienable share as a form of property (peculiar enough that Marx (1967 [1894]: 436) took joint-stock companies to herald "the abolition of capital as private property within the framework of the capitalist production itself"). Because shareholders own shares and not corporate assets they are in effect able to assert agency only by selling shares. Shareholders are de facto speculators whom directors can keep attached to the corporation only by increasing the value of shares and/or dividends, even if long-term strategy recommends otherwise. Performance-based compensation for directors exacerbates the dynamic, encouraging risky if not reckless activity to generate immediate returns. Accordingly, this perspective comes to the fore at times when corporate excesses (Enron, AIG, etc.) attract public censure and raise questions about the accountability of an entity that enjoys not only limited liability but also some of the basic rights of natural persons.

From either perspective, irresponsibility appears to be built into the corporate form. One perspective focuses on directors and managers who disavow their obligations to shareholders; the other perspective focuses on speculative shareholders (and their agents) who disavow all obligations other than to increase their own wealth. The corporate form, one of the most consequential technologies of the last century, undoubtedly promotes capital accumulation. But it equally promotes stunning indifference toward debt, whether debt to non-shareholder participants "inside" the corporation such as workers or to all the non-shareholder participants "outside" the corporation whom we call Society At Large. CSR is thus ultimately oxymoronic. If corporations are legal vehicles for disavowing debt, then it follows that, as their influence expands, who owes what to whom becomes a question of dire urgency.

Acknowledgments

This essay also appeared as an article in *Social Anthropology* (volume 20, issue 4, 2012). Thanks to Ira Bashkow and Holly High for their comments on an earlier draft.

References

Berle, A. A., Jr. 1931. Corporate powers as powers in trust. *Harvard Law Review* 44(7): 1049–1074.

Berle, A. A., Jr. 1932. For whom corporate managers *are* trustees: A note. *Harvard Law Review* 45(8): 1365–1372.

Dodd, E. Merrick, Jr. 1932. For whom are corporate managers trustees? *Harvard Law Review* 45(7): 1145–1163.

Dodd, E. Merrick, Jr. 1935. Is effective enforcement of the fiduciary duties of corporate managers practicable? *The University of Chicago Law Review* 2(2): 194–207.

Friedman, Milton. 1970. The social responsibility of business is to increase its profits, *New York Times Magazine*, 13 September, 32–33, 122, 124, 126.

Godelier, Maurice. 1986 [1982]. *The making of great men: Male domination and power among the New Guinea Baruya*. Trans. R. Swyer. Cambridge University Press.

Ireland, Paddy W. 1996. Capitalism without the capitalist: The joint stock company share and the emergence of the modern doctrine of separate corporate personality. *Legal History* 17(1): 40–72.

Marx, Karl. 1967 [1894]. *Capital, Vol. 3*, F. Engels, ed. New York: International Publishers.

Strathern, Marilyn. 1991. One man and many men. In M. Godelier and M. Strathern, eds., *Big men and great men: Personifications of power in Melanesia*, pp. 197–214. Cambridge University Press.

Robert J. Foster is Professor of Anthropology and Professor of Visual and Cultural Studies at the University of Rochester. His research interests include globalization, corporations, commercial media, museums, and material culture. He is the author of *Social reproduction and history in Melanesia* (Cambridge, 1995); *Materializing the nation: Commodities, consumption and media in Papua New Guinea* (Indiana, 2002); and *Coca-globalization: Following soft drinks from New York to New Guinea* (Palgrave, 2008). His current projects include a comparative study of the moral and cultural economy of mobile phones in Papua New Guinea and Fiji, funded by the Australian Research Council (with Dr Heather Horst).

INDEX

DISLOCATIONS

General Editors: August Carbonella, *Memorial University of Newfoundland*, Don Kalb, *University of Utrecht & Central European University*, Linda Green, *University of Arizona*

www.ingramcontent.com/pod-product-compliance
Lightning Source LLC
Chambersburg PA
CBHW070915030426
42336CB00014BA/2424